Broken

By,
Ruth Aron Kyle

Dedication

For my Mother

And My Two Sons

Acknowledgments

There are many people who I owe a debt of gratitude to. Those who helped in the only ways they could, for instance, by helping me survive to make it to the other side of this and live to tell about it and those with the patience and contributions to make this book finally come to fruition.

My sons and my mom have been here through it all. My mom has been as supportive as she can possibly be without being sucked back into the tragedy and trauma of all this. She is very strong, and it has been her strength that has gotten me through just as much as it has gotten her through. The pain, trauma, suffering, and abuse, as well as having to be without my help on other projects during the time I've worked on this book, my sons and my mom have stuck with everything. I would not have had, or have currently, a roof over my head, nor would my sons, without my mother. She has been supportive in countless significant ways.

My sons have always supported my writing of this book, never have they tried to talk me out of it for any reason at all.

My aunt supported me through court hearings, traveled up north with my mother and me for those hearings, and went by herself with me for them. She has been a great support and ally. My brother, who is a mental health professional, has given me advice regarding my sons, as well as me, throughout all these years. There's never once been a time that I asked him for advice that he wasn't available to give it.

My attorney, who provided advice and support, as well as excellent lawyering and advocating for my sons and me, is truly a treasure, one who sacrificed days, weeks, months and years working exceedingly hard on our case, with both his intellect and his heart.

The Court Appointed Counselor Coordinator began as the 'family' psychiatrist. He worked with the entire family for several years committedly. He put blood, sweat, and tears into our case, just as our attorney did. Like my attorney, he believed my sons, as I did and wanted them to be protected. He worked and worked and gave of his time on a pro bono basis and has been a support and a true friend since.

The renowned child sexual abuse expert whose clinic conducted an assessment on my sons was invaluable as well. She sat for hours of deposition, which I don't believe the referee ever bothered to hear, as I can't imagine how she could have come to the conclusion she did had she listened to this expert. This expert is irreplaceable. She was kind, empathetic, and understanding of my sons. I will always be very grateful for her nature, as well as her knowledge and experience.

My therapist, whom I have regularly 'seen' (now it's over the phone because she has moved) for well over 9 years, has been invaluable. She has helped with the process of writing this book as well, she has listened and knows our story probably more than anyone other than me. My best friend stood by me for years, listening to my pain and the horrible impacts of the multitude of dangerous and incompetent decisions, one right after the other. Since I have saturated myself in completing this book, we have had limited contact. I'm hoping that will be rectified soon.

My best friend from high school also reached out to me after we lost contact for many years. The same is true of my contact with her. Again, I'm hoping to rectify that. My sons began getting their haircut by a great woman when they were in middle school. Castiel will not have anyone else cut his hair! She is a fantastic and supportive person. She has made a significant positive impact on Castiel, who has struggled with severe social anxiety, among other things. He connected with her, and she has been understanding and communicative with him. She is the only person who read this book, other than the editors, prior to it being published.

Castiel's trauma therapist has been understanding and fantastic and has worked very well with Castiel. Our psychiatrist has been understanding and wonderful as well. GTPAC has been a Godsend. Our lead, and our director for this group have been phenomenal, as well as the members of the group. I have made invaluable and treasured friendships.

There are many others who stood by and have been supportive, whose hands were tied, but they stayed around. Such as my employer has been such a kind, generous, and empathetic soul.

My grandmother didn't make it to see this come to fruition. She recently passed, I miss her and am thankful for all the years we had with her in our lives.

There were a multitude of professionals, friends, and family members who wrote letters in support of me. I appreciate every single one of these people who has been there and listened and tried to do what they could.

Clawing my way out of the entanglement of despair
And the heartbreak of agonizing trauma
Can be worthwhile knowing
I'm using that despair
And heartbreak
To create
change
To help others

There are people just as evil -if not more evil, than those who carry out these horrendous crimes against children,

They are those who stand by and do nothing to protect the child/ren.

They are those who allow the abuse to occur and look the other way.

They are those for whom it is their very job to protect children from harm, but they don't.

-Me

Section One

Our Story

Dear Gabriel and Castiel,

I'm sorry for all the pain and suffering you two have endured. If you feel I abandoned you and that I failed you, I understand. I will forever feel that I failed you both. However, I never abandoned you. It's abusive, archaic, destructive, and criminal to abruptly take two very young children away from their primary caregiver and protector, their mother and me.

For many years, I was prevented from protecting and parenting the two of you. As the loving mother that I am, you can't possibly understand how paralyzingly deep and profound were my feelings of sorrow, anger, and loss. I think of you both all the time. I always wonder what you're doing, if you're safe, if you're alright, is there a smile on your face or not? We've lost so many years, we've lost countless experiences together, and we continue to not have experiences we would have had, and we continue to suffer. We lost spending your childhood together, and you lost having a childhood altogether.

Your "childhood" - your innocence was ripped from you. Your trust was crushed to bits. All that has been done to you and committed against you has cost each of you your past, present, and future. Indeed, what has been done to you has cost you yourselves. I, too, have been robbed of the great privilege of being your mother. I've been robbed of protecting what is most precious to me: the two of you. Our lives together have been destroyed, and our futures have been marred and shattered. Our life's course was severely altered and set on a trajectory that has been traumatic and deeply scarring.

I am writing *your* story for each of you and for every other child and protective parent who has or is still walking this painful path as we have done and still do. I want the world to know how horribly inept and criminally unjust our child "welfare" and "family" court system is. I want the injustices that have been committed against you to be known. All the pain and suffering that you have endured is not going to be for nothing. It is my hope, with every thread of my being, that change will come of this, change for the better so that no child will ever have to live the cruel insidiousness that each of you has.

All my love,

Mom

For my most precious sons

And my mother

Like water,

Time and turmoil menacingly

carves new paths

leaving the safe and loving paths

forgotten and buried

-Me

It was January in Kentucky, and not cold for a Michigander like me. There was a little bit of snow on the ground, whereas in Lexington, that defined cold as well as winter. I felt a strange, deafening chill that morning. I remember looking in on my sleeping sons; I did not wake them to say goodbye; they were so beautiful, and they were peacefully and contently asleep. I will never forget their faces that morning, the peace and calmness over them took me to a place in my mind that I have not been since. I didn't know that once I left, I wouldn't be seeing them again for months, and I certainly could not imagine the terms and conditions under which I would next be seeing them. I didn't know that morning things were going to change that very day, and they would never, ever be the same for us again. Neither would the three of us ever be the same as we were at that moment.

Gabriel and Castiel would go to their preschool that day, where they knew everybody there and were safe -or so I thought. But police officers would come and pick them up and turn them over to their paternal grandparents -people they had not seen in over a year, people they did not want to see. I was with my attorney at an office nearby in Lexington, taking depositions. An officer would come and take me out of the room to tell me they had taken my children into custody, and they would not tell me when I would be seeing my children again.

They weren't thoughts of myself as I collapsed to the floor in a mangled heap of sorrow, pain, fear, and heartbreak. They were thoughts of my children. It was of them crying and me not being there to hold them, to take care of them, to console them, to protect them. What were my sons told? What was the explanation for this sudden and drastic interruption in their lives? All the things they had told me about their father and their paternal family were flooding my head. All the very disturbing and sexualized behaviors I had

5

witnessed, the sexualized interactions and verbalizations that I had been screaming and banging my head against the walls trying to get someone to acknowledge, do something about, and help them with; they all echoed and bounced back and forth in my head like several pinballs in a hopped-up pinball machine. I had never been so angry, fearful, lost and broken in my life. Of all the people I had gone to, none of them had been able to help -many thought I was foolish and hysterical and dismissed my concerns as overly protective and dramatic, mother-blowing trivial actions and statements out of proportion. Most didn't listen to a word I said. Some did but didn't try to help in any way. Many made things worse. Most kept their heads buried in the sand. Of those who listened and believed, they were professionals in the field of child abuse and child sexual abuse, but they weren't able to make changes to the course of action, and those who could have made changes didn't listen to those professionals either.

Heartbreak can cause death. What kept me alive after my sons were taken was only a thread of hope and an act of God. Hope of us being back together like we were before January 15th, 2008. That never happened, and none of us will ever be those people again. Instead, a huge dark sadness and emptiness began filling my heart. That dark sadness and emptiness stays with me to this very day. I worried and worried incessantly about my sons; I had no way of contacting them. The boys were ages six and three when they were abruptly taken from me -their primary caregiver and mother -and their safety. They were taken from love and sanctuary and placed with a sadistic and cruel family and in perpetual danger.

The reason my sons were abruptly taken from me was based solely on a custody evaluation completed in Ann Arbor. This one man who completed the evaluation is responsible for so much pain and heartache; he, in fact, set in motion the thundering of fallen dreams for three people: two innocent boys and their naive and trusting mother (me). My mother's life was sadly turned upside down as well. This evaluator called upon many to follow in his path; most did, all did not, for those that did, the harm they caused is great and unforgivable.

I did not get to say good-bye or even talk with my sons. I did not get to hug them or console them. Nothing. No I love you, or I'm sorry I can't fix this or change this or make this go away. I couldn't warn them that I could not stop anybody from sticking a "stick" up their butt where they were going, but then again, I alone couldn't stop that from happening anyway. Year after year, I was unable to prevent anything from going into their butts, gaslighting, physical, emotional, and mental abuse, stalking, threats, manipulation, group shunning and shaming, or stop the bombardment of bullshit and lies from going into their heads. They suffered horrendously, and nobody was there to protect them. When the paternal family got custody of my very young sons, they took away their identities. They changed their first names and their last names; they shaved their heads, and then the indoctrination began. They would not let me even speak to my sons, then when the court ordered it, they put the calls on speaker phone while the entire family sat around them to know what I said and to influence and control what they said. Remember, these are little boys who were abruptly taken from their mother and the home, routine, and safety they had known. I could tell how much pain it was causing my sons to have that short and monitored phone call with me that I came to not want to do that to them. I still did; I wanted to hear their voices -even with how pathetic they sounded, I wanted them to hear my voice. I decided it was better to at least maintain some kind of contact with them, even if it was brief and strained. I made the calls brief.

Where to begin? Family Secrets. Physical Abuse. Emotional Abuse. Undeniable Child Sexual Abuse. Domestic Violence. A PPO. Extreme mind fuckery. The Fucked-up Court in Northern Michigan, and the fucked-up family courts in general. The sorely incompetent and biased Washtenaw County CPS. Corrupt police officers, hateful and vengeful caseworkers, and police officers from Kentucky to Northern Michigan. A misogynistic custody evaluator is playing God. All the experts, and..... all the *"experts."* Polygraphs. A GAL deficient of a single moral code. Money, and lack thereof. Child *"Advocacy"* Clinics. Child *"Protection"* Services. My sons have been sexually acting out since before they were 4 and 2 and continuing for years, having been introduced to pornography at these very young ages -beginning porn addictions for both. Emotional and behavioral problems were ignored and covered up by their small-town school and their paternal family. Attorneys, judges, and referees. Lies and more lies. The *entire case file* having been sent to Washtenaw County - completely sealed by some unknown authority in Antrim County. Attorneys with integrity are getting screwed, and attorneys without integrity are getting everything. Hmmm? This isn't a start at the beginning and end at the end type of book. For one thing, this story hasn't ended.

My heart is an ever-growing black hole.
All my hopes have gone there to die.

My sadness grows darker and heavier,
pulling me deep into this endless black hole.

This sadness, I fear, will win.

-Me

In a closed back room of a northern Michigan courthouse, the fate of my young sons was decided by men who knew nothing about child sexual abuse, not to mention domestic violence, post-traumatic stress disorder, trauma, incest, or basic child development. Of those contemplating their fate were my ex-husband's malevolent and sleazy attorney, whose only ambition was to win his case at all costs. The GAL is absent of any sense of purpose or moral character and one who will take the easiest route to the finish line. My attorney, even armed with the knowledge he had, the massive amount of research and contacting of experts in the field he did, had the defect of integrity; he didn't have a chance. But he fought like hell. There were several different judges throughout our case. In retrospect, it was unrealistic of me, not only naïve, to even think that my sons could have had the opportunity to have been protected. How can anybody make reasonable decisions when they don't understand what it is they are hearing, seeing, and supposed to conclude on? If they don't fully understand domestic violence, natural child development vs. what an abused child may display throughout their development, child abuse, child sexual abuse, recanting, incest, and on and on, well then, they will not make very good decisions on cases that have those factors or allegations at play now, will they? The other major factor is our system is set up for failure in these cases. There are longstanding, ingrained beliefs that defy the truth, but they have been there so long that it is not only customary; it is natural for judges to lean into these biases and falsehoods. They haven't had to live with these consequences yet, and it seems until they do, they are unable to wrap their aloof heads around it, and they decline to try to understand.

The immediate or short-term effects of sexual abuse vary from child to child (Deblinger, Lippman, & Steer, 1996). The more severe the abuse, the more likely the child will be symptomatic (Kendall-Tackett et al. 1993). John Meyer concluded on the impact of sexual abuse that "molestations that included a close perpetrator: a high frequency of sexual contact; a long duration; the use of force; and sexual acts that included oral, anal, or vaginal penetration led to a greater number of symptoms for victims" (Myer, John).

Our divorce was final at the end of June 2006; I was awarded primary custody, with X having every other weekend parenting time. The boys and I lived in Kentucky at that time, and their father lived in Northern Michigan. He wanted to combine his parenting time for July, combining two weekends, his birthday and Father's Day, allowing him to have the boys for an entire week. (I didn't learn until much later that the court doesn't care about parents' birthdays; I am embarrassed at how naïve I continued to be). I very reluctantly agreed.

I called to check on them that week, as we agreed I would do. Their father never once picked up when I called. If he called back, he placed the boys on speaker phone to talk with me. It was disturbing to me how they sounded. I heard terror and pain in their voices. My mother's instinct, so far, has never ever been wrong. I knew something was wrong then, as I suspected earlier. Unfortunately for me, as well as for my children, I was, and still am, undeniably spot on in my sensing of something wrong, of my sons being afraid or being hurt, and of their feelings of terror and pain. I instinctively knew they were not okay.

I kept myself as busy as I could the week they were gone. They had never been gone that long from me before. I nearly worked myself to death. I tore out the carpet, I moved furniture, I painted, I cleaned, I repaired faucets, and I took a lot of sleeping pills at night, a lot of them, a habit I have maintained to this day.

At the end of the week, I met their father to pick the boys up somewhere between our home in KY and where they were in MI. I couldn't have possibly been happier to see them. Their eyes were empty, seemingly soulless, having the 'deer in the headlight' look. They were not the same boys I dropped off a week earlier. My youngest son had a huge knot and bruise on his forehead above his eye. I would learn later that his father kicked him in the head to stop him from climbing a ladder behind him.

Sometime after we got home, Gabriel went into the bathroom. I was doing the dishes in the kitchen, and Castiel was already in bed. I heard Gabriel yell from the bathroom: "mom, it hurts. I can't poop. Dad stuck a stick up my butt." Gabriel didn't poop. He also didn't look like he needed emergency medical attention (I probably should have taken him to the ER right then, anyway). I waited and took him to the doctor he knew in the morning instead of taking him to an emergency room on a Sunday night with a bunch of people he was not familiar with.

We went to the doctor's office the next morning. While at the doctor's office, Gabriel said his dad had stuck a stick up his butt, and his butt hurt. He pointed to his anus and said it hurts "up in there." Later, Gabriel would become very constipated, so his doctor took an x-ray to show him there was nothing still stuck up his butt and prescribed a laxative.

A couple of weeks later, I put a movie on for the boys, which ironically was "The Rescuers," and I went to take a shower. I came out of the bathroom and discovered that Gabriel had taken Castiel's clothes off and was attempting to put his penis in Castiel's bottom. I didn't have to ask but I did, and I knew the answer before Gabriel answered: "Where did you learn this?" he mumbled that his dad taught him. This memory will be forever singed and frozen in time in my head. I will always deeply regret the way I handled this incident.

This is just one of the thousands of memories and flashbacks that haunt me daily, hypnotizing me into deeper despair, spinning round and round my head, choking my hopes and dreams. I attempt to redirect my mind to all of our wonderful times in Kentucky, but sadly, they are rapidly overtaken by traumatic ones, leaving me with guilt, anger, and sorrow. As the memories replay themselves, the emotions grow the tremendous grief for my sons and all they have gone through, their bodies and their minds. Their confusion, anger, pain, and mistrust. My sadness, anger, and guilt for mishandling situations such as the one above, and my relentless guilt that I have not been able to protect my sons.

I will never forgive myself for scooping Castiel up and leaving Gabriel alone, sitting on the floor with his feelings to deal with as such a young child. He must have felt so shamed; Gabriel, too, needed 'scooped up,' as the reason he had done what he did was clear; -he too had been hurt and, indeed, raped. My sons were ages 4 and 2 when this incident happened.

Please do not judge my sons, especially for their sexualized behavior. This is what sexually abused children do; their brains are not developed enough to understand what has happened to them, so they re-enact the abuse for at least a couple of different reasons. The first reason is they are trying to make sense of it, it is their brain's way of making that attempt. Second, they want to gain control over it. In these circumstances, it is not being done to them against their will. It's not exactly their choice either, as it is because of the original abuse trauma. I ask you to keep this in mind as you read this and remember my sons are now adults, that was their past. Is it still affecting them? Damn right, it is. However, they are survivors, and they have already beaten unsurmountable odds. I am very proud of both of them.

Damn right, I'm a maniac.
You better watch your back.
'cause I'm fuckin' up your program ....

Just give me somethin' to break.
How bout your fuckin' face
I hope you know I packed a chain saw what?!...
A chain saw what?!...

A motherfucking chain saw-what?!...
So come and get it

-

Limp Bizkit, Break Stuff

My sons shed their innocence long ago. However, my boys didn't "shed" it as a reptile grows out of its skin and into brand new skin or like a butterfly metamorphosizes from a worm into a beautiful, winged creature. My sons had their innocence taken. They had their innocence cruelly, sadistically, and brutally ripped away by a man they were supposed to be able to love and trust, their father. Then, they were further abused by the entire "system" that is supposed to help them. There isn't anyone or anything who can ever right that wrong.

"What's This Life For?"

Hurray for a child
That makes it through.
If there's any way
Because the answer lies in you
They're laid to rest.
Before they've known just what to do
Their souls are lost.
Because they could never find

What's this life for

-

Creed, My Own Prison

13

When there was a disclosure of abuse, and the boys were in the custody of the paternal family, my sons were forced to endure group intimidation, humiliation, and shaming by the paternal family. These are some of the classic textbook behaviors, maneuvers, and tactics incestuous families utilize to keep their secret and keep up the facade they have created. I have learned of many of these tactics for years while my sons were in their primary custody. The paternal family works together, similar to a cult. There are many, many layers of abuse that my sons have endured. It's difficult to conceive, even for me, who had been "in" the family for several years. The teamwork of this family was like other mammals such as hyenas or troglodytes, who work together in hunting, but they also target a weaker member, engage in infanticide, etc. It seemed all so neatly polished as if they had been doing this for generations. It is my speculation, and that of several professionals, that this is indeed the case; -it has been going on for generations. As I look back to when I first met the family, little did I know at the time that I, too, was being groomed. Hindsight seems to always be the best lens to look through and discover many truths that were not seen at the time. There were so many red flags that should have sent me running.

From Goodwin: "Psychotherapists regularly encounter patients who describe an incest experience matter-of-factly, sometimes as an aside to a more "important" memory or problem...Few psychiatrists would argue about the damaging potential for children who grow up in the most extremely disturbed incest families, where a psychotic parent sadistically abuses the children physically and sexually. The perpetrator's use of physical force, death threats to the child or to other family members, the child's fears about his or her own physical sensations, the absence of any mirroring or comforting parent figure, the confusing quality of the rationalization or paranoid thinking used by some families – all of these increases the traumatic potential of the incest experience." Sexual Abuse, Goodwin P.).

"This" has been going on for so long. It's really all they know. It *is* what is normal.

"The world breaks everyone, and afterward, some are stronger at the broken places."

- Ernest Hemmingway.

Gabriel's scariest moment: he wrote in a journal that was being taken from me. Mine too. After all I've gone through, car accidents, being trampled by a horse, everything their father has done to me personally, my spotted history with different traumatic events: By far, the most painful, destructive, and traumatic was when my sons were taken and the abuse by their father and the paternal family that was allowed to continue. Nothing could come close to that devastation.

My oldest son, Gabriel, was always afraid of his father. He was afraid of him from infancy. He would cry whenever I would pass him to his father, but not when I let my family members (such as my mom) carry him. He usually didn't cry at all with my mom holding him. In contrast, even when his father came driving in the driveway after work, he'd begin to cry, and he'd stop whatever he was doing and run to me. What an idiot I am that I didn't leave him then, right? Yet, I'd console him; his father would come in and get angry that I was consoling him and start firing off questions about what I had been saying about him during the day. My son was less than two at the time, and I most certainly was not complaining about my husband to my two-year-old son while he was away at work. I remember that specific cry from Gabriel. It was a fearful cry; he would run and cry and cling and cry; it was a horrible position to be in as a mother, and I can imagine a much more horrible position to be in as a young child. I just couldn't put the pieces together at that time. But these experiences built the foundation of the horror that was to come.

My sons were taken from me and given back to me incrementally, only as shells of their former selves. Not only that, inside of these shells held thousands of new wounds, hurts that have never been tended to because nobody cared or was allowed to -or were tended to properly, ex. Getting stitches when they needed stitches. Those shells became armor of a sort that assisted them in becoming completely different children: very angry, traumatized, sad, and in pain. Both are doing things that they never would have done had they been left in safety. It is important that I speak for them. There are laws that need to be changed and policies created in this country for the states to protect children more effectively instead of unilaterally working against each other and against the children they are supposed to protect.

The nights and days turned into weeks and months. Then months turned into years. I worried about what my children were doing and what was being done to them. What were they learning, and what habits and morals were being imprinted onto them? Nights came and went; I had to learn how to go to bed without reading my sons a bedtime story and tucking them in. It took a lot of sleeping pills, a lot then and still to this day, but I was finally able to fall asleep some of the time. Every night, my brain rehashed traumas in the form of nightmares, which also continue to this day. Rainbows came and went without them, and sunflowers bloomed and died, as did the rose garden I planted for them. Two of their dogs died -as well as a cat and a horse. Papa left and moved to Florida. Storms blew and shook our house, lightning flashed, and thunder crashed. Tornadoes touched down nearby. Wars were waged in other countries -how I longed to comfort my sons.

January 15th, 2008, my sons were suddenly picked up from the safety of their preschool and placed into the custody of people they hadn't seen in over a year; the longest time they'd ever been away from me was when they'd spent an incredibly traumatic week with their father in which they had obviously endured despicable incidents, to say the least since it was why we were in this mess, to begin with.

I have fought CPS and the family court system for the privilege of protecting my young sons since 2005. My oldest son first made an allegation (although I didn't quite realize it at the time) of sexual abuse against his father when he was 3 years old (2004); he is now 22. My sons, one or the other, or both, have individually alleged their father has stuck a stick up their butt, stuck his penis in their butt, stuck his penis in their mouths, made them put their mouths on his penis, said that he has "peed" on their backs and in their butts and in their mouths, and many more similar statements. My oldest son also demonstrated with two anatomically correct dolls, the father doll anally penetrating the son doll, and drew on anatomically correct boy pictures exactly "where" his father hurt him on the front of his body and the back of his body, mouth and penis on the front, bottom on the back while meeting with his therapist in Kentucky (while he was 4, this therapist would later turn on us like a rattlesnake and contribute to my sons being placed back with their abusive father). My oldest son also told a psychoanalyst his dad laughed at him when he screamed; this was when he was describing his dad putting his penis in his butt and that it hurt; his dad apparently thought that was funny. These are only a fraction of the sexual abuse allegations. There are many more physical abuse allegations and emotional and psychological abuse allegations. I was there to witness and experience many of them.

I was originally granted primary custody, and their father had every other weekend. He never wanted more. Until allegations of sexual abuse surfaced, then he decided he wanted full custody. We went through a long custody battle, which began with the allegations of abuse but morphed into the primary focus of the entirety of the case being on my mental fitness and whether my sons should remain with me for any amount of time at all. The Referee of the case, even though it was clear she had made her mind up at the beginning, after going through many tests, assessments, and the like, granted him primary physical custody, which he had until after my oldest son reached 18 and my youngest son was 15; -12 long painful and horrifying years. Initially, I could only see them in a supervised location (Yes, I had supervised visitation intermittently, at least 3 separate time periods). Then, the court ordered that I see them every other weekend and on Wednesdays after school until 7:00 p.m. Much later, it was every other week from Wednesday to Monday. It wasn't until my youngest son had charges pressed against him for destruction of property that his time was split (I had him half of the time), but only for him because their father would not agree to his older brother spending half of his time with me. He didn't agree to Gabriel staying that long with me until after we went in front of a reviewer, who actually agreed to lie on the paperwork -to appease X and reduce his child support, stating I made much more money than I did, so their father would only have to pay the very least in child support, and this only after I waived thousands of dollars in back child support (I agreed to the lie because it was the only way I was going to be able to spend more time with my oldest son as well). Then, X did not follow through on that until after the paperwork had gone through the entire court process, although I had already signed off on the thousands of dollars of back child support. In fact, Gabriel was already 18 when he was able to come to stay with me at half-time. That was not the first time X failed to follow through with a verbal agreement. Even though this one, he finally followed through, but it wasn't on the timeline originally agreed upon.

The pandemic came around the same time as the above was happening. I am thankful for the pandemic. Of course, I'm not thankful that there were many people who died, and it caused much heartache and pain for so many. What I'm thankful for is X will do whatever it takes to avoid getting sick -he used to send the kids to school sick just to get them out of his house. In the case of Covid, he wanted them to stay with me until it blew over. Fortunately for us, that took a long time, and neither of them ever went back.

One of the other times he had not followed through was many years earlier. The boys were still quite young, and I was still fighting in court for custody of them, pulling my mom into depths of debt we were still trying to climb out of. At that time, he told me if I pulled my parenting time and custody case from further court action, he would agree to a 50/50 parenting time arrangement at that time. He never ever followed through with that. Day after day, month after month, became year after year, that he kept making one excuse after another as to why he wasn't agreeable to that at that particular time - even though he had already said he was agreeable. As critical time passed, he continued to make excuses as to why the boys could not be with me half of the time. The excuses included that the place I lived in was too small, I did this and didn't do that, and on and on. Time was narrow and restricted from the court for my sons and me, as was reminded to me by my sons' father and his wife frequently. So, consequently, that never happened. Since I had continued to be naïve, I never had gotten anything in writing, so there was no way of fighting him on that.

The court and the caseworkers followed many years-long repeated failure after failure to protect my sons, a precedence set by Washtenaw County CPS, which seemed to be in large part based on a discredited custody evaluation that was exploited by my ex-husband. There were many other reports that were ignored by CPS, even an assessment by a renowned child sexual-abuse expert and clinic, giving their findings that my sons had exhibited behaviors demonstrating they had been sexually abused by their father. She (the expert) also witnessed physical abuse perpetrated by their father in the clinic right in front of her. CPS had also been given a transcript of my son disclosing to a psychoanalyst - giving many details, as well as a report by a renowned psychological testing evaluator and an intensive report by the Court Appointed Counselor Coordinator, who was also the psychiatrist who had seen all family members, even extended family members. None of the reports that really mattered, mattered to the agency that was charged with the task of "protecting" children.

My mind jumps back in time, back and forth to different time periods, as it frequently does, and my body steps into each of the houses in which X and I lived. Every day, floods of flashbacks and memories I don't want to remember to rush through my head. I'm always overcome with emotion; usually, it's anger or rage or deep, deep sadness. Other times, I feel sick to my stomach, my head starts to spin and ache, and my chest pounds, and as hard as I try to redirect my mind, it keeps coming back to whatever has gotten me worked up, to begin with. Music helps as a distractor and exercise, too. But there is nothing that ever stops the flashbacks and floods of memories.

I've decided what might be helpful at this juncture for both you and me is for me to 'get out' some of these incidents that interrupt my thinking, my mood, and basically me being who I used to be and who I wish I could be again-which was a thoughtful, caring, fairly carefree and happy-go-lucky type of person. As were my sons, so sweet, generous, loving, kind, joyful, innocent, carefree, and happy. If I write all of these incidents as they flowed, you would be looking at an encyclopedia rather than a book. So, I'm saving us both from that!

There were plenty of huge warning signs that I did not heed regarding X and his family. To think that I could have spared my sons any of this torture and madness had I done anything differently always delivers a huge, powerful punch in my gut.

So, the following are some brief, some lengthy incidents in a bullet point format, that are listed in a loosely followed chronological order. Often, many things happen so close together that, admittedly, they may be a bit mish-mashed.

I remember more from when we lived up north -the last place we all lived together. It had escalated so much, and there were now two children, a very big, hostile, violent, and demanding man who only seemed to gain more and more strength in those characteristics every day. Then, there was the week the boys spent with him after the entry of divorce. I heard from them about that week and saw the shape they were in when they came back to me. There are, of course, many things from the years X had custody, and I saw them very little and their descriptions of their living conditions plus what I saw on their bodies that matched those descriptions, many investigations, and the boys being taken from me repeatedly. Then, spending a bit more time with them and how they acted, looked, what they said, what they did not say, fears and behaviors, I knew what was happening at the other house by their actions, all the actions and inactions taken by the school; stuff I was informed of, the plethora of things I was never informed of, all throughout these years, then there were court actions on both boys. Theft, destruction of property, etc., each boy had probation at different times, and there were juvenile court hearings. Now that both of them are older, they realize they have a choice, and they choose to have nothing to do with any of the paternal family -immediate as well as extended. They also validate the things they told me when they were younger, and to my great dismay, I find that the things I felt in my gut were happening but had not yet had verbal confirmation were spot on, and with some other things, what was going on was even worse than I had intuitively felt was happening.

Storm Brewing

- I first met X at the bar his family owned and ran. I waited tables and I was a bartender. Honestly, at this point, I felt sorry for X because it seemed that his sister was favored by his parents, and he was 'stuck' cooking at the bar, which he claimed he didn't want to have anything to do with.

- I noticed X would chastise the locals coming in and call them crude names. He did this in the back while he was cooking. He never did this to their faces. However, it was a small restaurant, and I really don't know how they couldn't have heard him. He thought he was so big and bad, even as he cowered in the kitchen and blurted out negative statements. Admittedly, at first, I thought it was a little bit funny, but it didn't take me too long before I realized it was mean and cowardly.

- X and I began hanging out on Fridays and Sundays, as the Tavern was closed on Sundays.

- Shortly after I began dating X, I was at a nearby local small-town bar. The bartender and owner of the establishment (who was always there and seemingly 'knew' everything about everybody; he also was friends with one of X's ex-girlfriends) made an interesting comment to me once he found out I was dating X; "just don't drop the soap" several people at the bar laughed like they knew something I didn't.

- I was thrilled when X's father told me they had a horse a long time ago. I had horses all my life -until fairly recently.

Having had that privilege afforded to me by my parents is, in large part, what shaped me as a person. But then X's father laughed and said they "shot it" because it bucked X's mother off once. Because he was laughing, and because I didn't know them, I sincerely thought he was joking (not a very funny joke, granted, but I didn't think it was true). That was unimaginable to me. However, he wasn't joking.

- I got pregnant once before we were married. The paternal family pressured me and basically forced me to get an abortion. I didn't want to get that abortion, but now I know why they pressured me so much. I could have had a baby, then left X, and he may not have had the legal rights he had being married to me, at that time at least. They said it was because I didn't have insurance. But I worked for them. They could have easily rectified that problem. Had I known more, I could have gotten Medicaid, and I'm sure I would have qualified. They also said, "it just isn't the right time." I know what that meant now. They wanted rights for the child. I fainted immediately following the procedure. The staff revived me with smelling salts. X never asked me how I felt emotionally or physically following the procedure. He knew I wanted a baby and that I wanted to be a mother. He was so robotic and unemotional I don't know how I didn't see it. X and his family had ulterior motives and a lot to say prior to the abortion but offered nothing after, no support, no empathy, nothing. This was my loss to deal with on my own. In fact, it's a bit ironic, isn't it? A red flag was on fire before we were married. Even before I had children, they ripped away my dream of having children.

- The paternal family thought I was dumb, like his sister. But I learned to play dumb to placate X. At least it stopped many temper tantrums and rages from him, even before they began. He had a superiority complex, and he enjoyed thinking I was dumb and he was smart and running the household. But I certainly wasn't dumb. There were things I knew that he didn't know I knew, and there were also things that he had successfully kept hidden from me, mostly because of technology, and I didn't care enough about technology to figure it out! However, the main point is there were things I knew that he couldn't have imagined I knew. I just didn't quite know how to get the evidence of his lowly endeavors.

- X's adult sister, when she was about 25 or 26, told me at the bar that she had some kind of bugs biting her or a rash between her breasts. She said she had a bunch of red dots underneath and in between her breasts and that she showed her father and her brother to see what they thought it was. She had quite large breasts, and she usually had a lot of cleavage showing (which was admittedly always a pet peeve of mine; I just thought it was gross). The fact that she went to her father and her brother with her red dots between and underneath her breasts rather than her mother, a female friend, or, for an even more shocking idea, maybe a doctor, is very strange to me. I thought about it and put myself in her shoes and would have never even thought of going to my dad or my brother about something like that, much less, showing them. If one is really looking for clarification for these red dots, I would say a medical professional would be the best bet. Needless to say, I was appalled. (X had never mentioned this to me, interestingly). But these are the same people who watch vulgar, gruesome, and savage deaths of people together and watch pornography together, and it was also my suspicion that there were cameras hidden in the bar that they watched together, especially since X had them hidden in our home and we later found out that the boys were being viewed on camera by X in their father's house. I don't think behaviors such as this simply pop out of

24

nowhere. I think they are learned, normalized, continued, increased and metastasized.

- I would come home from work and find him and his sister viewing pornography together.

- Interestingly, when I got home or came into work while they were viewing sordid, objectionable, and inappropriate shows or videos on the bar TV, his father and/or his sister always seemed to have to go. They never watched whatever they were watching with me present. I would never have watched that anyway, but they saw me and very suddenly turned it off and 'had to go.'

- Prior to being married to X, elder members of both sides of his family took me aside individually and told me to be a 'good wife.'

- Shortly after, I moved into the house next to his parents, when it was clear I was getting more than meets the eye, but I was not heeding any of the red flags. There were several incidents. His parents had a middle-aged dog, a golden retriever, who was a very sweet dog. He was at our house one summer day, and I was petting him. He had a terribly offensive smell; I found the cause for the smell to be maggots that were in a wound he had. I washed him and washed all of the maggots out. I was pretty upset that this was the shape that he was in. They never let him inside, even though there were plenty of ways they could have done that, and he would not have had to go into the main portion of the house if that was what they were worried about, but they didn't do that. He was terrified of storms and would travel miles to try to escape a storm. They were never concerned - they said he'd find his way back eventually. All they had to do was to care a little bit for him, keep his wound cleaned out and dressed and take even just a little better care of him. They didn't do any of that. They chose instead to have him euthanized. He would have lived years longer if they had just taken care of him. All they had was one dog: -him. Anyway, they replaced him within a week or so with a new golden retriever puppy. I just felt very sad thinking of the puppy's future. So, you know, I find euthanasia the most kind and compassionate alternative for an animal in many circumstances. I have had to make this very difficult choice before, and it is no less heartbreaking now than it was then. However, I think when an animal is healthy and fairly happy, to choose euthanasia simply because one has grown tired of the animal is not ok.

- Before I had met them, X's sister somehow got tickets for a Republican National Convention. (-I'm going to bite my tongue and keep my politics to myself!) It was held in Texas or maybe Louisianna, I think. She was given an extra ticket and could take whomever she wanted. She didn't take her best female friend with her, she didn't take her boyfriend with her, she could have taken anybody, but alas, she chose to take her brother with her. Years after, she was still joking about how drunk they got, how he held her hair out of the way when she got too drunk and was throwing up, and about how many people thought they were husband and wife or girlfriend and boyfriend, and how after a while, they just let them think that. It seems rather strange to me, but she thought this was just hilarious -especially the 'letting them think that' part.

- We got married. I admit that I really wanted to have children, and I felt that my time was quickly running out. So, I just wanted to get married. I think it could almost have been anybody.

- His family came and went in and out of the house we lived in regularly. However, it was where I lived, too, not just X.

My family never barged in on each other, ever. Wherever we lived, we respected each other's privacy. When I lived in apartments or in houses with friends, we always respected each other's privacy as well, I never expected anything less. So, I was used to a bit of privacy, and I would go to the bedroom from the bathroom wearing just a towel to get my clothes, and I didn't worry about it. That was until his father barged in, and I was in the shower nearest the front door. I had left the bathroom door open to let the steam out. Consequently, his father caught me getting into a towel. I was angry and felt violated. No boundaries in that family. His whole family just came and went as they pleased, no matter the time, what we were doing or planning on doing, nothing. None of them knew much less respected boundaries.

- Regarding his father, he and X were discussing some things about a particular bedroom that we were all in. -A big tree fell against the house in a storm and moved the entire house on its foundation, so there was a lot of damage - and I worked my butt off on that stupid house. We were discussing work in that particular room, and I was sitting down on the bed in the same room with my legs crossed and up on the bed, leaning back on the wall. Suddenly, his father jumped right on top of me as I was on the bed. He didn't get right off either. He thought it was the funniest thing, as did his son. I did not find it funny in the least.

- So, I bitched enough about the 'catching me getting into a towel incident' that we moved to the small apartment on my mom's property; it was alright to not pay rent to my mom, despite him having paid his parents rent for years (I wonder what he did with all that extra money?). X's family gave me the cold shoulder for a while after we moved, even though

X said he had told them that he would "tell them later" why we moved when his father asked, but his father made a shitty comment about having to get an invitation to come over to see us. So, I'm sure X told them lots of things about me and why we moved out. -All because of me, no doubt.

- X told me that when he was younger, he and his dad had taken his sister's cat 'down the road' and 'dumped it.' They didn't like the cat. Apparently, it didn't matter that she did, as much as she could like an animal anyway. All these years, they've let her think it ran away.

- Stray cats would come around occasionally, and X told me that if ever a stray cat was on his porch, he would pick it up, throw it against the side of the house, laugh, hiss, and run after it. I saw him do this on one occasion. When I say he hissed at the cats, that's exactly what he did. He made this loud hissing noise, he'd have a wild expression on his face, he'd wave and reach his arms up and all over, and chase and stomp after them as if he was going to attack them. When I say I saw him do this on one occasion, that's in reference to throwing a cat up against the house. I saw him kick, stomp and run after, terrorize, hiss, and yell at the cats frequently.

- X's sister 'handed down' to me her underwear and bras, with the comments between her and her brother. I never wore any of those, even if they would have fit. She never 'handed down' any other clothes, just those underwear and bras. It wasn't about them being used items. So you know, I haven't purchased a new piece of clothing in a very long time (for myself anyway). I always buy used ones. Thrift stores are my thing! It's just that these were her bras and underwear, and after the comment at the bar, I felt a bit uncomfortable wearing those items of clothing. Also, I am significantly smaller than her. In the big picture, when I look back and consider the relationship between her and her brother, I find it strange.

- X is a pathological liar, a sociopath and a narcissist. He's controlling, abusive, mentally, emotionally, verbally, psychologically, physically, and sexually. He's an addict. He's a sadist. He enjoys inflicting pain and watching someone or something (animals) suffer. He gaslights and manipulates, and he can make you and others think there is something wrong with you rather than him. His family helps him and are contributors to these abuses. They are 'good' at mind games in that they are successful in attaining their goals. They are controlling, demented, diabolical, incestuous, and abusive themselves.

LIVING AT MY MOM'S, IN THE APARTMENT ACROSS THE DRIVEWAY:

- Gabriel was born while we lived in the apartment next to my mom's house. I really liked that my mom was there, and I liked the place.

- After Gabriel was born, my mom came up into the apartment to see him and check on how we all were doing. She noticed his darkish-yellow skin and how quiet he was. I just thought he was content and hadn't noticed his skin darkening because it happened slowly, and I always had him in my arms. She was shocked. She said he needed to go to the hospital right then because he was jaundiced. She probably saved his life. I did not know. X nearly refused to take him to the hospital because he couldn't stand the thought of my mom being right and him being wrong. He said she didn't know what she was talking about, she didn't know anything, and that Gabriel was fine. I finally got him to go because of

29

how lethargic, dark, and uninterested in food Gabriel was, I'd never had a baby before - so I didn't realize how abnormal it was until my mom came over. We got to the hospital, and they got him right in. His bilirubin level was frighteningly high; he needed a double-volume blood transfusion. He had to be in an incubator with lights on him all the time except to eat. He was so small. He was there for what seemed like forever. X never wanted to go to the hospital, and I just wanted to stay at the hospital, but I knew he wouldn't have taken care of the animals at home. I always wanted to be with Gabriel, but it was as if it was a hassle, a pain in the ass for X to be with our child in intensive care. It was killing me not to be with him. X would say things like, "he doesn't even know who we are, he doesn't miss us, he doesn't know we're not there." Astounding and shocking, to say the least.

- Soon after Gabriel came home after spending time in the NICU, whenever he would cry, X would say how much he couldn't "deal with his crying." X said he cried too much and that he hated listening to the sound of a baby crying because it irritated him so much. I tried to always be caring for Gabriel, as X would get very angry, hold him too tightly, shake him, yell at him, and I was afraid he would hurt him. On this note, a few years later, after Castiel was born, it was the same thing with the crying. I always took care of all things child and household, and it was only if I had something else I needed to take care of at that moment that X would need to be responsible for a child, but that was incredibly difficult, as several times I caught X holding Castiel tightly, yelling at him, shaking him, and even holding his large hand over his mouth to muffle the sound.

- When I had Gabriel, I did not want to leave him and go back to work. I also feared for his safety if I left him with his father while I was at work. So, I told X I didn't want to go back to work. I wanted to stay home with Gabriel. He was furious and complained incessantly. He made me sell my car to stay at home. There was nothing owed on that car, so it was only costing insurance to keep it. It was purchased several years earlier. Of course, I got rid of my car. I don't remember seeing any of the money, but I did what I had to do to stay home with my son. However, X was going into the office at that time, so I was left in a rural area with an infant and no transportation in case of an emergency. Eventually, my mom would purchase another car and give me her previous one as she did not want us to be without a car.

- X killed one of my elder cats while flying out of the driveway at my mom's house. He didn't stop. He never showed any empathy or sympathy or was ever apologetic. The cat's name was Genisis, I found him at a park my friends and I were at while in high school. He was very old and had been with me for a long time. Of course, I was terribly upset.

MUNITH:

- X threw the boys up high in the air even when I asked him not to do that -repeatedly. Really high. You could see that it scared the boys. It wasn't fun or funny to them.

- "Dada spank me," Gabriel said tearfully as he came running towards me; I had just come home from the grocery store when we lived in Munith. Of course, his father very tersely responded, "I did not, no, I didn't, don't believe him, he's lying." He had never been 'spanked' before -that I knew of anyway; he was a toddler. How did he even know the word 'spanking,' or what a spanking was, if he hadn't been spanked?

31

- I didn't want my sons to ever be spanked, but he spanked and continued to do it, and then it got worse when the boys were at his house (after being separated from me) because it was not only him who was spanking them, at the very least, it also included his father.

- X would live trap animals and tell me he was going to release them but kill them instead.

- When I was pregnant carrying Castiel, I was really sick and had migraines constantly. X's stress, attitude, and contempt made it all that much worse. I jokingly told him not to tell me where his guns were because I was so miserable I didn't trust myself when I was in that much pain. I never would have ended my life. Not for a millisecond would I have left Gabriel. I knew that. However, I'm not sure X did. So, the very next day, X said he wanted to show me something down in the basement. His 'office' had been down there, the laundry machine was down there, etc. so I didn't think much of it. This was when I was at least 8 months pregnant. He walked me over to an area and told me to look up. There, out in the open and just resting on low ceiling beams, lay all of his guns within easy reach. I was shocked. He saw the expression on my face and added, in case of an intruder or something. The very next morning, after X left for work, I noticed a couple of boxes and a bunch of loose bullets on the kitchen counter right next to the stairway downstairs. I had never seen loose bullets sitting out, ever. Not in that house or any place we had lived prior.

- When I was pregnant carrying Castiel, X had come home from work. I had supper made. He said he wanted canned pineapples (it was out of character for him to especially request any fruit, and it was odd; it's not as if pineapples were a favorite fruit of his). He kept pushing the pineapples on me, and I don't remember him eating any pineapples. I thought that was strange. I suddenly went into labor the next morning after he had left for work. My 2-year-old son Gabriel was so calm, and he got me the help I needed. I tried calling X many times and could not get a hold of him -trying that many times and not being able to get him is rare. I think it was Gabriel who called my mother and 911. When 911 showed up, Gabriel led the EMTs to the bathroom, where I was on the floor. I didn't find out until a bill came in the mail from the ambulance company that while I was upstairs in labor at the hospital, X was downstairs arguing with the ambulance staff about paying the bill. He had told them he was not going to pay for it and was yelling and swearing and being belligerent to the people around him. In fact, if it hadn't been for Gabriel and the ambulance, I would have been in labor by myself at home. I didn't know about any of this until I called regarding the bill. The lady who answered knew all about it and she told me, I was embarrassed and appalled. She felt bad for me and waived away the very large debt.

- Both boys were born with higher-than-normal bilirubin levels. As I've stated previously, Gabriel had to go back to the hospital and go into intensive care, have a double-volume blood transfusion, and stay in the NICU in an incubator under bilirubin lights. Castiel and I went to a different hospital than where he was born and had to stay in the hospital. He, too, was in an incubator under bilirubin lights. He was sent home with an incubator and a Bili blanket.

- While I was in the hospital with Castiel, X had Gabriel. We were only in there for 6 or 7 days. But in that short amount of time, Gabriel was mimicking his father smoking a cigarette; he mimicked many of his father's very harsh facial expressions, and he had acquired his rude and aggressive attitude. Fortunately, that didn't stay with him long, at least that time.

- While living in Munich, X's father came to see X. They were outside looking at a lawn mower or some other gas-powered piece of equipment. Gabriel was outside with them. I looked out the window once and noticed X and his father talking and laughing, but I didn't see Gabriel, which caused me concern. Shortly thereafter, Gabriel came running inside crying and had a baseball size burn on his calf. X and his dad were hee-ing and haw-ing and not paying one bit of attention to where Gabriel was or what he was doing. They didn't notice he was too close to an extremely hot surface; they didn't even know he was crying because he had gotten burned. They didn't even bring him in to doctor his leg. Seriously. He had a big burn that he had gotten from the exhaust. I doctored it, and I never trusted the two of them to pay attention to my children again. -However, there wasn't much I could do about that when X gained custody.

- When Gabriel was very young, between 1 and 2, X wanted me to take a picture of his little butt -he liked his little butt. Granted, that may seem petty, but knowing the context of what came after, it doesn't sound petty anymore.

BELLAIRE:

- X would get angry with me when our oldest son would get up the stairs and go into his office, which could happen when I was changing Castiel. But guess what he had in his office? Chocolate and other candy. I did not know this initially, but once I figured out he was giving him candy, well, there you have it. Of course, he's going to go up there.

- On an almost daily basis, when he would come down after work -or during work, X would check my phone calls. I didn't have a cell phone. The only phone I had was a landline (he had a cell phone, though). He would look at the call received history, ask me about phone numbers that he didn't recognize immediately, who they were, and then he would hit redial to see what the last number I called was. It was intimidating, which I'm sure was the point.

- My grandmother and mother came to visit us in Bellaire. They locked the door to the bedroom they stayed in because they were afraid of X. My mom also said she never wanted to come back because X was so rude to them.

- Our arthritic dog was laying, stretched out in the large kitchen floor - where it was easy to walk around her or step over her. However, X didn't like anything or anyone to be in his way. Instead of walking around or over her, as most people would do, he kicked her and yelled, "Move," "MOVE, GET UP, MOVE, MAGGIE, MOVE," and continued to kick her until she pulled herself up off the floor. He did this on many occasions.

- X frequently yelled at Gabriel, who was two-three when we lived up north. I remember being on the phone with my mom on many occasions, and she would hear X call Gabriel a "fucker," "little fucker," a bastard, and other similar names. She was appalled; I tried to call my mom as much as I could for reality checks (although she didn't know that). I stopped calling her as much, though because X would follow me around to listen to what I was saying, and I didn't want her to hear how he yelled at us.

- X wanted supper to be ready and on the table when he came downstairs from work. Sometimes, I could do that. Sometimes, I couldn't do that. There was one day that was forever etched in my memory. Castiel was in his chair at the table. He was crying because he was hungry. Gabriel was mostly beside me while I was getting food, or he'd go over to the table by Castiel. My anxiety immediately jumped as I heard the thundering footsteps coming downstairs from an angry-sounding X. He plopped himself right down at his seat with a very impatient and dismayed look on his face. So, he brought his extra negative energy into the room while Castiel was already crying, because he was hungry. Castiel did not yet have words to express what was going on, and unfortunately, his father never chose to use words rationally. He got what he wanted by using brute force. I could see X's face reddening, his veins popping out of his temples, and his fists clenched as he slammed them down hard on the table. "Shut up, SHUT UP, CASTIEL, she's getting it, SHUT UP, SHUT THE FUCK UP!" X went on. I wish I could say it was like nothing I had ever seen before, but that wouldn't be true. Castiel was around 6 months old then. I put food on the table to calm the biggest baby, and then I immediately got Gabriel and Castiel's food for them.

- Stressful is not a word to describe that experience. I think trauma best describes it. We had two children under 3 years old and X wanted everybody to be quiet at supper time. Ridiculous.

- We were in the living room (the boys and I). I believe Gabriel was watching The Wiggles on TV. Castiel was sleeping in his bouncy seat. I was standing because I had been dancing with Gabriel, but I stopped because I knew something was coming. X came stomping down the stairs -which you could see from where we were. He was clearly very angry and was charging directly at me. X got right up into my face, yelling about something. I remember his face being red, his eyes steely, and his arms and fists tightened and clenched.

He raised his arms to push me, and Gabriel immediately got in front of me.- in between us, X knocked him down, throwing him clear across the floor. Gabriel began to cry, and I immediately rushed to help him up and make sure he was ok. Castiel was abruptly startled awake from his peaceful sleep, afraid and crying. X stormed off upstairs and continued yelling obscenities, calling Gabriel a mama's boy, a sissy, a pussy, a baby, and saying how fucked up Gabriel and I were, etc. Gabriel was around 2 1/2.

- Now that I've introduced name-calling and obscenities, X had many choice names for the boys, as well as me, and some humiliating catch phrases, too. It began with me prior to us being married. For the boys, it began shortly after they were born. Some of these included little fucker, little bastard, little shit, snowflake, loser, dummy, retard, idiot, moron, crazy like your mom (me), wiener, stupid, lazy, worthless, piece of shit, weakling, pussy, sissy, mama's boy, baby, loser, nuts, he told them to shut the fuck up regularly from very early on (especially when they were very young and were crying because they needed something and they did not yet have the words, and Castiel had delayed speech), he yelled at them like he would the dog and the cats, MOVE, get out of the way, and more. For me, he always called me fat, and as I would move around the house, he made loud beeping noises like what heavy machinery makes as it backs up or moves. He called me lard-ass, chunky, loser, cunt. He made noises as I bent down to pick up the boys or clean up toys, and he called me weak and lazy -especially when I had a debilitating migraine. He had no compassion, which served to only make my migraines worse. He never helped, so even when I had a migraine in which I literally could not see or hold my head up, I had to keep going. I would go in to get some of my migraine medications and find the bottles empty because he had taken all my medications (to get a buzz from). He would deny it and gaslight me, but I knew I didn't leave empty bottles in the cabinet. He said and did a lot more to us, but I think you get the picture.

- I'm not sure how many bank accounts he had in total. I learned he signed my name on the taxes for at least a couple of years. I was too busy being a mom to even notice, but if I ever asked about the taxes, and I did at least once, he said that we barely got anything back, and I didn't even question that. Come to find out, he had at least 3 bank accounts, and more than "barely anything" tax refunds were put into his PayPal account for him to gamble with (online) or whatever else you pay money for online.

- X hit my breasts while I was lactating and breastfeeding Castiel. This hurt terribly, as most women can imagine. I believe it's why my body stopped producing milk so soon after Castiel was born. If I didn't know where he was, I was on edge because I never knew if and when I would meet him in the house, he was going to block or barricade me from getting to one or both of the boys -which he frequently did, especially if someone was crying or if he was going to hit me hard in the breast or the crotch. When I said it hurt, he always denied that he hurt me. He'd call me a baby, wussy, or the like. Then, when there were bruises from him doing that, I would sometimes show him, and he would deny they were from him. He reacted the same to me anytime I said what he was doing was hurting one of the boys or me, and then he'd deny the bruise was a result of him. He even tried to blame me for the bruising on the boys sometimes.

- Most of the time, he touched me solely out of anger or to humiliate me in some way.

- X grabbed my wrist and jerked me towards him. I had bruises from that. As well as he would also grab my wrists and just squeeze very hard. He did that on my forearms and upper arms as well; those always left bruises. He squeezed very hard and left bruises on the boys as well, on their arms and legs.

- He repeatedly tried to get me out of the house; he'd suggest grocery shopping, biking, walking, and whatnot. Then, when I didn't bite at his repeated suggestions because I didn't want to leave the children with him, he wanted to take Gabriel with him when he dropped movies off at the video store or when he went to get cigarettes. Gabriel cried and cried and did not want to go, which infuriated X more. So, stupidly, I thought it would be better at the time for Gabriel to go with him than to stay with me based on how I thought X would treat him if he hadn't gone. He clearly wanted time between only him and Gabriel, and the farther away he could get from me, the better. At the time, however, I wasn't seeing it clearly for what it was. I should have listened to Gabriel and trusted his instinct.

- X made it very difficult for me to use the computer at any time, wherever we lived (hiding something?). In Bellaire, every once in a while, when he would go to town for a pack of cigarettes If I could, I'd try to get on to look up whatever it was I wanted to research very quickly. After doing this a couple of times and especially after x asked me about why I was looking up whatever it was, I was looking up -usually horses, I figured out he was checking my history.   Then, I became a bit smarter about my very brief computer time; I used my time much more wisely. I looked at *his* history (once I figured out how to). There was a tremendous amount of disgusting porn, very young people -too young -they looked like children. There was a black screen with titles continuously rolling that apparently one could click on, the titles to view whatever it said it was -they were mostly regarding incest and familial porn and again titles insinuating very young with older people type porn. Etc. Then, I looked at the log for IMs. I found very interesting conversations between X and his father, x and his sister, and X and his colleagues from work who were working from different locations. X, of course, worked from home in a rather rural area of northern Michigan. I had been getting suspicious and was trying to put things together, and many things were happening all at once. The instant messages included conversations with his father asking him if he "still had control of the money" and for him to purchase whatever kind of vehicle he wanted, despite what I wanted -that I could "just Flintstone it" or "thumb it," and "it's your money, right?". Also, conversations with his sister where again he complained about me being a "nag" and his sister telling him that she "will do WHATEVER" he needs her to do. Also, in conversations with his colleague at work, they had pet names for each other, "poopie." He had particular names that he had for me and only used those; he never used my actual name. Instead, I was referred to as the "ball and chain," "the warden," "nag," and more unpleasant names. Furthermore, he told her he was drinking alcohol (long island iced teas) and getting drunk while working, that the neighbor's dog pooped in our yard all the time, and he was going to shoot it. I never saw a dog that wasn't ours on our property. I don't think the neighbors even had a dog.

- He was a pathological liar. He lied to employers, colleagues, family, and 'friends.' Although, I don't think I can refer to them as friends because they really don't know who he is. They know who he wants them to think he is. He lied to them about owning the house next to his parents, he didn't, he rented it. His parents demanded rent, and when we discussed purchasing the house that his dad had purchased

40

dirt cheap years earlier, his dad wanted to get someone out to appraise it, and the cost for us would be based on the appraised value. He lied to them about the Tavern, claiming he had some stake in that, too, which he didn't. He lied a lot about money. He lied about all kinds of things, even just silly things that he seemed to come up with off the cuff as he was talking with somebody.

- Bellaire was the house of horrors, how many things and what things it took for me to realize our lives were in jeopardy and that I needed to get us out of there is embarrassing. My mom was always there for the boys and me, I didn't want to impose on her and her new husband, but she would have never turned us away.

- I always tried to put myself in between X and the boys and X and the animals when he was going to become abusive. I tried to anyway, I just didn't always make it there in time.

- X complained of chest pain. He wanted to go to the hospital. But I had the boys to get ready, the diaper bag, all of that. If he was really worried, he would have wanted an ambulance, right? No, he wanted me to drive him to the hospital. It was a distance to get there, and there was this long straight stretch. X suddenly said pullover, pullover, I think I'm going to throw up. So, he got out of the car and stood near the front right passenger tire well. He looked around and looked back at me as if why are you not getting out of the car? I had two babies in the car, and if he was going to throw up, there wasn't anything I could do. I needed to make sure the children were alright. However, it was very odd. X kept looking around and looking back at me. I had a very strange feeling, and against my better judgment, I got out and walked around the front of the car. There was no throwing up, no salivating as if one is going to throw up, but still

41

strangely looking up and down the road. I know when I'm legitimately sick and feel as if I will throw up, I'm not looking around at anything, I've got saliva coming out my mouth, and then, if I'm going to, I'll throw up, feeling miserable and not wanting to think about or look at anything. However, X had a deviant and malevolent expression on his face. He no more appeared as if he were going to throw up than I appeared to be waltzing in the middle of the road. X, just as normal as ever, said, well, I guess I'm not going to throw up, and turned right around and got back in the car. We went on to the hospital. When he came out, he had been told it might have been a panic attack -which he'd had before, and he knew what it was and what it felt like. So, taking into account all that was going on in the house of horrors at that time: threats, the knife incident, the bathroom door incident, etc., it is my strongest conviction that his chest didn't hurt. He never felt as if he was going to throw up. His plan was for us to get out on that stretch of road that I am over by him all worried (that kind of concern had flown the coop a while ago) and wait for a car to come along for him to push me in front of. It may sound extreme, but that was the answer that "fit." My instinct is always reliable. I've counted on it for a long time now, and it's always correct. This wasn't the first time I felt my life was in danger, and I have been correct about it.

- X used to run out of the house, into the front yard, side yard, whichever, then pull his pants and his underwear down around his knees or ankles, or without them at all, and run and jump around aimlessly. He laughed hysterically and maniacally. He was giddily enjoying this activity. We didn't get a lot of traffic by our house up there, but there was traffic, and when somebody drove by, they would get to see this spectacle of events (everywhere he and I lived together, we lived close to the road). He did this everywhere we lived, but especially here.

- One time, we were all in the large kitchen up north. X had a large butcher knife in one hand and a candlestick in the other hand. He had a crazed expression on his face as if he was losing it again. He was waving both the knife and the candle around, saying he needed to cut the wick of the candle and he was going to do that with the butcher knife -which, of course, made no sense. If the candle wick actually needed to be cut, there was a drawer with a pair of scissors in it immediately to his right. Gabriel was behind him to the left, and Castiel was behind him to the right. All I could think of was how do I get to both of my sons if he is going to crack. It was very frightening. Never in my life will I forget his expressions or the crazed look in his eyes when he is 'losing it.' I'm sure my sons have had plenty of those expressions ingrained in their minds as well. The situation dissipated by him 'deciding' that maybe the wick did not need to be cut after all, he set the knife and the candle both down on the counter and went back upstairs to his office.

- X went on a 'work trip'; it was winter in northern Michigan, and right after he left, we ran out of propane, which is what the house was heated on. The house very quickly became cold. I had an almost 3-year-old and a baby only a few months old. We were all very cold. Of course, I focused on keeping the boys warm. Since X wanted to be in charge, he was in charge of paying the bills, so I was clueless as to who to even call regarding the propane. I called repeatedly, trying to get a hold of X. Once I finally got him, he yelled at me for interrupting him, even after learning of the problem. He eventually got around to calling the propane company. Despite his lack of concern, and because of the kind-hearted people at the propane company, once they learned from me there were two young children in the house, the propane company came right out as soon as they could to get our heat going. Thank God for them.

- Gabriel wasn't even two years old when X began to "roughhouse" with him. He would always hurt Gabriel. Then, it eventually became the same with Castiel. Then it was Castiel, who usually was the one who got hurt (this was relayed to me by Gabriel).

- X frequently grabbed me by my neck and jerked me towards him. Every single time, I asked him not to do that because it hurt. I often reminded him I had been in several car accidents, but one in particular injured my neck very seriously. He kept doing it anyway. He thought it was funny.

- Up north, while I was changing Gabriel's diaper, he looked at me and asked, "Finger up butt?" "Thumb up the butt?" I looked at him with a very confused expression on my face. He answered my look with, "Daddy do". Then he turned over and put his bottom up in the air.

- We only had one vehicle for several years because X 'made me' sell my car when I wanted to stay home to be with Gabriel. That was until my mom gave me her vehicle because she didn't want me to be without a vehicle with the boys, especially in an emergency. This was the vehicle I used to finally get away from him with the boys to my mom's house. The boys finally had a short time of reprieve.

WHEN THE BOYS AND I WERE STAYING WITH MY MOM:

- After the boys and I left Bellaire, I went back up there to get A few of our things, and X was not there, which was a pleasant surprise. He had put a padlock on an outbuilding, and I could see through the window a tall stack of my years-long collection of CDs. I also saw a lot of what I presumed to be my CDs broken and crushed on the same table, with a hammer right next to the crushed and broken CDs. A lot of the tools in there had been my father's (who is deceased), such as the hammer he used to crush my belongings. I never got those tools back to pass on to my sons, as I had planned. I saw a big pile of clothes on the floor, all of them mine. I assume those were the ones that were burned in front of my sons while they were there for that week-long visit, which would happen later. I could clearly imagine the psychotic expression on his face and his wild and crazed eyes while he was destroying my property, piling up my clothes, and then burning them, and burning and throwing darts at pictures of my family, friends and me - while making my sons witness it all and take part in aspects of it, it's terrifying to think about. I have seen that expression several times before, so I know exactly what it looks like. I'm getting chills and goosebumps simply thinking about it. I went inside the house because my name was still on the mortgage, and there were still a lot of my sons and my belongings in the house (that we never got). I discovered he now had a police scanner. I wonder why he felt the need to have a police scanner? Bellaire was a very small town, so having a scanner only made sense if one was solely concerned about police movement for a personal reason. There was also a black lab in a crate that was way too small for the dog. The dog didn't bark. He only looked afraid. -I know how that entire family treats animals, so I just felt very sad about it. I took the computer. I had pictures of the boys on that computer, which I wanted and was entitled to. Sadly, I have no idea where any of those pictures are now or if I even got them. I had newspaper articles that

I had written on that computer from a couple years earlier. But the main reason I wanted the computer was to have a computer specialist analyze it to see what was on there. I knew what I saw of pornography, so I could only imagine what was there that I was unaware of.

- Once, while we were staying at my mom's, I offered to meet X with the boys at a hotel in Grayling that had a pool. I said I would pay for it, and we could see if we could resolve anything. This was one of the dumber things I've done. The boys and I arrived, I put them in swimsuits, and we swam for a while. X got there eventually. He interacted with the boys very little; while we were in the pool, I was with the boys -of course, because they were so young, and he was off swimming somewhere else by himself. I'm pretty sure we got pizza -that I paid for, I'm not sure if Gabriel ate that or not. I know I had to feed Castiel something different. X ate and then went to the hotel bar. He came in after we all had gone to sleep. He woke in the morning and was headed out the door without saying anything to anyone. I asked him if he was going to say anything to the boys. He turned back around, said something briefly to Gabriel and was out the door. What a model father, wouldn't you say?

- My mom and her husband bought a house in Kentucky, and the boys and I went with them to Kentucky. I had been showing X homes in Kentucky online, and I very much preferred the weather there to northern Michigan. He worked from home so he could live virtually anywhere. X and I had previously spoken about living in Kentucky; he knew my mom was moving there, and their house in Michigan was placed on the market, and the move was made to Kentucky. X, at this point, never called to see about the boys. However, I still provided him with occasional updates.

WHEN WE WERE IN LEXINGTON:

- There were a slew of disclosures and sexual acting out when we lived in Lexington, especially after their week-long visit to Michigan.

- Gabriel told me, "Dada showed me icky stuff on the 'puter."

- I discovered that both of the boys were putting toys up their anus, especially in the bathtub, and I hadn't seen this behavior prior to their week-long stay with their father.

- Gabriel initially saw a psychoanalyst when we arrived in Kentucky, Dr. Gahndolph. Dr. Gahndolph wrote several letters to CPS reporting his strong suspicions of sexual abuse. I didn't realize at the time how much he was aware of what was going on with Gabriel. Unfortunately, the boys and I moved to Lexington and went to a different mental health worker.

- The social worker in Lexington, Judas, was one to whom Gabriel repeatedly disclosed. He was graphic and detailed in his disclosures. He used anatomical dolls to show her what his father did to him, and he showed her pictures of a naked preschool boy where his father had hurt him. She wrote letters of her strong suspicions of sexual abuse to CPS, the police, an Antrim County Court Judge, and then a month before depositions after speaking with the custody evaluator Mulefucent, and X's parents, (which she was not going to do either of those), she did an about-face. I should have known when she suggested that I spank my young children, something I was adamantly opposed to. After hearing and witnessing all she did for the years she did, she let the voices of liars (X's parents) and a terrible and misogynistic custodial evaluator talk her into something she knew was not right.

She let their voices outweigh the very strong, heartfelt, and compelling voices of my sons, who were pleading for help.

You Fucking Idiots, Look What You've Done

WHEN THE BOYS WERE TAKEN:

- When the boys were taken and lived with X. Their environment was drastically different than it was when they were with me, X and his family made it as much like a prison as they could -as if it wouldn't feel that way to them anyway. They installed a 6' privacy fence around the entire yard. They installed an alarm system, and just like in Bellaire he placed cameras all over the place, mostly inside of the house. This was not to keep people out. Although, I'm sure he explained it away to people by saying it was because I was crazy that he had to do all those things. It was mainly to keep the boys in, and to watch them and monitor their whereabouts and what they were doing constantly. -And not because he cared about them, or was concerned about them, or wanted to make sure they were safe, but so he kept complete and tight control of them also because there isn't any privacy there.

- Immediately when the paternal family gained custody of my sons, they set out to change their very identities. They changed their names from Gabriel to Gabe and Castiel to Cas. X's father wanted to call them by shortened names when they were only 2 and an infant. I told him I didn't want to change their names and that when the boys got older, then they could choose to shorten it. Should they so desire, that would be fine, but I wanted it to be their choice. X's father brought this up two Christmases prior, the one in which he threatened me. They did it immediately when they got them anyway, Gabriel told me he didn't want them to call him that, but they didn't care what he wanted. They did what they wanted. They cut their curly and beautiful locks off their head, and not only cut it - they shaved their heads. Then X humiliated Gabriel for his ears. X said they were big, and he called him Dumbo, as did other paternal family members. Both boys' ears then became used as weapons against them as X and his wife pulled them by their ears. They also changed their last names; they have a hyphenated last name, but they only used the paternal name of their last name. The school fell in line behind them. So, when they went to school, they began school with these new identities.

- In short, they first changed their external IDs. Then, they set about to change their internal identifications.

- The boys were made to do all the grunt work. It's as if they were treated like slaves. Their jobs were the garbage, picking up the dog poop, doing all the dishes (that they just piled in the sink with food still on them), all the cleaning -such as the bathrooms, vacuuming, and all the grimy jobs that X and his wife were too good to do - everything. On top of that, they constantly bitched at them about anything and everything about school; the boys had to put their rooms back together after X had gone through everything and threw their rooms upside down and all over the place, searching through it for the main purpose of instilling fear in them and making sure they knew they had no freedom or privacy, the boys had to do any hard labor outside - they had no choice in these matters, as they were punished harshly if they did not do as they were told. They were not given any respect in any way, they did not have choices, and their voices and opinions about anything did not matter.

- X monitored the boys' whereabouts continuously. He had the Life 360 app installed on their phones, followed the paths of everywhere and anywhere they went and would question them about their every move; he even questioned them about places they went when they were with me. He did everything to instill fear into them and let them know that he was always watching. The boys woke up to this and were tired of the questioning and would turn their phones off sometimes. If they were with me, X would text me to ask why their phones weren't working, and they ended up getting punished for trying to escape his stalking of them.

- The boys would sneak out at his house, sometimes at night, sometimes during the day. During the day, they would ask me to meet them down the road from that house, which I always did, but it made me very anxious, especially for them. Sometimes, they snuck out at night to go with their friends somewhere. Some of those times, they came to our house. Of course, I was thrilled to see them, but I always feared what would happen to them if X found out.

- He tracked them at school with the assistance of school staff, parents, and other members of the community. A lot of these people had gone to the very same schools along with X and his extended family members as my sons were attending and bought into his lies, so they told him everything they knew as well. They even looked for something to tell him. X and his family had made me out to be such a horrible person, and they were so blind (and a bit dumb) that I think they thought they were doing a good thing by giving him information. Maybe they didn't know how he was using it. All these people had grown up in this small, isolated, smothering town. It seemed to be such an incestuous community; everyone was related to each other somehow; they weren't fond of outsiders such as me. However, they were fine with keeping tabs on Gabriel and Castiel, what they did and didn't do, who they were with, when and where.

They always told him when I was at the boys' school or in town. So, when X told the boys he knew what they were doing at all times, he could actually back that up and scare the boys to death with information to prove it. This was one way he gaslighted them, controlled them, and brainwashed them. He knew when they were taken out of school early or dropped off late when they were with me. He would obtain the records to show in court. On the other hand, he would send them to school sick, especially on days they were coming to my house, then, look, oh my gosh, mom picked him or them up early again -no mention that he or they were sent to school sick in the first place.

- There was only one time in all the years that Castiel was at his father's that X let him have one friend over. He never let Gabriel have a friend over. He never let them go anywhere. He kept them isolated. On the contrary, the boys frequently had friends over to our humble abode, even though they were probably embarrassed by our small and meager home. We also did a lot of things together and went to a lot of places.

- He punished them for anything he could that had to do with me.

- He punished them for talking about me in a favorable light, which meant he would have overheard them, as they knew better than to directly say anything positive about me to X or his wife.

- When he once found out that they had ridden their bikes to see me down the road, he punished them. I think that was the last time we met down the road.

- He wouldn't let them keep anything I gave them, and he'd take it or use it as a form of punishment.

- He only let them talk to me on his phone, on speaker phone, with him present. Once they got their own phones, they would call me, but he went through their phones and if he found they called me, they were punished. If they deleted their call to me, he'd find that, too, because he went through deleted calls, and if he found them to me, they were punished. Then, they discovered an app and downloaded it. From that app, they could call me, and it wouldn't register the call. It always came up as a different number for me, though, so it took me a while to figure out it was them; I had so many bill collectors calling me that if I didn't recognize the phone number, I usually didn't answer. However, once I realized the numbers they would call from were all different numbers, I began answering every call!

- The threat that X's father said to me that Christmas time was as they were walking out the door, he told me, "You've got a good thing going here, don't screw it up." X, X's parents, and X's sister were there for Christmas -and they were there for that comment. They had ignored me the entire time they were there, going off to different rooms to talk if they were in the house, frequently they were out 'sightseeing' though. After the comment, and they had all walked out the door, X actually spoke to me. He said, "What was that all about?" as if he didn't know.

- Soon after the boys were taken, X went to the Social Security office to get the boys SSI payments redirected into his already large bank account. I'm sure that money did not go for the boys as it was supposed to. Personally, I think there would be many, much more important things to be doing at that time than spending hours at a Social Security Office, like taking care of two little boys who were transplanted into a completely new environment. I could not afford coats and shoes; he just didn't get them. However, frequently, when

I broke the bank and took the boys to get something like clothes, shoes, coats, or a backpack. X would suddenly decide he didn't like that they were wearing something that I bought them, so he would somehow find money in his bank account that he could use on them and go get the boys the same things I had just purchased them. Then, he wouldn't let the boys wear or use what I had just scraped for, even though they would like what I got them better, as it was their choice what I got them, not just, "Here, this what you're wearing/using and that's it."

- I learned much later that the boys were made fun of wearing the clothes that their father purchased for them. When I could purchase clothes for them, we would go to Plato's Closet or a similar type of resale store. Neither of the boys was too proud to wear used clothing. However, X forbade them from bringing anything from my house over there, which included clothes.

- When Castiel was older, still living with X, though, he tried to get help from the sexual acting out being somewhat pushed on him by his brother (who was only reenacting his trauma). He went to his father (he had nobody else to go to, and his father knew about it all because he did it to them). X first told Castiel that because it's between two boys, it's not sex. Then he told him that because it's family, it's not sex, and there's nothing wrong with it.

- X is cruel. The intent of his punishment is cruelty, instilling fear, sadism, and manipulation. However, he is able to switch to a relatively decent person when he wants or has to. He can cry on demand, or at least act like he's crying -he'll even put a big show on for you, but it's just bullshit. He hides his cruel monster from 'outside' people. Unfortunately, the boys and I got to see it every day.

- I was at a softball game watching one of my sons play softball. His game ended and his brother was out a distance playing with one of his friends. I watched and heard X's wife whistle as if whistling for a dog. She loudly whistled for my son to come back so they could leave. You know that really loud whistle that you put two fingers on each side of your mouth to do? The one that hurts anybody's ears that is standing or sitting anywhere nearby them. That whistle.

- At a basketball practice, X's despicable wife yelled loudly for all to hear Castiel, "Stop beating on your brother. We all know you're going to win, and he's going to lose, and then he's going to cry, and then we'll have to listen to him cry, so just stop it." She has a big mouth and is a heinous person; she and X are two peas in the same pod.

- I did not know who X was or who the family was. Initially, I had a very different impression of the family; I thought he was only 'misunderstood.' Even with the bright red flags, I kept telling myself, don't listen to your gut. You're overreacting. But I wasn't overreacting.

- X called me fraudulent because I hadn't done anything with my son's SSI payments they got from my social security disability after they were taken. As if taking care of X was top of my priority list after they had deceived everybody and taken my sons away from me to punish them, as well as me. Furthermore, he wanted me to be as poor as possible so I could not fight him anymore in court. Even later, much later when the boys were spending more time with me, I approached X about the SSI payments because I needed them directed back to me since, of course, I was not receiving any child support and should have been -and I should have been receiving those SSI benefits for my sons care anyway. With his usual contempt, he stated, "You can have them.

They put me in a higher tax bracket anyway."

- The 'family' would do anything to keep their secrets from getting out, which meant they had to make me look bad or crazy and keep my sons very controlled and anything the boys said and did that was disturbing or destructive, they blamed on me, even when the boys were solely or primarily at X's house.

- At basketball practice in Chelsea, X's wife said to me, X "didn't do what YOU said he did," …as if that was all there was to it, something I said and nothing else.

- X's wife also barricaded me from getting back into my car after an exchange when I took the boys to X. So, the boys were in the back seat of X's truck watching as she yelled and screamed at me, demeaned me, called me names, threatened me, and so on. She was about 4 times my size, and all she had to do was sit on me to crush me. It took me years to figure out the obvious; she was baiting me. She wanted me to assault her in some way so they could call the police and then use that in court against me. All the judge would have seen and heard was that I assaulted her, not that I was just trying to get into my car. I was going to file a report, but it was Michigan State Police who had jurisdiction and that area, and X had previously told me he had connections within the Michigan State Police. That could have been untrue, and he was saying it to threaten me, but it also could have been true. It certainly would explain some things if it were true. I wouldn't have punched her or done anything like that anyway, I would not have wanted my sons to see that (at least then), and I'm not that type of person. I don't like confrontation. But now, as I look back over all this, I wish I had socked her right in her face. My sons probably would have actually gotten a kick out of that!

- "Kids are imaginative," "Boys will be boys," among many other catchphrases making attempts to dismiss everything that my sons said and did, and the abuse they suffered because of X and the paternal family, by school staff etc., has been outrageous and ludicrous. I really don't think the statements and disclosures they made fit in the category of an imaginative 4- and 2-year-old, nor an 8- or 6-year-old. Moreover, I saw their expressions and heard the pain, anguish, inflection, and fear in their voices. On the other hand, I also heard them say it matter-of-factly, but it was still clear that their statements were true. They were just in a place in their minds where they needed to be guarded. All you had to do was look into my sons' eyes. But school principal PennyWise kept blowing off big deals and dismissing compelling statements and behaviors. Apparently, just to cover X's ass.

- Getting the boys back incrementally was excruciatingly painful, but at least I was seeing them for some amount of time. Admittedly, I was broken in pretty much all areas of my life. This includes my parenting ability. Having your children taken abruptly while they are so young is destructive to everybody. I was a damn good mom before they were taken. We did so many things together, we explored, we read, we were involved, and they saw their granny and papa regularly, and their uncle when we could. They had experienced trauma, and I was trying to get them help for that. Gabriel had just gotten glasses, and Castiel was getting speech therapy. They were doing well, and then they were abruptly taken. When I got time back with them finally, it was so short, and I missed so much of their lives. They had grown and changed, and there was a massive number of things we wanted to do together and things they wanted to do that their father wouldn't put himself out to take them to do. Our time was rushed. There was also the fact that I knew their father was abusing them, and I thought I would try to make up for that by treating them extraordinarily well; I admit sometimes I was more of a friend than a parent. I so badly wanted them to have happiness even if it was for a small part of the time. I knew how cruel, sadistic, and hateful X was. I knew they felt empty, and they did not feel cared for, certainly not loved or had a horrible idea of what love was from that house. I wanted to try to give them good memories, fill them with goodness, and make them feel loved and cared for.

- Gabriel also told me, as well as the Court Appointed Counselor Coordinator in a session, that among many waves of abuse, X made him take "hot, hot showers," "too hot."

- At one supervised visit, I learned that 7-year-old Gabriel had been put in a diaper because he had an accident in bed the night before. You will learn in the next section that it is common for sexually abused children to have accidents. I'm sure that wasn't the only time, nor the only child; they did that too.

- Thinking of that, I was in a store once, and I went down an aisle and saw my son Castiel in a shopping cart. He was being pushed by X's mother. This was gut-wrenchingly painful. We met eyes, and neither of us knew what to do. I saw his deep sadness, and he saw mine. X's mother was taking her time looking at stuff. I could immediately tell that Castiel needed a diaper change and that he had been in that dirty diaper for a long time -too long. I knew she was taking her time to punish him and making him have to stay in a soiled diaper for as long as she wanted. My heart broke into a million bits. It took all the strength I had to tell Castiel I had to go and then tear myself away. It was truly brutal for both him and me.

- There were times at supervised visitation when the boys had to go to the bathroom, and the supervisor had to take them, and when one or both were wiped, there was blood on the toilet paper or blood in the stool that they showed to the supervisor.

- The boys talked about sex during supervised visitation. They would say one or the other was having sex with 'somebody.' There are many such details written down in the supervised visit reports. Since there were oodles of supervised visits over 2-3 years, there is a massive amount of visit reports. I included a couple in section two, but each report had something in it that was concerning. I spared you about a ream of those.

- There were many reports made to CPS by the supervisors from this specific supervised visit location as well.

- The boys, individually and together, brutalized animals occasionally.

- The boys were attention-starved. They would come to my house, both desperate for my attention. I knew it was because they didn't receive appropriate and certainly not supportive or positive attention from their fathers. Additionally, they only saw their mother a scant amount of time.

- They crave approval in most anything they do. They mainly grew up without attention or approval at their father's house. Instead, they were demeaned, demoralized, humiliated, and criticized.

- They still desperately need attention and approval -they were neglected and harshly criticized for so long.

- On the rare occasion that X would play catch with them, he would throw the ball too hard, and it would hurt them when they caught it, but he ridiculed them if they didn't catch it.

- X and his wife made them sit at the table until they finished their plates, whether they wanted the food or not, if they liked it or not, or if they were hungry or full.

- If food was ever found in the garbage, they would be punished harshly.

- They began throwing the food that they didn't want or couldn't eat out of their second-floor bedroom windows and onto the roof if they could get it out of the kitchen; otherwise, they were forced to eat it.

- A lockbox was placed around the thermostats in their rooms so they could not have any control over it. In winter, it was set at 62. In summer, it was set at 76, but the summer didn't matter. They didn't have central air, the sole air conditioner of the house was in X and his wife's room.

- Punishment for the boys, no matter how young they were or how old they got, always included a bare bottom spanking, kicking, hitting, slapping, squeezing a part of the body very hard (left bruises), humiliation, shunning, shaming, spitting at them, ridiculing, name calling, locked in their rooms, grounding, phones, tv, Xbox - all taken away, anything regarding me taken or thrown away, taking away activities, (once they were supposed to go to Florida, Castiel said something to X's wife that she didn't like: so...Castiel was left behind while the rest of them went on vacation, leaving his older brother miserable as well), mouths taped shut, they were locked in the barn, in cages, taking away food or drink - the boys already got the bottom of the barrel whereas X and his wife ate much better food made by "choice" manufacturers - they didn't eat the cheap shit, but the boys did, the wife and the entire paternal family joined in on the punishing.

- "Made me drink pee in a cup" was one of the statements the boys made several times over. The things 'professionals' took literally and the things they chose not to are astonishing. And the fact that just because something grosses a caseworker or the like out does not at all make it untrue. There are a lot of people who have done a lot of sick stuff in this world that was proven to be true -after many professionals thought it could not be. There are other liquids that come out of a man's penis as well, and the boys made statements when they were younger such as Dada peed on my back, peed in my mouth, peed on my butt, peed in my butt, stuck a stick up my butt, stuck his penis up my butt, made me help him pee, etc. If workers actually made a little effort to use their brains, widen the space in there, connect some of the dots, look at the bigger picture (this is why reading other reports would have been helpful), use some common sense, think outside of their teeny tiny little box, maybe, just maybe they would have come to a different conclusion.

- X took away any phone I would get for them, burner phones or regular cell phones with a contract.

- The phones were always the first thing that was taken from them as a punishment. Knowing it was our only form of communication, I would text and get no response. I'd worry and worry about them, wondering what happened -because they always got right back to me, and when they didn't, I'd worry about why they couldn't get back to me. Then I'd realize the phone must have been taken away again. X and his wife were probably sitting back and reading whatever I said, laughing that it wasn't getting to either of the boys.

- X went through their backpacks, phones, and clothes when they got home from my house and/or school, but always after they were with me, tearing things apart and dumping them all out. He would go through their rooms, most frequently when they were at my house, flipping the beds over, going through drawers, leaving their rooms as if the FBI had gone through them looking for some little something. What was he afraid of? What did he think he would find?

- Both X and his wife hit them regularly. I have frequently heard the boys talk about getting hit by X and his wife right on their heads, hard, smacking them on the side, back, or tops of their heads.

- Gabriel was humiliated and shamed by the paternal family about his ears. They called him Dumbo.

- X would also yell very loudly directly into both boys' ears, getting up close to their ears, right next to their faces, and yelling directly into their ears.

- They were punished if they said anything positive about me or complained and cried because they missed me.

- Personally, I think you can instill respect and better behavior without spanking and/or hitting. An opinion I freely expressed, but X chose not to respect. He probably did it even more because of my opinion.

- Gabriel and Castiel were outside playing with Nerf guns. X's mother and father came driving down the road after being gone for some time. Castiel, in a playful way, shot at the car with the Nerf gun he was using. Whatever kind of 'nerf' it was hit the car. No big deal, right? These are nerf toys. However, X's father immediately stopped the car, chased after Castiel, and spanked him. Both X and his father spanked terribly hard. Castiel said he ran inside, up to his room, crying.

61

- I later found out that with the boys in the vehicle, X would drive by my house. There are plenty of ways to go anywhere and not ever have to go by my mom's and my place. He was not going to ever stop. It was only to be cruel and to torture them to go by our house when they longed to be here, with no intention of stopping but just to drive slowly by. I'm sure he was hoping I'd be outside and that I would see them. That would be a double whammy. He'd be driving a stake through my sons' hearts, as well as mine. Cruelty was always his intent.

- Castiel often had to choose between getting a spanking or staying in his room for an extended period of time.

- The boys admit they were in their rooms most of the time. They were at their father's house anyway. They didn't want to be around X or his wife or any of the other extended family members, who I'm sure were there a lot of the time.

- The boys would take things from my house to that house just so they would have something to do, such as the Xbox, Xbox games, and DVDs. Their father had an Xbox of his own, but he would not let the boys use his Xbox.

- The paternal family had a lot of money. Unfortunately, though, they just spent it on themselves, not on the boys -other than on litigation to keep them from me. They had nice cars, nice houses, everything they needed to make their yards appear impeccable, etc. They focused on outward appearances. On the contrary, I had very little money, and I spent everything I could on my sons.

- Because I saw my sons so little, I tried to be involved at school as much as I could. Even though I hated the school, they treated me like Hester Prynne was treated in the Scarlet

Letter (book by Nathaniel Hawthorne). The school staff and the other parents were despicable and oblivious. I tried to have lunch with the boys as frequently as I could and then go out to recess with them. Depending on their individual lunch schedules, I couldn't do both for each child. While in the lunchroom and at recess, I was watched like a hawk. Then they reduced the number of times I could come to only days that I would be picking them up after school -hugely inconvenient, the school is about 30 minutes away, I couldn't come there for both their lunches, go home, and leave to pick them back up. Financially and time-wise, I could not do that, so that cut in on my lunches, and I am sure it was the paternal father who pushed for that. When I did have lunch with them and just stayed the entire day in that gossipy, inbred town, the lunch monitors monitored me more than any other child while I was there in the lunchroom.

- Castiel told me that his father had grabbed him by the neck and, while holding him up by the neck, slammed him against the wall and yelled at him for being in his way.

- Rest assured that I am not mentally ill. I've been depressed (who wouldn't be?), I do have anxiety, and I have complex PTSD, but I do not have a 'mental illness' as far as the labels that have been attached to me initially by the custody evaluator. The terms he used weren't even mental health diagnoses as defined in the DSM-IV, which he used at the time of his writing the report. I could list out all the schools and universities I have been to, all the papers I have written, what I studied at U of M and other Universities, all the various demanding positions and roles I have held, the volunteer work I have done, and so on, but I'm not going to do that because I don't think I should have to.

63

COURT NOTES

- In court, X and his family claimed the boys were uncivilized, that they didn't even know how to brush their teeth when they came there. Funny how when they were with me, they brushed their teeth, and they were sweet, smart, and helpful; I could go on and on. Maybe they should have pointed the finger back at themselves as being the reason the boys were acting so chaotically -they were living in chaos, they didn't want to be there, they were severely traumatized, and they wanted their mother. Eventually, that family created robots like themselves, completely brainwashed and under their control. They did this by being harshly strict and using brutal and cruel punishment, physical, emotional, and mental abuse and neglect, by shaming, shunning and humiliating them, and they did those as a group.

- CPS didn't return phone calls to specialists and professionals who were experts in this type of abuse and case, and these people were trying to reach them. I have the call logs to prove that. These experts also provided them with reports and documents that completely contradicted Mulefecent's custody evaluation. But the only report that was ever referred to was that custody evaluation.

- All Washtenaw County CPS caseworkers, except one, whom I only spoke with once briefly, approached me with a clear bias and prejudice. They were incredibly rude and judgmental, and they never listened to what I was trying to tell them regarding my sons' history of disclosures and behaviors. Most unfortunately, they did not listen to my sons because they wrongfully claimed that I had coached them.

- CPS caseworkers prevented my sons from being protected. Their decisions kept my sons in a notoriously abusive household. I hold Washtenaw County CPS -especially these specific caseworkers, as they all spoke with each other, a sole custody evaluator, numerous useless and deluded police officers, a worthless GAL, an unfathomable turn of a spineless therapist; Judas, who had been disclosed to repeatedly, but she chose to act as if none of what she had seen and heard ever happened, and an oblivious, power-hungry referee, completely responsible for the massacre of my sons lives, my life, my mom's life, and the annihilation of the relationship between my sons, and their relationship with me, my mom, and with the entire maternal side of our family. Caseworkers were dismissive of me and the seriousness of the allegation. They blatantly lied, misled, and showed a clear prejudice in every single one of their "investigations" and reports. The fact that they received a plethora of reports regarding my sons and chose not to investigate and continued to unsubstantiate the allegations is outrageous. It was a vicious cycle; they all fed off of each other's incompetencies, and each of them fueled more and more horrible decisions, each impacting my sons' lives more and more negatively. Individually, growing more and more blind to the facts, more and more willing to compromise the lives of two young boys -especially if it made their lives easier with less work to do and less and less caring altogether. Once they saw an opportunity to throw the case away, they all jumped on board. We were doomed.

- X and his family lied on the stand in court, he lied, and they lied about how he treated the boys, what kind of father he was, how he treated me, what kind of husband he was, how he treated animals, the intimidator's name, world trade center and people falling to their deaths and his reaction, X's use of pornography, he and they denied he even ever looked at porn (laughable) when they all knew otherwise, his sister had watched it with him, his father most likely did as well, he had huge boxes full of pornographic magazines and DVDs that they all saw and even helped move. They said he didn't have an anger problem, even though he admitted it when he was fighting my PPO in court., and they all had experienced it for years. In short, they all lied repeatedly, without the blink of an eye. They lied on obvious issues, things the referee should have easily known they were lying about, if not for anything else but from previous court actions.

- MSP (Michigan State Police) destroyed the DVD from Lexington CAC (Child Advocacy Center), and they also destroyed most or all of the corroborating porn found on his computer that was directly connected to him. That in nature was sadistic, brutal, young with older, incestuous, bondage, pain inflicting, grotesque, etc.

- The custody battle went on and on. We had a computer expert analyze the data on the computer I had taken out of the house up north. He emphatically testified on my behalf. They tried to make the case that it was my brother's. But I knew it wasn't his -he lived out of state, and most obviously, he never accessed our home computer, which X then used for work to do ANYTHING on, much less to view PORNOGRAPHY. That is absurd! But, absurd or not, if it's something they can somehow make fit into their warped brains, it'll do the job. Even more, the computer expert could prove it was X's because everything was time-stamped. There were the articles I wrote for the paper, porn, another article or two, more porn, some of X's work, and so on. It was never possible to be anyone else's but his or mine and I sure as hell know it wasn't mine. The computer expert, who, as you can imagine, sees all kinds of stuff because of his job, said there were many downloaded images (not just viewed) that he had to look away from because they were so horrific. Since we are talking about graphic, sadistic, bondage, 'young' looking people with older people, and cruel pornography, one can only imagine what he would have had to look away from. And X had downloaded thousands of these images to his computer.

- While Referee Teera Nichol was the acting 'judge.' She made her decision (the final decision) based mainly on the extremely flawed custody evaluation. I foolishly had initially trusted the custody evaluator to use common sense when he asked for my notes, and I sent them to him. He never called me to ask questions about them, he never asked me what I thought about things I wrote down, ever. He (and the judge) did what they accused me of doing: made assumptions, jumped to conclusions, and then made accusations without ever getting any context at all. Historically, I've kept notepads and pens out all over the place (I still do this today). It began when the boys were infants solely to monitor their medical health, but then it became more of a necessity. (Now, it's because I have a lot of things on my mind and lots of things to try to do, and I can't remember it all!). My notepads were irreplaceable while the boys and I were in Lexington because of things I heard them say to each other and what they said to me, and at such frequency. I would not have remembered all of it had I not written as much down as I could have. I also wrote down behaviors that I was witness toor even things my mom saw or heard. I heard many statements that confused meor I didn't understand at that time, but I still wrote them down; it didn't mean I took them literally. However, I felt like it meant SOMETHING. But the custody evaluator and the referee took everything I wrote down, and they read as if I meant it all literally, yet nobody discussed with me what was going through my head or asked me why I wrote it down or what I thought about it. Nope, they just blindly assumed that I took it as a literal fact. Based on some of the things I remember writing down, I think that makes them delusional, not me.

For years, our very souls lingered,
saturated and drowning in pools of torment,
heartbreak, anger, and misery.

-Me

We could feel the sharp claws of ignorance and apathy,
We were draped in a thick, choking hatred and denial of the truth,
The darkness of despair wrapped tightly around us,
Smothering and killing anything good that was left.

- A few years ago, Gabriel attempted suicide (not the first time). I took him to the emergency room, and from there, he was taken to an inpatient facility, where he stayed for around 12 days. I visited him as frequently as they would allow visitation. He and I had a meeting with one of the therapists, and I learned -because my son told me that he blames me for all the years of abuse he has endured from his father and the paternal family because he thought I didn't care, and I had abandoned him and his brother. He thought this partly because this is what he was told by the paternal family but also because that is how it appeared to him. I was there, then I was gone, I was protecting them, then they were being constantly abused, and I was nowhere to be found. I understand how he felt this way. I think of all the times, in all the years that he was brutally victimized while a young child, either by himself or with his younger brother, and all he can think of and feel here is my mom? I will never be able to fix that. He will be haunted by those feelings for the rest of his life. And I will be haunted by my guilt for not being able to protect them.

■ I researched and researched, read, read some more, took courses and workshops, and learned about preventative care, even though it was too late for preventative care in our circumstances, although we briefly had home care in Lexington. We played therapeutic games, they met with mental health professionals, and I took a workshop in Virginia called Sexual Abuse and Behaviors, in which case it confirmed all my instincts; everything I had seen and heard was a result of sexual abuse and the many other sordid abuses. I took a 3-day course in Clinton Twp. Through TLC, that too was very goo. It was about trauma, the impact of trauma, and how to help traumatized children -in which case, I tried to utilize some of the tools I learned for my own children. I have been in therapy with the same therapist for about 9-10 years now, and I am very thankful for her. She is wonderful. Both boys have had therapy, some therapists haven't been horrible, and some have been complete quacks. The trauma therapist my youngest son has now is fantastic. He has connected very well with Castiel and is excellent with him, and Castiel works very well with him. All those prior to him that Castiel had were not great. A few of them did more damage than good, and unfortunately, that is all the experience with therapy that Gabriel has had. There are a lot of bad therapists out there. Do your homework and make sure if you are looking for a therapist for these types of issues that, you find an informed trauma therapist that they have experience with the specific abuse or trauma you/your child has experienced and who is a good match for your child and/or you. If your child does not feel safe with them or comfortable speaking with them, therapy from them will not work. And just because they might not be a good match for your child doesn't make them an inadequate therapist. It only means that it is not a good fit. It's not personal, especially when you keep it professional!

- I finished my degree at U of M through self-directed courses and working independently with truly wonderful Professors studying child welfare and welfare reform locally, statewide, nationally, and globally. I also have personally researched these many contributing and affecting issues intensively; mental health issues, various forms of abuse and abuse characteristics, every single year since I discovered my sons and I have dealt with these issues. I am a forever learner. These subjects happen to be what I focus on the most, especially since they have been most impactful to the lives of my sons and me. It also helps to be educated on these mental health conditions as I feel I can communicate better with a mental health professional, know what they're talking about, and know when they don't know what they're talking about. In this case, I wish I'd had a lot of this knowledge many years ago.

- Fighting for my sons while simultaneously earning my bachelor's degree at U of M was very challenging. However, I sincerely thought that the judges/referee would acknowledge what I had to say more by having this particular credential. That never happened. They didn't care one bit. However, I earned my degree and continued my fervent research. The more I researched, the more it validated what I believed to be true and what my sons had been telling me all along -that I never doubted, to begin with, but it helped to have confirmation.

Having said all of this, I have made it my mission to turn our tragedies into positive change. I am incredibly passionate about child welfare reform. My ultimate wish is for a world in which children are heard, believed, seen, valued, and protected. I wish that had been the world my sons could have experienced.

For this book, I have gone back through boxes and boxes of documents. All of it has been painful. Not that I forgot any bit of it, but seeing it all again on paper, all together, takes me right back to each of these moments. None of it has "healed" for me, but times that were beginning to scar over have become broken and raw again.

As you know, my sons and I saw each other through supervised visitation. The supervisors keep very detailed notes of those visits; it's their job to do that. I think those have been some of the most painful documents to read. It was many years ago, but when I read those accounts of a visit, I remember it as if it were yesterday. I remember on several occasions when each of the boys was taken to the bathroom individually, they came back and told me about the blood on the toilet paper when they wiped their bottoms; they had shown it to the supervisor. I remember the tearful hello's and the tragic and terribly tearful goodbyes. I remember times in which one of my sons would refuse to leave me, saying he was not going back to his father. I remember one of my sons bringing something that he wanted to show me that the supervisor had to take from him and him asking over and over again throughout the session to please not give it back to his father because he was going to get spanked and get into A LOT of trouble. I remember each of my sons telling me they cried themselves to sleep at night because they missed me. I remember their very young faces, their tearful eyes, and the tears streaming down their faces. I am deeply saddened, with tears in my eyes right now, remembering these heart-wrenching events out of the multitude just like them. I didn't tell them I cried myself to sleep at night, too, and I took strong sleep medication to get me to sleep. I still take medication to get to sleep. I also have music, nature sounds, a podcast, or MSNBC playing on my phone to distract my brain from ruminating and recycling bad memories so I can get to sleep.

When my sons were younger, we made the most of every moment we had together. We had fully enjoyed our time together before they were taken; I intensely regret any moment that I was not with them when they were younger, especially when we lived in Kentucky. I loved seeing the wonder in their eyes when we were exploring or doing something new. We dug in the dirt, studied rocks, stargazed, did crafts together, made playdough, watched movies, ate our meals together at the table, frequented parks, walked our dog, and I loved reading bedtime stories to them. If I had known my sons were going to be taken, I would never have left their sides. It's very upsetting. My counselor at that time called it "self-care," but as I look back, I call it deprivation of what was most important and valuable to them and to me. I'm not saying that to discredit her. She was great and never steered me wrong. It's just that every second and every minute is so critical to me, then and now.

When they were taken, and even now, I feel like a prisoner. Everything that was taken from us. I was, and still am, continually thinking about as they grew up without me. The pain, the suffering, the bruises, severe complex PTSD, severe anxiety and social anxiety, rage, OCD, depression, cutting, burning, scars, descriptions that only a child with direct experience could have, and the excruciatingly painful goodbyes when our brief 'visiting time' had come to an end again.

We remained as close as a family could, given the circumstances. When I finally got a little time with them in Michigan that wasn't supervised, I loved taking them skateboarding, scootering, and swimming. We threw a football back and forth. They drew and painted. Best of all I loved and still love hearing them laugh. It's the best sound in the world to me. I love to see them smile. It's not like it was, and it will never be that way again, but seeing them smile always makes my heart glow. Their laughter will never sound the same, the 'giggle' is long gone. That was another thing that was taken from them, as was their childhood. Years ago, they were curious, interested, and innocent. Their innocence for them was short-lived, as it was torn from them while they were so very young. After all, they were raped and viciously abused, ripped from me, and thrown to monsters, and all of it was sponsored and approved by the state of Michigan.

Originally, I was awarded primary custody with their father having every other weekend. The first time he saw them after that decision was when our lives began a drastic transformation that I couldn't have imagined at that time. He wanted to combine his weekends, the 4th of July, and X's birthday. He manipulated and pushed me around so well that I didn't even question if the Fourth was "his" holiday, and it wasn't until later that I learned that it's not court-ordered that we see our children on our birthdays. However, I was so happy that I had primary custody that I reluctantly agreed to this arrangement. Albeit, the boys and I had never been separated that long before.

It was in July, and I worked myself near to death that week; I had to keep myself distracted, or I would have been a basket case. I had tried calling and calling to check on the boys, as X and I agreed I would do -he never answered, though. X only called back once, and I immediately knew something was wrong, I could sense it, I could hear it. Of course, he put the boys on speakerphone so he could keep control of the call, and the boys sounded miserable, weak, and vacant. I could tell they were in a very sad state of affairs and that something was terribly wrong.

When I picked them up after that week, the boys looked terrible. They were zoned out, their eyes were glazed over and empty, their faces vacant, and they appeared severely traumatized. They were very quiet. Castiel had a huge knot and bruise above his left eye. Gabriel told me his father had kicked him in the head because he began to climb up a ladder after his father.

After we arrived home, Gabriel was in the bathroom the evening we came back. He yelled from the bathroom, "Ouch, it hurts, I can't poop, dad stuck a stick up my butt," among many other things. Shortly after Gabriel said what he did, I called X and said to him, "I know what you did," he asked repeatedly and rather frantically, "What did he tell you? What did he say? Whatever he said, he lied."

After the boys came back from that week and we were driving from Lexington to Cynthiana on a very beautiful stretch of road on a very sunny and warm day, my oldest son said: "It smells like burning animals." I, too, could smell fires burning as we had the windows rolled down as we drove. I asked him how he knew what the smell of burning animals was like. He answered, "Because when we were at Dad's, we burned animals."

Another thing the boys told me in a very disturbed manner about when they were in Bellaire and I was in Lexington was that I 'was there.' They were very much missing me and crying for me -they had never been away from me for such a long time. I'm sure X and his family did not like them missing me. So, allegedly, they told them I was out in the woods waiting for them. They ran as fast as they could to the woods. It sounds as if it was beginning to get dark, but I am not certain of that. When they arrived in the woods, they were met by a person wearing a dress and lots of lipstick. Apparently, that was supposed to have been me, and they made them think it was me who then chased them around the woods, screaming at them. I was horrified when I heard this. Seriously, I don't care how creative and imaginative a 4- and 2-year-old could be, but I do not believe this is anything they could "imagine." Let's be realistic and use common sense. Admittedly, it may be easier for me since I know how cruel and sadistic the paternal family can be. Incidentally, I like to wear dresses, and I used to wear lipstick; it was the only makeup I wore.

Well, God forbid you ever had to walk a mile in his shoes
'Cause then you really might know what it's like to have to lose
Yeah, then you really might know what it's like
Yeah, then you really might know what it's like
Yeah, then you really might know what it's like
To have to lose

-

Everlast, What It's Like

Gabriel told me when he got back after the weeklong stay with X and the paternal family that X had held his head underwater for a terrifyingly long time. He also spoke of being buried.

Never A Buoy

I lost custody of my sons. They were 6 and 3 when they were taken, and their father, their 'alleged' abuser, was eventually granted primary custody. CPS in the State of Michigan continued to keep them with their father despite their growing level of maturity, the advancement of their allegations, and the continual display of behaviors that matched the allegations that they had been making for years. There was also a report made by CPS in which there are statements from my oldest son stating, "My dad stuck his penis up my butt," in that same report, the caseworker states that he (Gabriel) is a liar and that I coached him to say what he said. This last part was not stated as an opinion. It was stated as fact. It was most definitely not a fact. Not only on that report is it falsely stated that I coached my sons to say what they said, but it also falsely states that my sons are liars.

I was so empty without my sons. I had no purpose. There were many times I felt I couldn't go on -when I was overcome with hopelessness, and when I saw the boys in tiny increments of time in which I could see very clearly that they were becoming mini-X's, and it was evident they were continuously being abused. It was sickening. I felt I was in a corner and any possible option I saw of re-gaining custody was already blocked or was nearing being blocked or broken. I made countless calls, sent emails, and went to different attorneys, all to no avail. The referee in our case had so tightly ruled against me that she made it impossible to fight her written decision. I wrote letters and emails and made phone calls to senators, house members, and other state and federal representatives. None of it got me anywhere. I was shriveling up inside. In fact, I was dying, both literally and figuratively. I was becoming hardened, yet somehow remained naïve. I felt like nothingness. My sons were everything to me, and I was without them.

One selfish and stupid thing I did was to try to fill the void, which was impossible, if it wasn't my sons, it wasn't going to fill my emptiness and give me back my purpose of raising them and protecting them. However, somewhere in the small part of my brain that was functioning outside of my sons, I decided I needed a boyfriend. Maybe that would make me look better in the eyes of the court. Maybe that would make me look better in the eyes of CPS. Maybe it would somehow help me get my sons back to me. As you can already see, I'm a very bad "picker" of partners. I pretty much always have been. Admittedly, they were not all bad men. However, if they were decent, I found a way to ruin it. There was one decent man after the boys were taken, but he couldn't bring himself to understand why I didn't have custody of my sons, no matter how many times I explained it to him. This has been something I ran into a lot. Many people who have not dealt with the family courts or CPS have a misconstrued image of these agencies in that they do not make mistakes, especially not deliberately, or make bad decisions based on biases and bad information, as well as lack of proper training. However, intermittently, over the span of those many years,

I exposed my sons to three more idiot men. I fully regret that and will (and probably should) carry that guilt always. My sons had it terrible enough without exposing them to another loose cannon in the short amount of time we had together. Fortunately, at my insistence, those men were not around too long.

I believed what my sons told me was true, especially regarding their experiences with their father and their paternal family. I had something these caseworkers, judges, police officers, teachers, and evaluators did not have: I had time and experience with X and his family behind closed doors; I saw them when their masks weren't on, heard things that were 'off,' saw things that I knew weren't right, had very strong intuition and instinct that this family was messed up - unfortunately, I didn't listen to those instincts early enough. My instincts were telling me loud and clear to get my sons and get the hell out of there. Which I did, ultimately. The behaviors the boys described fit the man I had come to know; he is the personified definition of a sadistic sociopath. I knew him in a way that most others did not. The rest of the world only saw the mask he wanted to show them; the same is true of his immediate family. They all had masks, but behind closed doors, they were not the same people. Also, I saw the boys' behaviors, individually as well as together, and those told the story of their experiences.

I saw the blank, zoned-out expressions on my sons' faces. Frequently, when I caught them engaging in anything inappropriate or even at times when they told me about scary things that had happened, their eyes would glaze over, and it seemed as if they were in a different place completely. We know the boys were shown pornography by their father at a very young age. From my years of research, I know that children this young are unable to reenact these behaviors from being shown the images through pornography. They were, but these actions were done to them. They saw it in pornography, and they also experienced it. I had seen, heard, and experienced things people in 'the system' apparently couldn't fathom. In that case, it was easier for them to simply disbelieve it.

Those that I had previously trusted to do their part...no, those with whom it is their very job to protect children from situations such as this, failed them completely and failed me as a mother. My sons and I are not a small minority "who slipped through the cracks"; it's grimmer than that. There are many like us who have walked a similar tragic path throughout Washtenaw County, all of Michigan, every state in our nation, and every country in the world. The United States has one of the worst records of protecting children among developed nations.

This song is for anyone.
Fuck it, just shut up and listen.

I'm tired of all of you; I don't mean to be mean
But that's all I can be, it's just me

I hate to be bothered.
With all of this nonsense, it's constant
And all of this controversy circles me
And it seems like the media immediately
Points a finger at me
So I point one back at 'em, but not the index
Or the pinkie
Or the ring, or the thumb, it's the one you put up
When you don't give a fuck
When you won't just put up
With the bullshit they pull,
'cause they full of shit too

-

Eminem, The Way I Am

The last of the inappropriate acting out was a long time ago, they are older now. However, there are layers and layers of residual scar tissue. Their mere presence around each other triggers the other and/ or themselves of their painful pasts. They also have a trauma bond because they wouldn't have gotten through all that without having each other. There can be bitterness between siblings (or others) for acting out when, if one researches abuse, this is exactly what happens, their brains act it out over and over, trying to make sense of it all, even trying to conquer it and have control of it, as it had been forced upon each of them. When they were in X's custody, and they came to my house and acted out, it was always an indicator that something had happened at their father's house prior to my picking them up to come to my house, especially if they had not done it in a while.

One of the last times that I remember, the above scenario played out, and they confirmed to me that, yes, X had raped them again. This time, I went to the police first. This is not something I would recommend to anyone. Gabriel went with me and agreed to speak to the officer, who clearly had zero experience with something like this, and I felt like he also had zero experience with children as well. Gabriel volunteered information to him. He told him his father had put his penis in his butt. The officer stated to me that he would talk to the sergeant and then file a complaint with CPS. I don't know if he talked to the sergeant or not, but I do know he didn't file a complaint with CPS. When it was getting near time for them to go back to their father's, and the boys were afraid they were going to get into trouble for telling on him, yet I had not heard anything yet, I called to see if a report had been made - it had not. The caseworker asked why I was inquiring, so I told her. She said if I did not take them to the ER, she would charge me with neglect. Now that it had been several days since the disclosure had been made, who knows how many days since the assault.

However, I took the boys to the hospital, and there was a caseworker who met me there. I had thought she was the first and only understanding caseworker that I had or ever will have spoken with. However the worker assigned to the case was the same caseworker as the previous caseworker who unsubstantiated the last case. At the hospital, they took pictures of genitalia and found fissures on one of my son's anus (one time, it was Gabriel, another time, it was Castiel, and I think this time, it was Castiel). The doctor said she could not assert that a fissure was definitively from child sexual abuse, but instinctively, I felt it was. When the caseworker spoke with Gabriel, she asked him what the worst thing his father had done was, and he told her that he peed in a cup and made them drink it. Incidentally, I had previously, on several occasions, heard about X making the boys drink pee. I held my tongue because I knew nobody would believe a person was capable of such a thing. Nonetheless, that statement was not made in a vacuum; it was made among many such statements. And the man is demented. Furthermore, it struck me as interesting what the 'officials' chose to take literally and what they chose to believe as fabricated or coached. "Pee" could have different meanings; it could have been anything, and X told them it was pee (remember, basic goals for him were to instill fear, to be cruel, and to humiliate). The boys had regularly stated that Dada had "peed in my mouth," "Peed on my back," "peed on my butt," "peed in my butt," etc. Lastly, this strikes me as a possible action taken by their father. To a child who has been horrendously abused for nearly his entire life by this man, perhaps this was the worst thing or the most recent thing that stands out in his memory, or the grossest thing, or the most humiliating to him.

No one took statements that also came directly from the boys' mouths, such as "Dad stuck his penis in my butt," or any of the other very similar statements literally, other than experts. Yet, when it comes to pee drinking or the very shallow comment, mom told me to say it while he was at his father's house, without any details, within a mountain of very detailed disclosures made for years to a variety of people, in a variety of places and circumstances, it's those

80

that are going to be taken literally so they can disbelieve every other very detailed disclosure made prior to that. How extraordinary.

So, they refused to believe him when he told the truth, then chose to believe him in an isolated circumstance (while at his father's house) and said something he actually was pressured to say by his sadistically abusive father when he said his disclosure was a lie. For me, I look at this entire scenario from a big-picture standpoint and think, hell, these people didn't need a lot of extensive training. All they needed was fricking common sense. Seriously. All they had to do was to remove the lenses that they wanted to see this case through and see it for what it was. Why are these children afraid of their father and keep telling us they don't want to live with him? Especially along with all of these contributing statements. Hmmm, there might be something to that.

So, once again, I did not see my sons for an extended period of time, then it was supervised visits - again. Supervised visitation for children who want to be with their mother and their mother wants to be with them, and absolutely no abusive action has occurred in their relationship -only protection is a heart-wrenchingly painful experience. It was insanely incredulous. When I finally had the boys back to our place, they were constantly worried that their father was going to come get them because they were in trouble. Most especially if anything slipped out about X or X's family. My sons were afraid and frenzied, clearly not because of me, but I assumed, and I have learned I was correct in that assumption, they had deep fear instilled in them, the threats that had been brandished, and they were afraid of the treatment they would receive when, in a brief time, they would have to go back there. They were afraid of the questioning and badgering and the outrageous extremes he and his family would put them through to extort information about me. Once over there, they would go through everything they had: backpacks, clothes - -anything, to make sure they did not have anything I gave them as a keepsake or a gift so they could feel close to me. If they did have something, X or his wife took it and 'hid' it from them, telling them they would 'give it back' later, or they threw it away right in front of them. When the boys would get to their rooms, they would find their rooms had been 'searched' and turned upside down, as I have previously described. Since this happened every time they came to my house, one might think that someone might not even want to go away if they had to deal with that every time they returned. If you do not think that is outrageously controlling and maniacal, I'm sorry, friend, and maybe you should consider finding yourself a therapist. -Just do your due diligence in finding one!

My sons used to be each other's best friends and protectors. Gabriel was long a translator for Castiel, as no one but Gabriel and I could understand him. He was taken to Michigan with a very limited vocabulary. Then, more and more severe abuse happened. They would naturally act it out on each other. Furthermore, X and his family pitted them one against the other. They'd make fun of a shortcoming they saw in one, and if it wasn't a shortcoming in the other, they would make a big deal about their brother not having that shortcoming. By default (although the paternal family knew exactly what they were doing), they made them begin to resent each other. The family separated them regularly and placed them in positions where they'd be against each other, and the losing end was always ridiculed, and neither of them wanted that. The X's made them compete for everything. I had run our household very equally; they both had choices, and their choices equally mattered. It was not that way over there. If they were competing for Dairy Queen, the 'winner' was the only one who got the Dairy Queen. The other had to sit there and watch them all eat Dairy Queen. Anything they did became a competition. The boys were never competitive before. In fact, they went out of their way to support each other. But the X's needed to break that up; they didn't want them to be a team, and they didn't want one or the other child to have anybody else with which to go, to confide. So, they did their best to divide and conquer, and I'd have to admit, using their very cruel tactics, they were quite successful in dividing my sons.

The boys had a few interviews at Child Advocacy Centers: two in Lexington, Kentucky and at least two in Ypsilanti, Michigan. The two in Kentucky happened before the two in Michigan, but I want to tell you about one of them that happened here in Michigan first. The Child Advocacy Center, like Child Protective Services from my experience, is another oxymoronically named organization. While the child interviewers may have done an ok job, the police officer who was viewing the interview was a complete idiot. He should not have any job in 'public service' because he is solely self-serving and clearly displayed his ignorance on child development, child abuse, and particularly child sexual abuse. I had to argue before a room full of people, including the aforementioned officer and the caseworker who later placed *me* on the Central Registry and threatened to file for termination of my parental rights (because she had a power complex, because she hated me, because she could, and because she thought she'd get away with it), along with several other staff members - I'm really not sure why they were present. I argued for a solid twenty minutes for them to speak with my sons, and they decided to interview them. Still being unbelievably naïve at this point, I thought this was a good thing. Nope, this was far from good. All of those people had their minds made up prior to the interview, and thanks to an inept custody evaluation and a torrent of rotten people, they had the inaccurate idea that I was "delusional," and they believed I had coached my sons. My son disclosed in this interview, and apparently, he disclosed quite a bit. But the officer chose not to believe what was said. The boys had not seen their father in a while, and I told them to tell the truth and they would be safe. Never tell a child that last part if you ever find yourself in a situation such as this. You never know what will happen, and if something such as this happens, you've let them down. It doesn't matter if it was out of your control or not. The fact remains that you have let them down. Later, my sons came running out of the interview room to granny (my mom) and me, like they were free of it all and so happy to see us. But wait, then the cop came following right after and took me into a dark room off to the side and angrily stated to me: "I have never heard so much bullshit come out of a kid's mouth before." He proceeded to tell me that their father was already out in the parking lot with his girlfriend, waiting for the boys to be released to them. Clearly, evidence that they had their minds made up prior to the interviews. The faces of my sons as he took them to go to their dad, will never ever be erased from my memory. It brings tears to my eyes and a gut-punch feeling right now as I am writing this. It was heart-crushing then, and it is still heart-crushing and sickening now. As so much of this is, the pain is raw, and it's all still right there. Stunned, devastated, and speechless, my mom and I walked out of our car to go back home without my sons. That officer was still talking to X, laughing loudly and joking around, and there sat my children, fearful, angry, and horrified, watching from the back seat as Granny and I got in our car. Once again, I did not see my young sons for a long while, and it was at supervised visitation for a 2-hour visit when I did see them.

Seriously, think about what the cop said to me. He said he'd never heard so much bullshit come out of a kid's mouth before. Gabriel was 6 years old. The fact that he thought a 6-year-old could have been "coached" to make any disclosures is unbelievable. Much less 'remembering' whatever it was he was supposedly 'coached' to say. It's mind-blowing.

Welcome to a new kind of tension
All across the alien nation
Where everything isn't meant to be okay
In television, dreams of tomorrow
We're not the ones who are meant to follow
For that's enough to argue

Don't wanna be an American idiot
One nation controlled by the media
Information age of hysteria
It's calling to idiot America
-

Green Day, American Idiots

Later, I had to go back into that room where I had sat previously and argued for my sons to be heard. This time, they asked about a sum of money that Gabriel had taken out of his piggy bank earlier. They actually thought I paid Nathaniel to say what he said -whatever it was exactly that he said. I was told by a CPS caseworker that she was going to be filing a petition to terminate my parental rights because she believed the 'custody evaluation,' -the flawed and inaccurate custody evaluation, that I am "delusional," -not an official diagnosis, and even if that were true it is certainly not a reason for a parent's rights to be terminated, and that I am making my sons say these things, of which in the custody evaluation it was stated that he did not believe any of the allegations were originating from me! In fact, quite the contrary, the evaluation stated that my believing my sons was making them believe it. Which, of course, is just as ludicrous, but it is not the same as coaching, as they continued to state. First, if they were lies or coached allegations, there would not be any context or details, and the disclosures of abuse have lots of details as to where, when, who smells, etc. Second, my attorney asked at trial if the caseworkers had read any of the many other reports they were provided with, such as the Court Appointed Counselor's Report to the GAL (A Psychoanalyst who was charged with and then volunteered to see all members of our immediate and extended families was upgraded to this such title; he conducted extensive research and interviewing and also had an interview with Gabriel in which Gabriel made many graphic disclosures (there was a transcript made of this discussion, but CPS would not read this simply because I was sitting in the room. The Court Appointed Counselor Coordinator's report was to offer what is the recommended custody arrangement that would be in the best interest of the children. He advised primary custody with me, X only having supervised visitation, and the court was supposed to adhere to that, but it did not. Another assessment was conducted by the clinic of a renowned child sexual abuse expert and her mental health staff who saw the children for a duration of time intermittently, brought by each parent on three separate occasions, conducting play therapy among many other proven modalities to reach a conclusion regarding child abuse, especially child sexual abuse and if the child had been abused - they decided both of my sons had been abused in a number of ways, including sexually, and the psychiatrist even witnessed physical and verbal abuse by their father to my sons in her very presence, and a Psychological Evaluation Report from a well-known psychologist who looked at psychological testing results and how the testing results were determined and if the appropriate results were warranted and if the relevant data was interpreted correctly. His analysis was: -1. They were biased to favor the father, 2. The results were not warranted, and 3. The data was not at all interpreted correctly. None of these particular reports were ever read or referred to. When I later called to get these reports and the written final argument my attorney worked his ass off on d put so much of his heart and soul into, I was told that none of the documents I was inquiring about were in the file.

When the CPS caseworker informed me that she would be filing a petition to terminate my parental rights because she believed the custody evaluation, she believed me to be crazy and delusional and to be telling my young sons to say these things about their father; I was numb, shocked, and terrified. So, this is where trying to protect my children has gotten my children and me? I was kind of outside my body and looking down watching the entire scene unfold. I wish I'd had my wits about me to ask her if she thought I was telling my dear sons to sexually act out with each other. Was that because of me? I wasn't the only one who had witnessed those actions. Did I tell my sons to cut and burn themselves? Did I tell them they should talk about and consider suicide? Of course not. Did they think I could conceive of and make up any of their disclosures and then try to get my children help for something that wasn't even true? Who would do that? Someone in this scenario is not using common sense. Someone is burying their head in the sand, someone is getting the wool pulled over their eyes, but it wasn't me. My eyes and ears are wide open. The caseworker threatening to try to terminate my parental rights is the very same caseworker who got the call from the social worker at school. My oldest son had cut marks on his arm that he told the social worker was from his father and his father's girlfriend cutting him. When this caseworker called me and laughed because she had done some real detective work and discovered that father and father's girlfriend didn't do that at all, Gabriel had cut his own arms, she thought it was funny, not only funny that he did that but also funny that she caught him. The only thing I could think of was, "Well, aren't you a genius? Why aren't you one fucking bit concerned that this young child is cutting himself? (He was 6). What? Is this funny to you? A happy child, especially one this young, is not going to be cutting on himself, no matter what the circumstances are." I wanted to tell her to please quit her job; she was inflicting much more harm than helping anyone, and she needed to be stopped.

X enrolled our sons into a small-town community school system. The same small-town school system that he, his immediate family, and all the rest of the worm-infested leaves coming out of their extended cultish family tree all attended. That school system only protected X and only helped the boys' lives get worse. A plethora of concerning and sexualized behaviors and statements exhibited by the boys, in a very clear pattern, quite evident of abuse, were there for all the staff to see. If any of them had cared one iota, my sons would be in a much better emotional and mental state right now.

Behaviors such as 'mooning,' grabbing other's butts, hitting others in the genitals, peeing on the bathroom floor, rage, aggression, and attempts to view porn on school-issued computers repeatedly, to name a few. The principal had read several of the reports, so who was she protecting, other than their father, and why? And for what gain? All this information, all this knowledge....and zero action. What the Fuck? My sons just kept getting punished for acting out, detentions, in-school suspensions, and out-of-school suspensions. What the school did and didn't do did not work; it only made matters worse. The staff were not doing their jobs. These behaviors are happening on their watch, and they are turning their heads the other way or just burying them in the sand.

The custody evaluation that I have been referring to was completed by a man in Ann Arbor while the boys and I lived in Lexington, KY. This man unethically conducted and submitted a dishonest and misleading report to the court. It should not matter what his gender was, but in this case, it did, as I later discovered he had a history of demonizing women. He was misogynistic and probably should not be relied upon to conduct fair and reliable custody evaluations for anyone. The Dr. Mulefucent evaluation was refuted by at least three other professionals who were more credentialed than he was and found the report to be extremely biased, the psychological testing misinterpreted and misused, and different tests used on X and me (the one used on him were chosen to cast him in a more favorable light), he used a computer analysis system to analyze X's testing, and he personally and manually analyzed and scored mine, and he brought in a completely different individual to analyze and score some of the testing material as well; -it may have been the Rorschach Testing. Incidentally, I suggest reading The Cult of Personality - you will find it cited at the end of section two. In that, you will learn how biased and ridiculous these tests are. The Rorschach Test results are ambiguous, and the results can be interpreted differently by different professionals. I suggest if you can, refuse to take any of these "psychological tests," especially if you are a woman; they are not made for women. However, Dr. Mulefucent's report was very damaging to me, he claimed, and supposedly 'diagnosed' me as delusional, crazy, and mentally ill. None of which are terms used and defined in the DSM IV which is the manual that he utilized for our report. Not being an actual diagnosis did not stop him from using them on me in this very important report, as they were used to label me, and as long as he had those words associated with me, he accomplished what he set out to do. He used words that would alarm lay people and allow their perception of me to be distorted and, therefore, think the worst of me.

CPS and other officials have reportedly 'cleared' X of what the boys for years have said he has done to them. They have also accused me of doing something I have not done, which has cost my sons and me a horrendous price; my sons are not believed, and not just because their father told them to say they "lied" when they said what they said about him, but now anybody who has any interaction with the paternal family actually thinks they have lied all these years, all the times they have reached out to get help regarding their father. Can behaviors be misconstrued as lies? How is that explained away?

Let Me Be The Mom I'm Supposed to Be

When Gabriel was born; --so was I. My life truly had meaning in a way that was more significant than anything I had ever felt. I loved being a mother. There was nothing more important to me than my child and his welfare, and the same was true when Castiel was born. There was nothing less of that feeling to be had.

I cannot write about or describe how their father felt because I really don't know for sure. All I can describe is what he said to me and what I saw. He seemed to enjoy watching the gory details of me giving birth; it's not as if he was up by my head consoling me or anything. I remember it wasn't when my babies were born; it was the intensity of the labor, and he seemed to enjoy my being in pain. However, he was very put out by the demands of an infant. He didn't seem to enjoy being a father. Even though becoming a parent is a life-altering eventt for most parents, it didn't alter his in a manner that affected a change in lifestyle; he went on doing the same things as he always did. He became very angry and jealous of Gabriel; my attending to Gabriel, and later Castiel, took away from my attending to him, and he was demanding and wanted to be attended to. When Gabriel and/or Castiel would cry, X was irate. When he got mad, his face turned bright red, his veins popped out, he clenched his jaw tightly, and he clenched his fists. In fact, he said he "could not deal with it" and "could not stand to hear a baby cry," so he wanted me to always handle one or both crying babies. I shudder as I remember him asking, or more stating, can't I just put a pillow over his head? Yes, that gave me goosebumps at the time, but I thought, ok, he just wants to not hear it and that's it, but that's another thing that haunts me to this day. I loved taking care of my babies; crying, sound asleep, hungry, eating, changing diapers, giving baths, rocking them, singing to them, holding them. If I were with them, I would be happy. When Gabriel began to cry while X was right there, as I said previously, he would clench his fists, his veins would jump on his neck, his face would get red with anger, and his jaw would clench if, for some reason, he had to pick him up, he would squeeze him tightly and shake him. I caught him on more than several occasions yelling in baby Gabriel or Castiel's face when they cried to "shut up." I'd get to them as fast as I could. I was so afraid he would squeeze him too hard or shake him too hard. When X was just holding Gabriel or Castiel, they began to cry because they could feel his anger -and I think evil, and I'm sure just feeling his anger scared them. It did me. It's been over 22 years now, yet somehow, I can still feel that thick, dense choking anger from the boy's father, and in this case, it was simply because there was an infant who was crying, like all infants do, trying to tell someone that they need something, in the only way they could express it.

Soon, there came the time, when X came driving in the driveway, Gabriel would come running and crying to me. X came in the house yelling at me because Gabriel was crying (which, as you can imagine, his yelling as he walked through the door was very helpful in calming Gabriel down); "What kind of bull shit are you telling him about me all day long?" He would yell out. Gabriel was 2 years old when this happened; we weren't sitting down for an afternoon cup of tea with our scone and discussing the events of the day, and oh, by the way, what do you think of daddy? He's a real asshole, don't you think?

I remember finding bruises on the boys' legs. They were just like the bruises on my forearms and upper arms. I knew how handprint bruising got on my arms and wrists. It was from X angrily squeezing and forcibly holding or moving me. These bruises on the boys' thighs appeared after he had changed their diapers, even though I changed them regularly and always kept them clean. I knew he was rough, and so short-fused that I just wanted to try to eliminate chances for him to get rough with the boys. It wasn't until after I had left X and was working late on the computer while the boys were sleeping. The boys and I, as well as my mom, lived in Kentucky at that time. That's when it all became clear to me. A light shined above my head. I had just flashed back to a time I had been date raped and remembered the handprint bruising that was on my thighs for what seemed like months after that incident. The bruises were from him holding me. Then I realized that's the same reason the boys had handprint bruising on both of their thighs. I kept thinking he was holding them too hard changing the diaper, but it's difficult to change a diaper with one hand, much less no hands.

There was a court-ordered social worker who stated that our sons were "very angry." Really? Do ya think? I wonder why. The social worker gave some head in the sand -anything but the truth, crap justification of their anger as being from "their situation." He did everything he could to dance around the fact that the boys are, at the bare minimum, severely traumatized and very unhappy with their lives. It's as if he believed and was insinuating that the boys were so angry because X and I couldn't get along, that we were fighting over them, and basically that I was being non-compliant. If I would just go away, all would be well. He is just another incompetent individual who had an opportunity to help my sons and did not.

Let's think for a moment about what my sons might be angry about -and please forgive my tone -as I, too, am angry about these things as well. Perhaps they are angry about their dad raping them for years, and to add to that, they have done what they are supposed to do; they've told police officers, CPS caseworkers, social workers, and psychologists -their mother -they just keep getting handed back over to their dad for him to do the same thing to them again. It's as if, especially in the eyes of my sons, all these so-called 'professionals' just keep handing them back over to their perpetrator and saying here they are, go ahead, do whatever you want to do. They are not important enough to us for us to get involved. The boys have even disclosed this despite being threatened by him that he is going to kill them and me. Yet, I used to tell them that they should simply tell the truth, and they would be fine, that they would be protected. Now, I am the piece of shit parent that can't be trusted because, in their eyes and worlds, I lied to them; they weren't protected at all. In fact, the opposite of that was true. How else are they to interpret that? How could I even expect anything different from them?

Gabriel stated he was laughed at by his father when he screamed because it hurt when his dad stuck his dick up his butt. Maybe the boys are angry because one time when, X's girlfriend left because they got into a fight, and they were yelling at each other, and she was crying. She got in her car and left. So, X immediately went upstairs, got his pistol and fired shots off the front porch into the air while the boys were right there playing in the front yard and very afraid. They told me X did 'his thing' to them later that very day. It sounds like, for the latter period of time, he would rape only when the girlfriend/ later wife was not in the house. Maybe they are angry because for all those years since they were taken from my custody and placed in the custody of the grandparents initially and then their father, they have told the grandparents what their dad does; stick his penis up their butts; and the grandparents laugh at the boys and tell them that is not true, that he doesn't do that to them. I'd say the grandparents are delusional, too, but I know they know and are just lying. Or maybe my sons are so angry because they were taken from the only safety they ever knew and the care of their mother, abruptly, 4 separate times, to be handed over to their dad and the rest of those sick fucks, and to only see me in a supervised setting.

I, too, have anger, hate, and rage. Seeing on paper in a CPS report that I coached my sons to say these things is devastating. We are going to go off track here for a minute. It is incredibly rare for any child, especially a young child, to make up these kinds of allegations if they are not true. Furthermore, for the child to be able to give any sort of details only adds to the credibility of what the child is saying. I mean, think about it and simply use common sense and look back on this entire picture. When the boys said they had been told to say what they said, it was while they were with their father at his house; the second time, it was in the school setting in which their father professes and often truly knows "everything they say and do" within those walls, and there were no details as to where, when, or what time of day, etc. in which I told them to say something that wasn't true - because that didn't happen. On the contrary, while in others' custody or care, they gave elaborate details, where, when, how, who, smells, times of day, day of the week as to when the abuse occurred, details of feelings, etc., do you really think a 4- or 5-year-old child could even think of all those details to 'make it up'? Do you really think someone could have given a child all those details of all these separate events and the child be able to keep them straight to repeat them? No, the answer to those questions is a resounding "No!" Everything the boys said their dad did to them came from them having those experiences, not from me. The only thing that was said that was untrue was that I told them to say what they've said, which, of course, their father told them to say. -They had to do that for their own self-preservation, and I certainly do not fault them for that; their living conditions were miserable. However, I doubt they received whatever was promised to them, as X never followed through on anything. Once he gets what he wants, that's all he cares about. So, it served only the needs of their father, and I know that left them with a lot of guilt, pain, and anguish.

My children and I were kept from real, meaningful contact for over 12 years. Instead, they were with a man they have alleged of sexually abusing them, physically, emotionally, psychologically abusing them and neglecting them. Many people, including me, had witnessed him abuse them in many ways and know what he is like without the mask. Other than their father, they were surrounded by people who didn't support them in the least and contributed to the abuse.

It is unnatural for children to be separated from their mothers, especially at a young age. Children need to be nurtured and cared for by their mothers. Not only is separating children from loving, safe, caregiving parents abusive and criminal, but it's also destructive to all parties in many ways. For the child, trust in anyone will be a lifelong struggle for them. It severs the bond between parent and child, it dramatically changes the child, and not for the best. Taking them from an abuser is a different story. Although some of these factors still remain at play, the child is protected from being abused. For me, I was unable to protect my children. In case you didn't know, that is one of a mother's basic instincts, and justifiably, it is a need for that mother to be able to carry that out -that was taken from me. I felt like I was locked in a cage, and my children were on the other side -they couldn't see me or hear me. Although I saw them being hurt because my eyes were held open, I couldn't get to them because my arms and legs had been cut off.

There were many times I had absolutely no contact at all with them. We were abruptly cut off from each other. When we were 'given' the privilege to speak over the phone, the call was always placed on speaker phone, for who knows who was listening in? Who was there bullying my children and chastising them for what they could say and what they could not say? I knew it was on speaker. I could tell in their voices that it was very difficult and even painful for them to talk to me. I damn near didn't want to talk to them -even if it was the only contact I had, because I knew how horrible it was for them. Knowing their sadistic father, he probably told them of other call times that were never arranged just for them to sit there anxiously awaiting a call from me that never came because it was never planned. He did that with other things; why would he not do it with phone calls?

I tried to communicate with them through FaceBook - and I am not a fan of FaceBook, or any other social media actually. I set Gabriel up with an account, I felt Castiel was too young, but X got Gabriel's password and closed the account. Within a few days, X set Gabriel up with an account, but we did not communicate through it because X was monitoring it. I tried getting the boys contract-free phones, but X immediately took them away. He even took them away if I got them contracted phones.

So, the only contact I had with my sons for a long time was supervised visits and then lunchtime visits to the school, and X influenced these as well. I'll begin with the supervised visitation. X was ordered supervised visitation at the very beginning -while we were in Kentucky and Kentucky, CPS was involved (CPS is called DCBS there). Incidentally, I think they would have done a much better job than Michigan did. I believe Kentucky would have actually protected my sons. X had the option to see the boys on many occasions, but he only chose to see them once. Even though it was supervised visitation, and I hated it, I made the best of it and went as frequently as they allowed me to see my sons. However, if you don't know anything about supervised visitation, there's at least one thing you need to know. The supervisor writes down everything that happens and everything that is said. Either parent has access to these notes at any time - which is something I did not know until much later. So, diabolically minded X could get the records and tell the boys, "So, I know you were talking about this, or you were doing that when you saw your mother," and this, my friends, is something he would do. He wanted them to think he was some kind of God who knew all and saw all, and with the cameras in his house, the 360 apps on their phones (once they got phones), and school staff reporting to him, he could terrorize the boys in this way. They always thought they were going to get in trouble for things they did anywhere they were. He was a stalker, as you know, he stalked me, why stop there?

Back to lunchtime visits. The school the boys went to -that their father wanted them to go to, was a construct of backward thinking, narrow-mindedness, judgment, and gossip. However, once I figured out I could see them more if I could stomach the fucking idiot staff and take them their lunches, that's what I did. It started out alright. I dealt with the office staff and the principal glaring and staring at me; the rest of the staff avoided me as much as they could, and the lunchroom staff, clearly being as fake as they could, were mostly friendly -but they asked a lot of questions. I smiled and walked on by these people in the hallways like everything was just fine, they didn't mean anything more than the dirt on the bottom of my shoes. At the elementary school, my coming in for lunch was very special for Gabriel and Castiel. Castiel was in kindergarten, Gabriel was in second grade at this point, and we rarely had the luxury of seeing each other. Castiel wanted to sit on my lap, I saw no problem with that, but eventually someone did, and I was pulled aside and told that he could no longer sit on my lap. Incredulous! So, I had to be the one that every time he tried to sit on my lap, I had to say "No" to my dear

5-year-old child, "I'm sorry, you cannot sit on my lap." Completely outrageous. Then, not too long after that, the principal informed me that X told her that I could only come in on days that I picked them up from school. Now, my head was about to blow off the top of my neck. Those were days that I didn't come in because I was already driving into that stinking town to pick them up, so now, if I wanted to have lunch, I'd have to go there back and forth twice. Since it was nearly a 30-minute drive, and I am a woman with limited financial resources, that made this quite difficult. The custody arrangement at that time, thanks to our fabulous family court system and the Washtenaw County CPS caseworkers, was that I got to see my sons only every Wednesday after school at 7 and every other weekend with a Friday after school pick up and a Monday morning drop off at school. So, with this I could only take them lunches on Wednesdays and every other Friday.

When I visited my sons at lunchtime, I either made them lunch or bought something and took it in. The principal at the elementary school ended up moving up to the middle school the same year my youngest son moved up to the middle school. I was very disappointed; the previous principal at the middle school, who had left, seemed to see through X and saw the bigger picture. However, the puppet principal, PennyWise, did not and would side with X any chance she got. She is also the principal who limited my lunch visits at the elementary school and is responsible for having the lunch monitors not 'allow' me to have my child sit on my lap during lunch. (In which case, I noticed when other parents had lunch with their children, for some very odd reason, nothing was said to them while their child sat in their lap. Strange, huh?)

Then came the time that Castielle was on probation for the destruction of another student's cell phone. The probation officer went to discuss and obtain 'family' information from Principal PennyWise. Which certainly was not neutral, but I guess he couldn't figure that out on his own. When the probation officer told me that

97

I *could not* take the boys' lunch anymore, he said that the principal complained that I was bringing it in for my sons, and none of the other students were getting any. WTF, right? How outrageously ridiculous is that? What idiot reasons like that? Since I'm bringing lunch to my sons, I'm supposed to bring it for the entire school? Or contact every single parent and ask if they would please take their child's lunch today so I can take it to my sons? It was completely irrational and controlling.

The other way I 'bought' my son's lunch was because I had food stamps and Medicaid, so my sons qualified for the free lunch program. Apparently, the program only entitles the child to certain healthy foods, not everything that is offered, but it was better than nothing, which was what they were getting. Even while they were in elementary school, hell, preschool, my point is they were very young when they were expected to make their own lunches. Nobody helped them at X's.

But, once X found out they were using the free lunch program that they were entitled to, he cut them off. He would not let them use that. He would not let them eat that food because they were getting it through me.

Whenever I think about the small-town pea-brained community and schools my sons had to deal with, it just makes me furious. Have you read The Scarlet Letter by Nathaniel Hawthorne? I really hope so because when I tell you I relate completely to the character Hester Prynne being in the small town or being in any one of the schools, you'll understand. I don't think I had as much grace as Hester Prynne, but I always tried to carry my head high no matter who or how those people were looking at me. I never did anything wrong, in case trying to protect my children is wrong. However, the 'crime' they would say I committed is I listened to my sons, and I believed them, and I always believed in them. Instead of Hester's large "A" she had to wear (for adultery if you don't know, as she was pregnant without a husband - -oooo the aberration!), I should have worn a large "L" for Listened or "B" for Believed.

The boys and I had a very tight bond, and we did everything together. We were a very content and happy family -until they were taken. I think back to the time we were in Kentucky, and although it is bittersweet, bitter because it came to such a tragic and abrupt end, it was sweet because other than the worst of it, I can see clearly my sons smiling and laughing faces. Sadly, those memories are overshadowed by the vile ending.

Our relationships were completely severed and altered not just because they were gaslit and lied to continuously and horrifically abused while becoming more and more like their father. But how they were treated and lied to at their school, not believed or protected by CPS, not believed or protected by police officers, the courts, and even some mental health workers. To top it all off, they thought I had abandoned them and were being told I didn't care about them anymore, that I didn't want them, and that I wanted to go out on dates.

All these actors have completely changed the dynamic between my sons and myself. They have also completely changed the trajectory of my sons' lives with all the extra years of abuse. My sons mimic their father in a lot of ways, they often treat me very similar to the way X treated me., and surely the way X treated them. I left him for a reason. It's devastating to see my sons have picked up similar characteristics and behaviors.

In many ways, my sons are only a mere wisp of their former selves. Of course, they would change because of developmental reasons. But these changes are not simple developmental changes. By observing my sons, it was as if you had a telescopic lens into X's house and could see how my sons were being treated.

CPS of Washtenaw County, MI, completely screwed up every single report they conducted, from the very first one, which was in

2004 or 2005, all the way through 2016 or 2017. The reports were biased against me and much of it was completely fabricated. In the very first one, it was recommended to me by the Child Advocacy Clinic in Ypsilanti to file a report with CPS. This was when I was changing the diaper of my oldest son, who was 3 at the time, and he verbalized the following question to me: "Finger up the butt, thumb up the butt?" I remember looking at him inquisitively, and he said, "Daddy do." Then he turned over and put his bottom up into the air. When the caseworker came out to the house -we were staying at my mother's home at the time, she told me to wait until they got a little older and they told somebody something at school! My sons were not quite 1 and 3. Are you kidding me right now? Is that seriously supposed to be some kind of comfort? Then, when I saw the final report, she had made it appear that my sons were wild and that I had 'no control' of my children. She stated, "The boys were throwing rocks". The truth of that is they were dropping pea gravel into a very small pool of water, and I was right there monitoring the situation. Another thing she wrote in the report was that there were mattresses on the floor as if we were leaving the area as if we were on the run or something. The truth was, and had she asked, I would have told her that my mom was moving to Kentucky, and I may have to take the boys with me and go there too since her house was going on the market, and I had no place else to go. X had not called in weeks to inquire as to how the boys were, but I had frequently talked about Kentucky to him in the past.

Incidentally, fast forward several years. When the police were looking for my sons in order to abduct them when they turned them over to the paternal grandparents, they went to our house and peeked through our windows. They noted and reported that we had several boxes as if we were about to leave somewhere. The truth was, we had recently moved into that house, and I was trying to be very organized, so I was putting things away in a very deliberate matter. I just couldn't believe the irony when I saw this assumption in yet another report.

In one of the investigations in which the boys and I lived in Kentucky, the same one I was referring to in the previous paragraph, this was immediately following the judgment of divorce, when I was awarded primary custody, and X was given every other weekend. After their week-long visit with X in Michigan, they came home with all kinds of disturbing details from that week. There were several reports filed with Kentucky DCBS. However, Kentucky investigates where the abuse happens, and Michigan investigates where the children live. So, both states were in direct conflict with each other; therefore, it went to the Michigan State Police, who never should have been investigating a case such as this. They were X's saving grace. He couldn't have asked for a more bungling and incompetent group of people.

It's infuriating how X could walk into a meeting with a 'mental health professional,' school staff member, most evaluators, CPS caseworker, police officer, etc., even while brandishing his smug, cocky, shittiness, and not hiding his contempt for authority or the mental health field, and he would still leave that appointment having the upper hand, somehow, despite his rudeness, although playing the victim card, he'd turn this person/these people in his favor. It was unbelievable. As he had done so many times previously, when he met with the Michigan State Police on this report, I would bet he turned on the waterworks and played his huge victim card, successfully turning these officers in his favor as well.

Playing the victim card was something he excelled at, and that certainly didn't hurt his ability to gain favor, no matter what. On the other hand, my hands shook, my voice trembled, my worry, anxiety, sadness, all of it was written all over my face and in how I carried myself. X was always confident, even if he was an ass, he was a confident ass, and he didn't care who he was being an ass to. He only kissed someone's ass if he knew he absolutely had to win their favor. Somehow, he knew that seeing a big man cry would work in his favor, or whichever emotion he had to fake would work for him, so he just brought it on.

For a very long time after my sons were taken from me, frequently even to this day, when I'm at a grocery store, or in town, at restaurants, or some other public place, I would see parents and adults treating children terribly. It was exasperating. Most of these people seemed to be the child's parents, yet there they were, displaying their abusiveness and cruelty right out in the open. What were they like behind closed doors? All I could think was, this person gets to have custody of their child, and they treat them like this, yet I do not have custody of my children, and I would never treat my children like that. It's sad that people do not realize the privilege and luxury they have to be able to raise their children and protect them. Perhaps if they did, they would treat them better. X has custody of our children, and he treats them horrifically. A clueless, mother-hating referee up north with her head up her ass took my children away from me.

The bruises and wounds have long faded from our skin, but the memory of the mark of each and everyone will never fade. Although some of those left scars, many of those have faded as well. Many of the scars that are left now are those that were self-inflicted by each of my sons. They were from cutting and burning themselves. Both of them cut their arms at different times, and at least one of them liked putting cigarettes out on himself. One of the times Castiel cut himself with a knife - I found the knife he used right next to his bed; I will never forget it. There were many cuts on his arm, some slanted one way, some slanted the other, some perpendicular -there was certainly not a clear pattern, just many cuts clearly self-inflicted with a knife. I was very upset and concerned about this, as any caring mother would be. I asked Castiel about them, and he said he didn't know what they were from. I saw it as we were walking out the door to get to school, and they were going to X's after school. The librarian at school saw them and took it up with the bubble-brained principal, PennyWise. PennyWise called X -not me, and X told her he wanted to see them before anything was done -of course - he needed to fabricate a story. Castiel went to his father's house after school that day. X decided the cuts had come from pages of a book by the way he was carrying the book. Who would believe that, right? Well, PennyWise and the rest of the staff at that school all bought into it. The boys were very young when they engaged in these behaviors. For the above incident, Castiel was in the 2nd or 3rd grade at the time.

My son's cuts, bruises, and burns have left a permanent blood stain seared in my mind. Before every new bruise, especially handprints, which continued to appear, especially on their arms (upper and lower), just as they had appeared all over my arms, wrists, and hands, it was as if I saw all of them at the same time again, I would see every single mark on their bodies he left, including raised bumps - which happened on both boys' heads. These 'marks' echoed Referee Teera Nichol's decision, and she wrote the decision in such a manner that it would be very difficult, if not impossible, to be overturned.

Each of my sons spoke of suicide as being their answer. Gabriel attempted it on more than one occasion. I have one suicide letter he wrote that I found, and I have kept it. Thank God he made it to treatment after one of those attempts and that I still have both of my sons with me. Struggling? Yes, they are. Still alive? Thank God that is a yes, as well. Incidentally, Gabriel wanted to go back to the hospital he was in for his suicide attempt rather than go to his father's when he was supposed to go there.

While the boys and I were stuck with supervised visitation and then our very limited schedule at home, I would give them things. Some I bought, some things were from home and were either theirs that I thought they would like and sometimes it was something of mine. They very much enjoyed getting these things, and I knew that, at least for the time they had them, it would make them feel closer to me. However, it did not last long. Especially if the boys really liked it or if they displayed a sentimental attachment to it, especially then it went right into the garbage at X's house or was hidden from them. My aunt bought long-range walkie-talkies in the hopes that we might be able to communicate with each other. Those *immediately* went into the garbage when they got back to X's after that visit. Anything from me, any kind of reminder of me, they had to eliminate it. I wonder, what were they so afraid of?

November of 2004, I secretly made a phone call to the Bellaire Police Department to inquire as to where I could take my young sons in the middle of the night should I have to urgently leave the house if I felt we were in danger. The officer was completely unconcerned; he told me about someplace in Grayling, I think. He never asked what was going on, never asked where we lived, never asked my name, never asked how many children or how old they were. Nothing. He never asked if I felt in danger right then. Throughout all those years, police officers never failed to disappoint me, just as the CPS caseworkers and the Referee et al. disappointed and disgusted me.

I left for the last time with the boys but knew I would have to go back for Maggie (our yellow labrador) and the cats. He was mean and cruel to them; I was not leaving them there indefinitely. I felt awful leaving them there without me protecting them for any length of time at all.

When I came back up north, I stopped at the courthouse to ask for a Personal Protection Order. It was granted. Then I went next door and once again asked a police officer for assistance. I asked for an officer to accompany me to the house to serve the PPO (yes, at least up there, one serves their own personal protection order to people they are afraid of hurting and their children) and to pick up the animals, my medications, and some of our stuff. What the officer said would blow your mind: "No, we don't get involved in domestic disputes," well, that was a new one for me!

Violated

When we were in Bellaire, up north -in the house that became the house of horrors -the Shining, there were many incidents that really frightened me. One happened at nighttime when I was in the bathroom downstairs -this bathroom had wooden sliding doors. X had been up in his office, either gambling, viewing porn, or any other insidious thing he did on his computer. Typically, when X came down the stairs, you heard it, not only because he stomped (he's a big guy) but also because the stairs creaked, and the bathroom I was in was directly under the staircase. I would have expected to hear him come down the stairs, there never was a time I didn't hear him, especially from the vantage point of that bathroom. Nonetheless, I was washing my face, brushing my teeth, putting on my pajamas, and so on. When I was done, I turned around and slid the door open to leave the bathroom, and was mortified because X was towering over me, just standing there in the doorway, blocking me from getting out, with a very odd and chilling expression on his face, his hands were behind his back. He stood there staring at me, not saying a word, keeping his hands behind his back. It scared the crap out of me, and when I reflect back, it scares me again. At that particular moment, I remember feeling sick to my stomach. I knew something was not right. There was rage in his strange expression and his ice-cold eyes. As I had learned a few years earlier, the way to bring X back from the edge was to say something funny, what will work the quickest is if I act dumb, foolish, and self-deprecating. It could be something I didn't believe, but any chance he got to laugh at my expense, he took.

Usually, I knew where X was in the house because he was more often than not angry, stomping around and complaining about something not done well or to his liking. Then he began to sneak around and creep up on us or just me more and more. My theory on this particular incident is as follows: intuitively, I think he had his gun behind his back, and he was going to use it on me. Since that first incident with the gun and the bullets being deliberately left out in Munith that I've already mentioned, this was not a reach. I saw how he talked about me, and I know how he referred to me while speaking with co-workers, friends, and family. I felt his contempt.

Playing a foolish woman was something that I learned well, and it was a skill I utilized frequently. I would act as foolish as I had to in order to stay alive for my sons (and my mom). My sons needed me to be with them (of which the bottom would fall out later). They did not need me to be buried 6 feet under in the state land behind our property. Somehow, I talked my way out of that incident, and I talked my way out of many similar incidents. When I see that chilling, sinister look in his eyes, that's all the warning I need. Never did I see what he had in his hands behind his back. Although I remember him backing out of the doorway rather than turning around -he seldomly backed up to let me through, and I distinctly remember he had to go down to the basement for something after I left the bathroom and the incident had diminished - the basement is where he kept all of his guns.

We had one computer. X was almost always on it. He used it for work, he used it for communication, sending and receiving messages from his family and work colleagues. He could be more secretive with his communication that way because I could not overhear a discussion, and he took full advantage of my technological challenges. If I ever had the opportunity to get on the computer, it would be when the boys were sleeping, and X ran into town for cigarettes or something. My time was limited, so I had to complete whatever research I wanted to do very quickly. Later, X would go through my viewing history to my face, blasting me with questions; "I see you're looking at Haflinger horses. Why are you looking at them? You're not going to get one, so why are you wasting time looking at them?" He would continue to badger and question me on whatever subject it was that I had looked up. He wanted me to know that he knew everything that I was viewing and everything that I was doing on the computer. Likewise, I did not have a cell phone at the time, he did, but all I had access to was a landline. If he heard me on the phone or just wanted to see if I had made or received any calls, he would stand right in front of me and go through the call history.- if he didn't know who a number was to, he'd ask me because he wanted to know, and he would check the outgoing calls in the same manner.

We had baby monitors, but I rarely used them as I was always with the boys. On occasion, I was not right there, though I did use the monitors, which is how I found out X had been using them regularly to listen to what I was doing and saying. He had turned the base monitor to face the wall so I wouldn't see the light and know it was on, and he kept the other part of it hidden from view in his office.

On that note, I also discovered cameras placed in the house. One was tucked in between the books at the top of the stairway in a bookcase. His office was upstairs, so I'm sure he wanted to be able to hide the tabs he needed to in case I was going to his office.

As I look back on all that now, not only do I feel intensely sick to my stomach, and my head begins to pound, but I also feel so violated, so infringed upon, so raw, and, of course, infuriated and very sad. I'm mostly very sad for my sons. They had to deal with all of this for years and years longer when he gained custody of them. He had cameras inside that house as well to 'monitor' them.

The world that I thought I was living in, even though madness was seeping through in places, and I knew X put on a show while speaking with professionals and changed completely right when we got in the car to go home. However, I still thought I had some semblance of control over my sons and my life, as well as I thought we had some sort of privacy. At that time, I certainly wasn't questioning our lives being in jeopardy. But soon, I would be.

X was smart in a sociopathic way; he wasn't super smart in common sense, but he knew how to manipulate people and lie to bring them over to his corner and leave them with the impression that they came to their conclusions all on their own. He was cunning, evil, and diabolical in his thinking and actions. On the other hand, I was naïve, trusting, and always wanted to believe there is good in everybody. Sadly, I found out the hard way that there is no good in everybody. I'm sorry to break it to you, but the saying "there is a little bit of good in everybody" is rubbish. Even though part of me still wants to believe that. But it's always for the wrong reasons: why am I making myself think there is good in this terrible person anyway? There are simply rotten people who bring more detestable rot into the world. I will admit that I don't believe there are rotten children, I believe all children have the capacity to become good adults. However, evil exists, and I think it can take hold of almost anybody if the conditions and environment are right to do so. I'm certain there are readers who may be cursing me for my professing of that. I admit, in the last 24 years or so, and even before then, I have come across abhorrent people doing abhorrent things, and by now, having had all of these experiences, I just cannot rationalize that any thread of their being is decent or genuinely good.

Dr. Mulefucent, the custody evaluator in Ann Arbor, is responsible for so much pain and heartache; he, in fact, set in motion the thundering of fallen dreams for over three people: two innocent boys, and their naive and trusting mother (me), my mother, and others in my immediate family, which my sons never had the opportunity to have relationships with. He called upon many to follow in his path; most did, all did not, for those that did, the harm they did is great and unforgivable.

There are hundreds of memories that haunt my thoughts, spinning round and round my head, crushing my hopes and dreams. My brain is trying its best to think of a good memory. However, the truth is there exists an overwhelming amount of anguish, grief, sorrow, and disappointment. Even by trying to access the good memories instead of the horrific ones, I see the others clouding and choking the good memories out. It leaves me in the clutches of guilt that will probably be the death of me, anger, and complete melancholy. As the memories replay themselves, the emotions stir and surface; the devastation for my sons of all they have gone through, their bodies and their minds. Their confusion, anger, pain and mistrust. My sadness, anger, and guilt for mishandling certain situations, and my relentless guilt that I have not been able to protect my sons. There is nothing anyone can do or say that will relieve me of that.

There was another time we were in the kitchen. I was about to prepare a meal. So, I had Castiel set up in his swing and Gabriel had been right next to me but wasn't at this particular point. He was behind and on the other side of X. X was standing at the counter with this incredibly bizarre expression on his face, those ice-cold and wild eyes. Then I realized he had grabbed a candle and a large butcher's knife. He kept saying that he needed to cut the wick on the candle, and he was going to cut it with that knife. By the way, there were scissors in a drawer right next to him that would have worked much better at cutting the wick if it really needed to be cut. He stood there waving this large butcher knife around and claiming he was going to use it to cut the wick. My main fear, at this point, was how to get to both of my sons, who were on different sides of him from me at the same time. I felt as if he was at a breaking point; his eyes were wild and darting, and he had a threatening expression on his face. He was nonsensical. No solution for my getting to my sons was appearing in my head. I was a bit frozen and unable to even call upon the dumb foolery technique I usually used. It's weird because when I think back, I only hear his yelling and his bizarre statements. I don't hear either of my children crying, I'm not sure if they were, and I have just blanked that out, or somehow, they had learned that their crying enraged him more. Eventually, he decided he did not need to cut the wick, placed both the wick and the candle on the table, and just went back up the stairs to work. This was just another scary event that the three of us had compartmentalized.

The best comparison I can make of what my sons' father was like to help people understand and look into our world a little bit, is if you've ever seen the movie The Shining. He is comparable to Jack Torrance, which was the character Jack Nicholson played; I frequently felt as if we were living in the Overlook Hotel. As the snow blew outside, X carried on with his strange, intimidating, scary rage fests inside. We all lived up north, away from our family and friends. I was finding my sons and me more and more in what seemed to be very similar to the plot of the movie The Shining (but worse), and this was happening for real and to us. It was terrifying, surreal, and shocking, yet I simultaneously felt as if I was watching it all unfold from above. Thinking back on that time, gives me goosebumps and makes my skin crawl, just like it did then. Incidentally, he told me that The Shining was his favorite movie.

On TV, he watched gambling shows, learning how to lie and mislead people and how to detect if other people are lying. X was a lot of different characters. He acted differently around his family, friends, and colleagues, and then again in the presence of a therapist. He is a chameleon but a devil disguised as a chameleon.

I was mostly happy-go-lucky prior to X. If there is a mental illness at all, it is due to living with a person who is a sadist, a pedophile, and about 5 other different people inside the same person, who everybody thinks is a great person. X is worse than Jekyll and Hyde; his family knows it, and I believe they are afraid of him. He could switch moods/emotions/people -whatever you want to call it, every 2 minutes, 20 minutes or much longer, you never knew. His behavior was peculiar. He came downstairs on top of the world; a couple minutes later, he was stomping and yelling to shut the fuck up if we were making any noise. He would throw things, slam things down, kick the dog, and scream at the boys and me because I was not "keeping them in line" and "keeping them quiet" he'd tell them to "shut the fuck up, you little bastard," and to me, "where the fuck is my food?" "where's my coffee?" etc.

I was getting supper ready, Castiel was in his chair at the table, and Gabriel went back and forth from being next to me and sitting at the table. X came stomping down the stairs and plopped himself into a chair. He charged, "Where's my supper?" Castiel began to cry harder because now, not only was he hungry, but he was afraid as well. The same for Gabriel; he sat quietly in his chair, trembling. Now X yells at baby Castiel, "Shut up., Shut the fuck up, your food is coming, SHUT THE FUCK UP, SHE'S GETTING IT." He pounded his fists on the table. X's face was bright red, his fists were clenched and slammed on the table, his veins were popping out of his temples and his arms, and his jaw was clenched tight. Castiel continued crying. I was dropping things. Gabriel continued trembling. I should have called the police; no, it was good I didn't. X was just mad...oh, and hungry. And the police in Bellaire don't get involved in domestic disputes - X didn't end up hitting anybody, at least not that time, right?

You may ask, why did I allow these and so many other things to happen? I did what I could to stop them when I was able to. Once we got to court and were dealing with CPS, X alleged that I "nagged" him. Saying anything to him, in the heat of the moment or not, about his temper created an instant rage. Saying anything to X about changing his behavior is nagging him. Of course, I tried to stop abusive behaviors when I could, mostly by putting myself in the middle -something I continued with my sons when they fought until they got too big. Whenever I caught it, knowing X, and having learned what doesn't make things worse for whomever he's hurting, I learned to be very calm and just move in and remove; so that is what I did whenever I caught the abuse and couldn't stop it any other way.

I heard Gabriel crying and saying, "Dada, kick me, dada, kick me," As he was running down the stairs. I was taking care of Castiel at the time. X came thundering down the stairs shortly after, loudly charging, "I did not. He's lying." "Whatever he says, it's not true. He's lying." Just like the spanking allegations made by Gabriel from a year earlier that X denied in the same manner, and exactly the same words that X would use when I got the boys back after their week-long stay with him up north when I told him over the phone that I knew what he did. I consoled Gabriel. A couple days later, Gabriel went back up the stairs to X's office;- it doesn't help that X keeps candy in his office - that *somehow* Gabriel knows full well about, and don't you think he's going to want to make that climb up the stairs if he's going to get some candy? This time, Castiel was ok to leave for a few minutes, so I crept up behind Gabriel and I poked my head through the railing, just to see how this would play out. Sure enough, within a few minutes, X is roughly pushing Gabriel out the doorway with his foot. When that doesn't work out so well, X begins to kick our 2-year-old son out of the door with his foot. There aren't words for how I felt about what I saw him do to my son. I calmly walked in, picked Gabriel up, and took him downstairs. Those were the days when I was still blessed with the luxury of being able to protect my children. That was before CPS and our family courts took that luxury away from me.

Nothing that my children have said their father has done or was doing has I doubted, nor has it necessarily surprised me.

At the Tavern, which was co-owned by X's parents and was where I met them, I may have just finished work. X's sister was there -she didn't work there anymore, but she hung out there most of the time -just sitting at the bar and blabbing. I sat down next to her for a moment because she was blabbing at me about something unimportant, but I didn't want to be rude and just walk out. X was in the kitchen, cooking something - I think it was for her. The two of them were having a disagreement. So, in her typical spoiled brat obnoxious fashion, his sister, sitting right next to me but talking loudly to him, put both her hands out in front of her and close to each side of her face, palms out -facing the opposite wall, with her fingers slightly bent as if she were holding onto something, and said; "Grab, spread, lick." She was talking about a butt, but I found that to be a bit descriptive and disgusting to say to anybody, much less her brother. Especially when, later in my life, I would learn this is exactly what is referred to as "butt kissing" by my sexually abused son, by the man his sister is making this comment to. I felt instantly nauseous.

I thought this was beyond grotesque, and even as I tried to blow it off, I asked myself, is that something I would ever say to my older brother? The answer was an immediate and resounding NO. That's not something I would say to anybody. I've thought of that comment so many times because of the "butt-kissing" episodes. It is that exact specific action she described in her comment.

X's wife claims that X cried once *when he had to spank*" one of the boys. First of all, the boys were ages 10 and 8, so he shouldn't have been "spanking" them at all. Second, they never should have been being spanked in the first place, period -my opinion, and that should have mattered since they are my sons as well. Second, as I've mentioned before, X can make himself cry and make a big scene on demand. Lastly, if he had never spanked, to begin with, he wouldn't have had to go through all that trouble of creating his 'crying spell'!

The logistics used by the family courts: judges, referees, attorneys, GAL, evaluators, a handful of the mental health workers, all the school staff, the small-town, small-minded parents, most of the police, and CPS caseworkers didn't utilize logic at all. At the very face of it, the school of thought that they bought into was that I was "delusional," -something that most all mothers tend to be accused of in these cases, interestingly, and I "coached" my sons to say things that didn't happen, which is another thing that supposedly happens "a lot" in these case, but in reality, it is exceedingly rare. When, in fact, the boys were crying out for help for things that were happening to them. The nature of the disclosures never changed. However, several of the disclosures became more mature as the boys became more mature. They grew up with this happening to them, as well as they had told a lot of professionals and had gotten sick of telling people and nobody doing anything to protect them. They were becoming hardened, as was I. The behaviors matched the disclosures, and early on they made a plethora of drawings that matched what they were saying and doing as well. But drawings are *only* drawings, right? It is completely preposterous and total balderdash to consider that they had been coached by anybody. The people who thought that only wanted to think that because it made their jobs easier and it was easier to stomach rather than consider the atrocities the boys spoke of as being true accounts. Then, when these particular so-called professionals had the ear of other so-called professionals who were weak and didn't want to believe it either (i.e., Judas), I'm sure it was fairly simple to talk them over to the easy side as well. They didn't have to challenge themselves; they then could keep with the status quo (that they created) and go on with their lives and not have to think of the horrors these children have suffered. What I'd like to ask them is, how did I get them to act out all of those behaviors? How did I get my son to not poop for several weeks? (And on and on).

Both boys were ridiculed, shunned, and humiliated at X and his family's houses. Gabriel was made fun of because he was shorter than his younger brother, and when he was younger, he had a little extra padding, so he was made fun of about that. (Incidentally, both X and his wife are fairly large people). Whereas Castiel grew to be quite tall and thin, so they humiliated him because they said he was too skinny. They made fun of Gabriel's ears. Of course, their father kept their heads shaved -in fact, they shaved those little baby's heads as soon as they got custody. I had not gotten Castiel a haircut at all, ever, and Gabriel, I had gotten him a haircut only once. I loved their hair; I still love their hair. They have great hair. It's not hair that should be shaved off under any circumstances unless it is to take a part of their identities away from them.

114

There was a particularly long stretch of time when Castiel was complaining that his butt was hurting; he said it was because of someone sticking his penis up his butt, but he didn't say who.

On Instant Messaging, X and his father discussed X getting a new vehicle despite us having a plan for a particular vehicle that would have helped the children. X's father told him to get whatever he wanted. He told him that I could "Flinstone" it or "thumb it" if I liked, even though I was the only one taking the boys to doctor's visits, dentist's visits, getting the groceries, etc. In the same text conversation, X's father asked him if he still had control of all the money. In their eyes, X's money was solely X's, and what he provided for the family was him doing us a huge favor -he didn't have to. He only did so out of his kind generosity. (Hysterical). X did as his father suggested, and despite our vehicle agreement, and without talking to me at all, he came home with a behemoth of a truck that I sure as hell didn't want to be driving my sons around in.

I saw an IM between him and a colleague where X stated all he wanted was a "beer and a lap dance." I had never heard him say anything like this, nor had I known of him visiting such an establishment. It was all new to me. But, as I was finding out, there was a lot to X I didn't know. As I look back, X never told me much about himself growing up, or as a teenager, or in school, really nothing. The only thing I remember him telling me was that the old guy who had previously owned the party store across the street from the Tavern sold him (or gave him) pornography when he was young. I assumed that was in high school, but it may have been earlier than that.

When 911 happened, and people were throwing themselves off the World Trade Center and out of windows to escape the fire, X was laughing. He out and out lied about this in court and denied laughing, but I will never forget. For most of humanity, this tragedy was traumatizing. For me, I remember the sound of their bodies hitting the ground or buildings beneath, and that being a shocking and terrible sound, but the worst part is what I hear after that. I hear the sound of X's laughing and the eerie wild-eyed expression on his face that is even worse. I am sorry to any of you who lost someone in that horrific attack, and I'm especially sorry if what I write next triggers you. I feel it is pertinent to include this cold, sadistic brute that I am trying to describe. X watched the live coverage of that day and watched it as it was being replayed over and over again. When there was a person falling to the ground from way up high, he would excitedly exclaim, "Oh, look, there goes another one," "And another," and so on. Then, he would continue to laugh at the sounds of innocent lives being taken in this truly tragic way. I tried to distract him, tried to get him to do something else, all to no avail. I would take my sons and leave the room to go anyplace else but there.

We had come back and forth a couple of times from up north to my mom's house downstate before I had left him for good. We would be gone for a couple weeks, then he'd call, turn on the waterworks, and I'd take the boys and go back. But, as much as he said he would work on his explosiveness and unpredictability, he never did. The last time we went back up north, he had made supper. But I don't remember us ever sitting down to eat it. The boys were excited to see their stuff and, naturally, a bit excited to see him. They hadn't seen him in a while. He was their dad, so yeah, they seemed happy to see him. Don't buy into the bullshit that an abused child is going to be afraid of their abusive parent no matter what when they first see him after a while. It's different for each child, each developmental level and so on -there's no set rule. If you are told there is, look at them and smile, and tell them, respectfully, they are wrong. However, shortly after we arrived, X freaked out about something with the TV, and he was very angry with one of the boys. Apparently, Gabriel interfered with him watching something on TV. Seriously, one would think that if you're so heartbroken…boo…hoo…and that you've supposedly changed for your family to be able to come home, you wouldn't be much interested in something on TV. You'd actually want to spend time, at least with your children you haven't seen in a while. We had been there probably less than an hour, which was long enough for me to have changed into my pajamas! I stayed in my pajamas and said fuck this......again, and took the boys and said we're leaving; this is never, ever going to change. And the boys and I left.

I got gas in Grayling, in my pajamas, in the cold, in April, in the evening.

Initially, I had met X over a summer when I went to work at the bar/tavern his parents co-owned. I had recently gone back to U of M and was weighing returning in the fall. I did not. I continued to work at the bar. Promising future there, huh? X hated that place. At least, that's what he told me. He cooked. He only worked during lunch, though. If anyone wanted food beyond the times he was there, we -waitresses/bartenders -which was one and the same, had to cook it -it was mostly fried foods in the afternoon and evening. The place was pretty small with high ceilings -it used to be a bank. The point of my telling you that is that voices carried. When someone would come in the front door, X would step back into the kitchen a few steps and then mutter nasty, mean, obnoxious things about them - calling them names, making fun of them, etc. But he'd do it while hiding in the kitchen, so it wasn't to their faces, yet he had to know they could hear him. If I could hear him from the bar, everyone else in the place could hear him, too. It was terrible and embarrassing. He thought he was so big and bad, even as he cowered in the kitchen and blurted negative comments about the patrons of the tavern.

It was an 'all X family' trait to be two-faced. X was always hiding behind something or somebody. There was very little truth ever in what he said or in who he was. He still hides behind a computer, or his wife, or his family. He hides behind his family as they have covered his ass his entire life. Lying in court came easily for him, his mom, dad and his sister since they had done it all along: "Oh,

117

yes, he's a wonderful loving father." Everybody's pants should have been ablaze by the time all was said and done, especially when these people know full well what kind of father X is: sadistic, controlling, heavy-handed, sexualized, and brutally cruel. Those people will go to any and all lengths to keep the boys silenced and with him and away from me. They would do anything to keep their secret from being exposed. The longer the boys were with them and away from me, the more likely their secret would be kept hidden a secret.

Bruises may fade, cuts may heal, scars may diminish, and knots and swellings level out again. However, all of them will remain as fresh as when they first happened, along with the pain in our memories. There, they don't go away. There, they remain forever.

The CPS, police, the courts, etc., have encouraged my sons to lie. They don't believe them when they tell the truth; they only believe them when they are threatened to recant their statements, and they do. Oh, now they will believe them, but none of the other hundreds of times they disclosed about the abuse that was happening to them. It never mattered when my sons said they wanted to be with me and that they were afraid of their father and did not want to live with him. That never mattered. They repeatedly told CPS et al. that they felt safe with me in my house, but they were afraid and did not feel safe at their father's house. Likewise, the boys told CPS, etc., about many of the abuses they have suffered hundreds of times, and then, 2 times, they said they were old to say what they said at the last interview or whatnot.

Sexual abuse perpetrated on a child by a complete stranger is quite rare. And of the cases that proceeded to court, were they actions against the alleged perpetrator or were they charges of another kind, such as mental abuse of the protective parent to allegedly "make" the child say something that was not allegedly true? The latter of those are even rarer. Yet, CPS claims to find them regularly. I call it hogwash, and that 99.9% of what they are labeling as "coaching" are true cases.

More than 90% of juvenile sexual abuse victims know their perpetrator in some way.

Childhelp.org

It is imperative for you to know that child sexual abuse is more prevalent than is acknowledged, and children are more secretive about this abuse than anyone would generally expect. Child sexual abuse is very damaging to a child, especially when it is perpetrated by a family member or someone the child knows and trusts, and over 90% of the time, it is perpetrated on a child by a family member, parent, and someone the child has come to know and trust.

Richard Gardner, the quack who brought us "Parental Alienation Syndrome," is known to have said: "There is a little pedophilia in all of us." Really? Because I disagree.

Children who have been abused in any of the many garden varieties of abuse that those having more control and power and over, have found to inflict upon our powerless, defenseless, and dependent members of society, and then those defenseless creatures have, therefore, found themselves, necessary or not, at the whims of a decision of a caseworker. These kids, most already -now forever; are different from the rest. And their lives' trajectory has been altered forever. Not simply because somebody has hurt them but because a system has failed them -the only system put in place to protect them. Furthermore, to qualified mental health professionals and to those who care, these kids stick out like a sore thumb -their behaviors - what they exhibit, and even what they hide -to the knowing is very revealing. It just takes those around the child/ren, who care - and who will act on their behalf to get them the change of circumstance in which they need. Most importantly, the addition of having those who are able to make those changes for the child/ren to listen closely to what they are being told by those who know what the hell they are doing.

The family court system and CPS have, in my opinion, perpetuated child abuse by their biases and ignorance. They add fuel to the fire when they disbelieve children and shun children when a child discloses abuse. Alarmingly, time and time again, the family courts have handed children over to the perpetrator. Most men who are not committing abuse understand that their young children, in particular, will be better off spending more time with their mother, and they don't contest this -these men are not abusers... the family court judges do not yet seem to understand this concept.

The Michigan State Police in Kalkaska actually destroyed and threw out evidence (one of the DVDs that Gabriel disclosed). In yet another CPS investigation, CPS caseworkers refused to read or listen to a transcript that was of Gabriel making many disclosures of all kinds of abuse by his father and paternal family. They only read one report by a custody evaluator who had very limited contact with the family and the children, and that report was the oldest. However, CPS was provided with several other reports that were more recent, and the professionals were more specialized in the types of abuse my sons and I were dealing with, as well as the professionals had much more contact with the children and extended family members. Several of these other professionals made many attempts to contact the caseworkers, but their calls were never returned. The caseworkers chose to only speak with one unqualified, long-out-of-the-picture custody evaluator, who had not even tried to reach them.

To add to the fact that our state and local laws and enforcement aren't protecting children the way they need to be at a state, intrastate, and national level, things are even worse. Frequently, state laws conflict with one another, as do their definitions of abuse.

So, when the boys were abused in many ways by different people, and the abuse took place in Michigan, but the boys resided with me in Kentucky, this brought all kinds of scandal and problems. The conundrum was answered by giving the case to the Michigan

State Police. I think you all know by now how I feel about police being involved with matters such as this. It may be different now, but it was a shit show then. The deputy that I talked to told me that she believed X did not do what I said he did, and she was going to administer a polygraph to "prove it," which, of course, is then what happened. Polygraphs and the questions that are asked, especially when there is intent to find a particular result, primarily lead to the results they are looking for; go figure. This very same deputy also stated on the stand to the referee, in my case, the same referee who had her head up her ass, that she thought it was very weird that I hadn't taken a shower for about a week when we had spoken very briefly on the phone (the one and only time we spoke). The reason why I hadn't showered was that after my sons had spent a week with their dad in Michigan, they were with me, and I had come out of the shower to find that my older son had taken the clothes off of his younger brother and was attempting to put his penis in his bottom. So, no, obviously, I didn't want to leave them unattended for any amount of time.

There was a police officer in Kentucky who watched one of the CAC interviews. He was as worthless as the officer who viewed the one in Michigan. After the interview, in which Gabriel disclosed, the police officer did not believe him -the first time this happened, the officer came out after the interview and, right in front of my children, threatened me, read me my rights, told me there is nothing worse than child sexual abuse than fabricated child sexual abuse. I took the boys and got in the car to leave, as did he, and the man followed me in his car for several miles. I thought to myself, so this is the kind of crap I have to deal with trying to protect my children, being doubted, threatened, etc.. I had no idea of what more was yet to come.

That particular detective came to the depositions to testify on X's behalf. He forgot a few of the main facts, though. When questioned about my children, he had their ages wrong and said they were quite a bit older than they were. He also stated that my children's genders were a girl and a boy rather than two boys and planted the seed by saying that the children (the boy and the girl) lied and said what I told them to say. I didn't and still don't even know what my sons said during those interviews, but I sure as hell know telling them to tell the truth isn't "coaching" them to say anything.

With the amount of police corruption, court screw-ups and CPS caseworker ineptitude, I'm not sure which one of those stacks the highest. MSP (Michigan State Police officer) once asked me: "Hey, weren't you hospitalized?" I don't think he even listened to my son plead with him for help about his dad putting his dick up his butt. He was still thinking about whether I was telling the "truth" about being in a mental hospital or not. That officer told me he would call and make a report to CPS, but he never did.

There has been a pendulous swing for children's rights, particularly sexually abused children. I feel a lot of this has to do with politics, as political shifts have either emphasized children's welfare or just ignored children's welfare and taken funding away from projects serving children.

We are one of the worst-rated developed nations with how we treat and take care of -or don't take care of our children. We are the one and only country that has not ratified the United Nations Convention on Children's Rights. We never seem to learn from our mistakes, always repeating the same cycles and crises over and over again. We are dependent on and use a massive number of resources. One of those resources that people typically do not see as a resource is our children. Most people undervalue children and treat them as less than others. If we don't protect them, listen to them, and do everything we can to keep them safe and with their families, we are only creating a future of more trauma. Why can't we get that?

"Believer"

And feeling belief grow
Rise above the obstacles.
People beseech me
But they'll never teach me.
Things that I already know (I know)

Dreams that have shattered
It may not have mattered.
Take another point of view.
Doubts will arise, though
Like chasing a rainbow
I can tell a thing or two (That's true)

You've got to believe in yourself.
Or no one will believe in you.
Imagination like a bird on the wing
Flying free for you to use (OK, baby)

I can't believe they stop and stare.
And point their fingers, doubting me.
Their disbelief suppresses them.
But they're not blind.
It's just that they won't see

I'm a believer
I ain't no deceiver
Mountains move before my eyes.
Destiny planned out
I don't need a handout.
Speculation of the wise

-

Ozzy Osbourne, Diary of a Madman

Mr. Tru Lee Valyent, my attorney, believed in my sons, and he believed in me. He was a rare gem in that he simultaneously was an attorney, was honest, had integrity, and cared more about the future and well-being of two little boys than he did a check in the mail -which was important, as the last of those was a small and rare happening, but he still stuck with the case.

I looked at Tru as sort of a father figure -my father had died in 1998, and before his death, we didn't communicate regularly. I respected what Tru said and felt he had our best interests at heart and was fighting for us. Tru put up a good fight, he did a lot of research, and he represented our case well.

X's wife was so much like X. She treated the boys abusively and endorsed and supported the crazy things X did. She, just like X, threw away things I gave to the kids, tried hard to get me out of the picture and supported the anti-mom agenda that had been propagandized by X and his family. They threw away shoes, belts, clothes, toys, keepsakes, gifts, etc., that I had purchased for the boys, no matter how much the boys liked them. How petty is that?

The boys were seeing a social worker in Kentucky, at the UK for a good portion of the time we were there, except for a psychologist, whom they had seen a short time earlier --whom I really wish I had stayed with. Stupidly, I didn't stay with him (he really was a good psychiatrist), but we moved on to the social worker who ended up letting herself be talked into an about-face change of heart and agreed to put the boys in harm's way, and she changed her mind about me. I cannot put into words how that betrayal of trust felt. Gabriel had disclosed to her graphically on a multitude of occasions. He even used anatomically correct dolls, one being the "dad" doll and one being the "son" doll (to represent himself), and displayed the father doll anally penetrating the son doll, and after he repeatedly disclosed to her over and over how his dad had hurt him after she repeatedly asked him the same questions over and over; even well over a year after the last incident, he still kept telling her the same statements, and in her words, he was annoyed by her asking; stating "I already told you about that." Don't you think a child would be annoyed? No child wants to talk about trauma over and over again, especially if nothing is being done to remedy the situation. Doesn't that go against mental health standards? That seems to me would be quite harmful for a child. It's retriggering a traumatic event. She should not be allowed to practice mental health for several reasons, and this is one of them. How many more children has she harmed in this manner? But when she asked for a custody evaluation, the X's parents made the trip down to meet with her, not to see the boys, like they hadn't done, but her, and not at her request, but at theirs, and she allowed it as she told me she would not do. In fact, she told me she did not want to meet with them because she thought they would try to manipulate her into believing the boys had not been abused and dissuade her of what she believed was true -seriously, those were her words. However, she went back on that, and that is exactly what they did. Or, I should say, that is exactly what she let them do.

When my sons were younger, they talked a lot about genitalia, poop and pee. They drew a lot of pictures of genitalia, butts, penises, and sex. They had knowledge of these topics that children at their young age should not have had. They also sexually acted out in many ways. However, I have thought a lot about this, and I feel like I should not elaborate on this point. Even though they were young, and they were acting out the abuse that had happened to them, I feel for their protection. I need to state this generally rather than graphically and hope you, my friend, will understand, especially for the sake of my sons. They were also abusive physically, emotionally, and verbally. In those circumstances as well, they were simply acting out what they themselves had been experiencing. They even had the same tone and expressions that X had.

If I combined my reading of books and academic articles, research on statistics, research from legitimate and reliable sources online and in scholarly articles and books, research from experts directly for my degree and my own personal curiosity, it would total years of thorough research. I have delved into every aspect of child abuse that exists locally, state-wide, nationwide, and globally, so I confidently feel I am qualified to give you information and quote some of the information that I have gleaned over the years. . Incest victims have their own unique set of symptoms. "Freud spoke of children's powerlessness in the face of adult demands and their discomfort at having to shift roles from lover to obedient child without explanation." (Sexual Abuse, Goodwin, p. 109). Another great book that looks at the state of child welfare worldwide, "An increasing number of evaluators are using certain behaviors of children as diagnostic tools. The most common behavioral indicators that are said to be suggestive of sexual abuse are precocious sexual behavior, seductiveness and knowledge of sexuality beyond what is reasonable given the child's age. .... Many sexually abused children experience intense pressure to retract their initial statements about being abused......sexually abused children go through five distinct phases: (1.) secrecy, (2.) helplessness, (3.) entrapment, (4.) disclosure, (5.) retraction, (Dr. Roland Summit). He writes that "whatever a child says about sexual abuse, she is likely to reverse it" and then goes on to describe the intense pressure a victim may experience to recant and concludes, "unless there is **special support for the child and immediate intervention to force responsibility on the father,** the girl will follow the 'normal' course and retract the complaint." (Hudson, Galaway, The State as Parent International Research Perspectives on Interventions With Young Persons, p. 273-274, emphasis added).

Abused children will behaviorally exhibit their abuse in lots of ways; through acts of aggression, fear and sadness, having nightmares, verbal expression, and drawings are just a few of the most common. Specifically, sexually abused children will sexually act out acts that have been done to them or things they were manipulated into doing, but very young children don't often act out acts that they have simply seen, such as in pornography, as they cannot quite make the connections from what they *see* and transform that into actions for themselves to *do*. Then there are those children who are either very quiet children by nature, to begin with, or those who are, on the other hand, very happy-go-lucky by nature, who simply maintain a seemingly positive outlook on the outside, and neither of these personalities "types" will appear as disturbed as they will not show outward behavioral symptoms of abuse at all.

I can think of times, facial expressions, things we were doing - where we were living -when my sons may have been going through different levels of these phases at different times. Earlier in this book, I pointed out what my children had said to me (and many other people) and what had been done to them. Hearing these statements was for me -as they would be for any mother -shocking, to say the least. The statements caused me great alarm, yet the things I caught my sons doing to each other were devastating. As you now know, CPS caseworkers chose to believe I 'coached' my sons to say what they said. Which, of course, is ludicrous, and we've already discussed that. What about the behaviors that went on for years? The behaviors changed over the years, but they didn't stop until they were older. (My sons have a trauma bond, but they also have this underlying element of anger and hate toward each other because of these behaviors). Did the caseworkers think I made that up? Who would do that? Who *could* make that up? Even worse, who would think that someone would make that up?

All forms of abuse, especially sexual, are extremely shameful and embarrassing for a child, and they don't go around talking about it, at the very least making it up, and think about it: if there were such a person that would try to "coach" very young children into saying these very acts, I can't imagine a very young child as being able to even repeat it if it were untrue. It's all so incredibly unfathomable. The argument that the boys were 'coached' is fundamentally ridiculous. The boys were so young. It would be impossible for a 4-year-old child to make similar statements, repeatedly, such as my sons have said, spontaneously, over a many years-long duration of time, to a variety of people, in different environments, and in a variety of circumstances.

My children became completely different people, and for a while, they turned against me. I can't say that I blame them. In their world, this is how they saw it; they had a mother who abandoned them, who allowed them to be hurt, even after they had told her of what was happening to them, time and time again, nothing was ever done to keep it from happening again, and worse, they were handed over to the people who inflicted this abuse, and it continued, although now, even more frequently and sadistically. They never heard from me. I failed to protect them -I continually did not come through for them. Not only did I not stop their dad from sticking his penis up their butt, but I also couldn't even keep them in the shelter of my own home. So, I didn't stop their dad, their grandparents, the girlfriend, the aunt, etc., from hitting them, from hitting them hard upside their heads, slapping their faces, humiliating them, tormenting them, criticizing them, changing their names, from yelling, screaming, grabbing, choking, pulling their hair, grabbing their ears, pulling them by their ears, making fun of their ears, grabbing them by the neck and lifting them up by their neck and slamming them into the walls, calling them names such as little bastard, little fucker, retard, moron, idiot, etc. bulldozing through them, ignoring them, minimizing them, forcing them to eat food they didn't want, not letting them have the food they wanted, locking them away from controlling the temperature setting in their rooms, humiliating them, spitting at and on them, shaming them, gaslighting them, mentally, physically, sexually, and emotionally abusing them, neglecting, shunning them, and on and on. I couldn't stop any of it; therefore, I allowed it to happen.

I didn't comfort them in thunderstorms when the rain was hitting loudly on the windows and scaring them, and the lightening flashed, and the wind was strong. I didn't help them to learn to ride a bike on two wheels. I didn't help them up when they fell down, I couldn't bandage the cuts they got or take them to get stitches when they needed stitches (which they each needed several times but were not taken to get), I couldn't stop them from falling and hold and comfort them when they cried; I wasn't there. Therefore, I didn't care. I couldn't carry them to bed when they fell asleep in the car after a long day of fun, exploring and traveling or after a day at the beach; I have never been able to take my sons to the beach. We haven't baked cookies together. All of this time, all of the opportunity to make and create wonderful memories was taken from us by the people who have made these abhorrent, ignorant, and tragic decisions for my children. Our lives have been fragmented. The futures of my sons have been altered forever. Essentially because of the decisions made, the futures of every person that crosses each of my children's paths have been altered as well.

Gabriel had begun to talk about his sexual abuse 'matter-of-factly.' At his last forensic evaluation, the detective watching the interview from a different room didn't believe him. he expected him to break down and cry. Then he proceeded to walk both my sons out to the parking lot and hand them off to their abusive father. When I read the following, my heart stopped for a second. An "adult" expects Gabriel and Castiel or any of these other unfortunate souls to break down and start crying or display intense fear of their parent who is responsible for the abuse; however, these children *living* this life may not do that. It's a way of life for them -they've developed a strong outer shell around themselves -especially about this. Abused children (and adult survivors) have suffered repeated trauma, and they have compartmentalized those traumas and may not show any emotion at all when referring to them. My friend, who is a therapist, told me she sees this all the time. Children and adults will talk about atrocities that have happened to them without expressing a single emotion. It's self-protection.

Instead of a solid foundation of loving and nurturing memories for my sons, theirs were filled with abuse, tragedy, loss, anger, violence and lies, scattered with superficial people who care little about who Gabriel and Castiel are and even less about who they will become.

"Freedom is never voluntarily given by the oppressor; it must be demanded by the oppressed."

Martin Luther King, Jr.

Clinical service ticket of Kentucky social worker Judas: "demonstrated with anatomical dolls father anally penetrating boy doll." Judas was referring to Gabriel having used these dolls approximately 2 weeks after having spent a week with his father up north in '06. I never knew dolls had been used. It wasn't until going through the notes after the boys had been taken from me that I learned of this. Gabriel was 4 years old then.

Gabriel disclosed to social worker Judas he had been hurt on his body, mouth, penis, and bottom by his daddy. Daddy hurt him with a "stick" or a "dick" and put his penis in his bottom, just like what Gabriel tried to do to his brother yesterday. (Her notes).

The social worker asked: "Did anyone hurt you on your body?" "Yes, daddy did." "Where did he hurt you?" "On the front and on the back." "Can you show me?" He pointed to the penis and the mouth. "What did he do?" "He cut me with a knife." The use of the word "knife" as a descriptor signifies very hurtful memories for children.

Remember, Gabriel was 4, and this social worker that he is talking to is the same person who signed an affidavit a little over a year later to turn them over to their paternal grandparents, who soon became their father.

"Where did he hurt you on the back?" Gabriel pointed to the buttocks. "With what, a knife, a dick, a stick. A dick?" "Yes."

"What part of his body did he hurt you with?" "His penis." "Did he ever bother the front of you with his body?" "He put his penis on mine."

"Where did he do this? Where were you?" "At daddy's house and at grandma and grandpa's house."

"Did this happen one time or more than once?" [I don't see the relevance of this question.]

"More times, maybe 1 or 2 times, can we play now?"

Incidentally, this social worker, who had heard a multitude of disclosures, as well as seen my son describe and 'show' the abuse he had received, turned completely around near the end after talking to the paternal family and the custody evaluator, testified that she really "struggled" with her decision. As if that makes any difference at all. She added that if every time my sons came to me with a disclosure, I overreacted and called CPS, then what would that do? It should have maybe protected my sons. Don't you think? First, I think I reacted pretty damn well. I did not ask leading questions. I was empathetic but not dramatic. I was concerned, yet caring. Second, how in the hell was I supposed to react? How would you react? So much of the thinking with many of these "professionals" was simply unrealistic.

Quick reality check: how preposterous is it to think this child has been coached or has some kind of active imagination? I would have to have known the future and all the questions that were going to be asked so I could "coach" my 4-year-old son on how to answer. Furthermore, A FOUR-YEAR-OLD CHILD COULD NOT AND WOULD NOT MAKE THIS UP. Fucking, seriously.

All the notes, the fact that she asked over and over, I hadn't been notified of these disclosures, and I think I should have been. I never knew about them or all that my oldest son had said to her. After she asked again for the umpteenth time, She wrote that Gabriel was "annoyed," and he said, "I already told you about that." Who wouldn't be annoyed? Hell, I would be annoyed.

On Mother's Day 2009, I took my oldest son to meet with the Court Appointed Counselor Coordinator. Who was described as having "God-like powers" by my attorney when he was put in place by the Antrim County Court, who then chose to never follow his recommendations or respect the authority that they had given him in the first place.

The reason for this meeting was because earlier that weekend both of the boys had individually disclosed the exact same information to me, and I had called this psychologist, Dr. Eryudite, and this was the first time he could meet. He asked me to have a tape recorder, which I did; Gabriel knew nothing about the tape recorder. I simply wore something that allowed me to have it in my front pocket. Dr. Eryudite had a transcript of the tape following the interview. He regrets that he recommended I take the boys back to their father on that day, as was their usual schedule. Dr. Eryudite filed a report with CPS. He called them repeatedly after his initial calls, but the caseworker never called him back and never read the transcript or his Counselor Coordinator report that he was attempting to provide to them. CPS conducted their own interview of Gabriel (another one) after X and the rest of the paternal family pressured Gabriel into saying what he said to the CPS caseworker for their interview over at X's house. After he had been shunned, shamed, humiliated, abused, threatened, and pressured to recant.

Over a year later the CPS caseworker admitted in court that she never listened to the tape or read the transcript provided by the Court Appointed Counselor Coordinator, nor did she ever call him back from any one of his repeated phone calls to her. She did, however, contact Dr. Mulefucent (the custody evaluator) because X and the paternal family provided her with the report written by him a few years earlier; Dr. Mulefucent had not seen the kids, but twice for an hour or so, and again that was many years earlier, and that was with both parents, each individually, no other extended family member. The reason given by the caseworker that she had never read the transcript was because I was also present during that interview. Had she bothered to ever discuss this fact with me, it more than likely would not have mattered that I was in the same room, as I said virtually nothing -which would have been apparent in the transcript and many of the disclosures I was hearing for the first time as well. I wonder if it would have mattered to the caseworker that I felt I was going to throw up hearing what Gabriel was saying, that the room was spinning and that my palms were sweaty during the interview? Listening to my son say these things made me full of rage for his father and the paternal family, as much as it broke my heart. I didn't want to hear those things. It's devastatingly painful to hear. What I would have liked was to have been handed a gun and a license to go kill the son of a bitch; after hearing those hings been told, I should not take them to meet X because Dr. Eryudite was going to file a complaint right then and there. Seriously, I never should have been told to take them to him, nor should I have done that.

I am human, and these are my very precious young sons we are talking about. There is a reason I don't own a gun; you might be able to guess what that is.

I didn't see my sons again for a couple of months because after that disclosure, when CPS went to 'interview' Gabriel at X's house, Gabriel had been pressured to say I told him to say those things -which is exactly what he did. He had to live with those people, after this interview, he was going right back to them, and he knew what punishment looked like from them, and he did not want that.

I'm hoping that you are seeing the pattern here, that when my son/s discloses they are taken away from me, they don't see me for an extended period of time, and when they do see me, it is under very difficult circumstances. Because, once again, when we saw each other it was at "that place," as we had come to call it, the supervised visitation location.

Historically, Gabriel gave spontaneous information and details regarding his abuse and has given elaborate details to many different people over the years, besides the fact that both of my sons do everything they talk about having been done to them. This couldn't have been stated about having been 'told to say anything.' Because it didn't happen, at least not from me -I have never told them to say anything that wasn't true. I have never given them any words to use. I would never do that. It's incredibly rare for anybody to do that. But they had been told to say that I did; otherwise, that would not have been said.

Seriously, it's not that difficult to figure out. Does it make any sense at all to think that a mother (any mother) can make her child make a variety of statements to a wide variety of professionals and family members over a span of many years while those same children are also behaving in a multiple of sexually inappropriate ways; sexually aggressively inappropriate ways, but then get placed in the custody of their father and make two shallow, non-elaborating statements - just at the right time, isn't there something wrong with this picture?

The three of us have been through trauma after trauma, a multitude of heartbreaks, and a plethora of pain, anguish, and despair. I've always believed if we rebuild where we've been broken, we will be stronger for it. That's what we have been doing, and we'll continue to do so moving forward. I admit that, at the time, many people, professionals, and agencies destroyed our relationships. They destroyed the trajectory of our lives and the peaceful path we were on. They destroyed the people we were prior to all of this abuse and turmoil happening. Yet we, Gabriel, Castiel, and I, were not fully destroyed. We're still here, still fighting, still picking up the pieces and putting them back together as best we can. We will overcome, and we shall be victorious.

"Injustice anywhere is a threat to justice everywhere."
-Martin Luther King Jr.

I received the Referee's decision through an email from X. I'm certain he had such a thrill in sending me the document that stated we had joint legal custody, but he was given primary physical custody, giving me only small increments of time with my children. This was an incredibly destructive decision. Her reasoning was based on all the bullshit she had been fed; she chose to believe the lies and take the easy way out; she didn't really have to do any work this way. She just followed the rest, who took the easy way out. It was a smaller pill to swallow and easiest for these people to wrap their fragile brains around.

hard-headed fuck you all-
hard-headed fuck you all-
hard-headed fuck you all.
don't hear a word you say, not a bit, and I don't give a shit
Soundgarden, Ty Cobb

-Me

This custody battle had spanned over 5 years. There were child protective service workers involved from two states, local, county, and state police (from two states), social workers and psychiatrists (from three states) 2, psychoanalysts (from two states), a Court Appointed Counselor Coordinator, psychologists, custody evaluators, a nationally known child sexual abuse expert, a GAL, medical doctors and medical staff (from two states), nurses, teachers and school staff(from two states), CAC staff and interviewers (from two states), a principal and other school staff, supervisors at multiple supervised visit agencies(one in which was quite active), a plethora of reports regarding abuse to my sons to CPS from a variety of professionals who knew what they were talking about, other court and legal staff, and multiple attorneys, judges and referees, and this was the "final decisión"; and my sons' fate. Countless people should have been struck down to their deaths on that day. My sons did not deserve this catastrophic sentence in any way, shape, or form. There has been one unbelievable judgment and horrendous decision after another on our case; for the better part of 22 years, anybody who doesn't know me almost doesn't believe it. But I'm telling you anyway because our story needs to be told.

Waking up throughout the night is a common occurrence for me. One night in particular, I was consumed by certain words. The following is the sensical containment of those words:

Time and adversity
Wickedly consumes
Our lives and souls
Brutally and viciously
crippling and
revealing to us a new trajectory
for our lives to be set, of which
We deplore
Leaving preferable futures
Buried
and beyond reach
What was hoped for
Becomes dusty, forgotten,
Abandoned
And out of reach
Into the depths and waste of trauma

-Me

CPS first became involved in early 2005, and they have made my sons' and my life a living hell on earth. CPS caseworkers used only what X's family put in front of them, and they only **believed** what X and his family put in front of them. Because of one initial caseworker's biases, prejudices, and incompetence, my sons are suffering. She began it, and every caseworker that followed fell right in line as if they were lined up like dominos, and they all fell, one right after the other. My sons' father was abusive to me and to them when we were married; -this is why I left this man. He continued to be abusive to them, and he continued to harass me. Nobody cared that simultaneously cared and had the power to do anything about it. My sons are now 22 and 19, and their father was given primary custody by the family court despite the fact that the boys 'alleged' he had sexually and physically abused them; I witnessed the physical abuse as I, too, tiptoed around in my own home not knowing what trivial move would cause his next blow up. My sons are still emotionally erratic, similar to their father. They, too, are aggressive and explosive. We all have severe, complicated PTSD, and I'm sure we will live with PTSD and flashbacks etc., for the rest of our earthly lives. Castiel takes medication and is seeing a great trauma therapist. Gabriel refuses therapy as he does not want to revisit any of his trauma as it is too painful for him. Both of them have had problems with pornography, drugs and alcohol. Gabriel is a formidable hard worker (too hard), and Castiel has been porn-free, nicotine-free, and marijuana free for some time now -something he has worked very hard at and a decision he made on his own, and he has stuck with it all on his own. I wish I could say our bond is back to the way it used to be, but I can't honestly say that. I dream of that and keep dreaming of that. I long for them to look at me as they did long ago, their mom, whom they loved, respected, were protective of, and always felt safe with and protected by. I truly miss our close and loving alliance. Reflecting back on what we had when we were in Kentucky, how all of our lives are now, all the pain, abuse and trauma they have suffered, and how trampled on our connection makes me sadder and emptier than anything else.

When I was younger and focused on boyfriends and all that, I used to say the only thing worse than feeling completely alone is feeling alone when you're with someone. That's kind of how this is, even though the massive emptiness, hollowness, and on the edge of death I was when my sons were taken, and for the many years following in which I was able to only see pieces of them, as they traveled through their brutal youth. They can be where they choose to be now, and I continue to feel alone and separated from them. I'm still advocating for them, still fighting for them, yet only still seeing only ashes. I didn't realize until this very day that in my head for all of these years, I have been holding on and waiting to get my little boys back, my 6- and 3-year-old boys, as I left them sleeping that January morning in 2008. We would just go on with our lives, happily living it as we were. Together and safe from further abuse. I still want to hold those little boys, those 6- and 3-year-old boys who were taken from me while their spirits were intact before they were broken; with all of my heart, I want that. My heart hurts for that, and my chest aches as tears stream down my face.

Ours is a simple, clear-cut example of what happens when CPS goes wrong. Everything else followed their decisions and went wrong as well. Unfortunately, it is unlikely, no matter what, given the bureaucratic limitations of CPS, that they will admit this glaring failure and the damage and destruction it has caused. Unfortunately, CPS goes wrong a lot of the time.

However, the state of MI is working to address the problems in the child welfare system in Michigan. There are many people I have met who are passionately devoted to making Michigan a better and safer place for children. I am the Vice-Chair of GTPAC (Guy Thompson Parent Advisory Council), we are a group of parents who have had to interact with the child welfare system or the adoption and foster care system in the state of Michigan. We work together on different committees, councils, and policies happening because of the Michigan Child Welfare Re-Design and offer our voices and input based on our experiences to create positive change. I'm very hopeful and appreciative of the Council and the Re-Design Unit. I am thankful to be a part of it.

As I began this venture -all my research into how differently the departments work from state to state and intra-state, I was justifiably shocked at how horribly this system works, not only in Michigan but across the board. Although Michigan recently enacted a policy where child fatalities due to abuse have to be reported - which is great because, for the longest time, that wasn't the case. Texas improved training for social workers on infant death investigations because of recommendations from child fatality reviews. Although many states require reporting of information on child fatalities caused by abuse and neglect, the detail of that information varies. Michigan, historically, has fared terribly, ranking high in abuse rates, low on academic achievement scores, etc. However, there is an internal push for child welfare reform. There are many councils and committees working diligently to improve different aspects of the child welfare system. As I previously mentioned, I have lots of gratitude for this. All of the people I've met so far are very dedicated to this cause.

I'm like a beggar with no luck. I'm holding street signs up
on your street corner steps,

like most, you try not to see me. You stare straight ahead,
ignore the responsibility,

Excuse me, Excuse me, Mr., I've been waiting in line,
and I'd like to buy some of your time. You've got things all wrong,
You make me feel like a crime,

Excuse me, Mr.

No Doubt, Excuse Me

-

No Doubt, Tragic Kingdom

139

There have been more fuck ups on this case between Michigan and Kentucky, and X could not have dreamt of more incompetent people. They fell right into his hand. If it wasn't a scandal, it was a damn perfect years-long run of what NOT to do to help kids in an incest and abusive situation, and one perfect coverup for a narcissistic, abusive, sadistic pedophile.

This System IS Broken, So Let's Fix It, Dammit

Some things we have a lot of control over, such as -what we eat and put into our bodies. Some things -not so much. How we deal with incest is indoctrinated into our culture as an icky thing we should turn our heads from and believe it doesn't exist. I like to think that as a group, we can change how our culture thinks and reacts to situations such as incest, child sexual abuse and all other forms of child abuse; we can't help them if we deny their existence.

The United States children are ranked one of the worst out of the developed countries when looking at abuse rates, poverty and neglect. Our country does not take care of our children. We care more about being at war in other countries and how other countries are running their governments than we do about our children, rich or poor. Wealthy people spend time and money trying to keep more of their money. Poor people work their asses off just to put food on their tables. In the meantime, children aren't acknowledged, children are 'in the way' of far too many people, and children don't even matter to many people. Consequently, they aren't noticed when they are hurting.

Interestingly, Michigan has allowed the courts to be opened up to the public during juvenile court proceedings: "Now states are beginning to unseal the doors to the other side of juvenile court-- the hearings at which judges determine whether to remove children from parents accused of abuse or neglect. Twelve states now routinely admit the press or public to such hearings. Oregon was among the first, opening the doors to all delinquency and abuse hearings in 1980. Eight years ago, Michigan followed, then New York four years ago." (Stack, Post-Gazette.com). It is important that this trend continues. A personal passionate pull for me is to see that children cease to be tried as adults, as is happening more and more today -they are not adults; no matter what the crime, they are children. The human brain is said to not be fully developed until we are 25 years old. We, as a society, are in large part responsible for any crime committed by a child. When children commit crimes, it is their history that should be looked at, and I'm not talking about their criminal history. I'm referring to their trauma and abuse histories.

Potential Answers

First, the funding for the services provided needs to be changed. Just as easily as Title IV and CAPTA have put children into foster care, a new law can re-route the federal dollars into preventative care and in-home services. "In-home services" could give a LOT of assistance to a lot of people -if there were enough caring caseworkers out there with the funding and the incentive to utilize the resources to help people in need. In-home services could be used to help people in poverty, and instead of using "poverty" as a means to remove a child from a loving home, if the funds were available, the family would stay intact, and there would be services to help them during a financial crisis; however long that is; -maybe giving them assistance to education that they never had would prove to be beneficial, assistance in finding transportation, etc.

Along with this, requesting funds to be delineated from out-of-home care and the states only being able to gain monetary funding for utilizing in-home and preventative measures; -there must also be added that the state child welfare laws be married together.

Currently, every state works independently, abiding by its own unilateral child welfare laws. Each state has different definitions for different types of abuse; for instance, Michigan will define child sexual abuse differently than does Kentucky - as an example, and so on. Sometimes, state child welfare laws will completely contradict one another. For instance, my sons were with their father for a week in Michigan while they lived with me in Kentucky. When they got back, my son was in the bathroom, and he yelled for me to come there (he was 4 at the time), "I can't poop. It hurts, dad stuck a stick up my butt." Kentucky investigates where the abuse occurred, and Michigan investigates where the child lives, so neither one would investigate the allegation. All the states have to work together and have the same laws and similar descriptions of abuse.

There has to be an educated front line. Caseworkers, judges, police officers -anybody who is going to be making decisions on behalf of a child has to be educated on child development, domestic violence, and all aspects of child abuse; sexual, physical, emotional, and neglect. 'Normal' child development vs. development occurring simultaneously with abuse. PTSD, trauma, ACEs, and what type of behaviors might be seen associated with certain types of abuse.

Ideally, there would be a "Child Court," separate from juvenile court, as this does not hear juvenile offenses but child abuse cases and custody cases involving allegations of child abuse. Family court is for divorce, the separation of property, and when there are amicable divorces where parties work out parenting time; -which does happen and frequently. I think child court should be a place where there are trained experts who actually know, understand, and care about the children in question and are willing to really work to find the "best interests" of the child/ren. Where attorneys work for the court, not especially for 'one side' or the other, it's not about winning or losing. It's about fact finding and working together to find the best solution for children. They would consider all professional viewpoints, yet ALL professionals involved have to meet specific training criteria.

Every actor in this court system is educated, experienced, and trained on all aspects of child abuse through all developmental levels and ages, and much more. That is what I would like to see.

Going back to my son's case, there were particular points during our case of the family-court-CPS-corrupt/screwed-up process in which there was a specific cause and negative effect. There are ways to address and fix that process. Through a lot of research, talking to others who have been down this road, and talking to professionals in the field (real credentialed professionals, not those simply claiming to be). While watching my sons completely spin out for many years, I have come up with these alternative solutions, and maybe someday I'll have the chance to present them to Congress. However, at the time of this writing, I don't see even if I had that opportunity right now it would make any impact or significant change on the dysfunctional congress at work currently. What has happened to my sons and me has literally sucked the life out of me, and for me, I actually have to do something to really impact change for the better in order to soothe some of my negative feelings.

We need to acknowledge that there is a very ugly patriarchal system at play, and this system isn't looking at what's best for children or mothers. I am unclear as to what the current goal is. Is it to try to 'make up' for the fact that mothers have been given the benefit of the doubt as being the better parent for young children? Generally speaking, of course, and men have created a pushback if you will -making up for lost time or some other ridiculousness. There needs to be a greater awareness of women, mothers and children themselves. The needed maternal bond is vitally important and needs to be kept intact for the child's sake as well as the mother's.

I also think there should not be a use of psychological testing. Or it is very limited, and interpretations cannot be ambiguous. Or not used until these tests and interpretations are updated to our current century, and not used until gender-neutral tests are created, and not biased against women and mothers. My reasoning is this; most of the data conducted around those tests show that men test better, that the tests are geared more for men, as far as if you are less emotional, you'll come out 'presenting better'. Most were created by men for men many decades ago.

Remove custody evaluators from their powers; one person who may meet with a family only a couple of times should not be able to decide their future. Each individual custody evaluator could come back with a completely different result -as was seen in our case, so how can we justify giving these people so much power, especially when they are not credentialed in the ways we need them to be. No way, that's absurd. I read in several places that family court judges tend to hang their hat on what a custody evaluator says to be the truth. Then why aren't custody evaluators family court judges? Why aren't family court judges qualified to make their own decisions?

Mandatory reporting should become a thing of the past as well. It seems as if reports made by "mandated reporters" are minimized; caseworkers (and courts, etc.) simply don't generally take them as seriously as they ought to -from the frame of mind that the reporter made the report simply because they *had to.* What good is that? That is not helpful. I say just do away with it. Also, mandated reporters don't report when they should, and since they rarely receive consequences, what is the point in making them mandated. Then there are the social workers and psychologists who understand how poorly their local CPS agency is performing that they refuse to report to CPS now anyway because, based on their many negative experiences, they believe CPS will simply make life worse for the child/ren. This happened with at least one professional in our case. Along with doing away with mandated reporting -yet still educating on the massive importance of reporting, CPS needs to take non-mandated reports more seriously. Get over thinking everybody wants to make life worse for others. Yes, there are those out there, but that's far from all the non-mandated reports. Obviously, it is the people in the home who know, see, and hear the most. That's not rocket science.

"In Sweden, Finland and Denmark, adoption is not currently viewed as an option in child welfare policy. Welfare policy in these countries concentrates on strengthening families and on preventative services. The rate of children entering care is very low. In Sweden, there is no provision for placing a child for adoption without the consent of the parents (Performance and Innovation Unit, 2000). Australia and New Zealand both promote working together with families, with an emphasis on early prevention rather than intervention...Thus, out of these Western countries, it is the UK and the USA that have the highest percentage of children in care, and which have focused on adoption as a permanency solution for children, even when the consent of the parent to such an erm... arrangement is lacking." (Adoption and Looked After Children).

The United States has a deplorable record when it comes to protecting children within the country's boundaries; it does not matter what a child's race, ethnicity, nationality, gender, or income bracket in which they fall; in the United States, children come last. However, it is an accurate claim that black and brown children's cases are moved to an investigation, and children are removed to a larger proportion than white children. It seems there is a war against children and a war against moms trying to protect their children when there are abuse allegations, especially child sexual abuse. Children are placed with their perpetrators, whether intentionally by some or not. I could see the judgment in the caseworkers' eyes as they were out at our home. I was an excellent, loving mother, although what I lacked was financial resources. The boys and I lived, and Castiel and I still live in an apartment over a garage on my mom's property. Yes, it is small, but certainly not unlivable. We had everything we needed. My sons love it here. Their father and his family had much more money, and a house etc. This was even pointed out in CPS caseworker reports. They weren't even hiding their bias. However, any day, at any time, my sons would have chosen our apartment over that house over there for many reasons, but mostly because they were loved here.

Currently, the rights for children to speak for themselves, be heard, and what they say to be actually considered are not recognized. When they do speak, they are minimized, laughed at, scoffed at, imagined to be crazy, making allegations up, or having been coached to say them. Kids sometimes get told and falsely reassured that it does matter what they say, and children tell where they want to live and with whom, but then they are shipped off to the other parent in the name of; "in their best interests" bull shit; in other words; kid, you just didn't give the right answer; I'm right and you're wrong.

Kids learn through trauma, abuse, and lack of protection that our entire system is fucked up; what else does that teach them? That they can't trust anybody, ever. Their country sucks, there is absolutely nobody, ever, who is going to protect them, and even when they desperately want to protect them, they are prevented from it.

Child abuse and politics should not necessarily go hand in hand, as far as it is partisan; unfortunately, however, that is the case. Where politics should be involved is to create legitimate legislation that will prohibit these horrible decisions from being made by biased and uneducated legal participants and caseworkers. Maybe there are too many players in each case now, but at the same time, one decision from one of the key entities influences the rest of them. There are many ways this can be remedied, or at least out-of-the-box thinking needs to occur at the legal level, as they frequently have the final say. When they don't know what the hell they are talking about and take someone else's biased and poor judgment for their own decisions, that's how we get generations of trauma. A particularly well-trained court to handle these cases is what I advocate for, especially in cases of incest.

As far as politics go, I'm not trying to persuade anyone to any side of the political aisle. I'm just stating a fact. Local, state-wide and national administrations give and take money from and to certain "causes," when Republicans are in charge, money is taken from child protection causes. When Democrats are in charge, more money is dedicated to children and child welfare causes. Instead of using Republican or Democrat, it could be stated as Conservative vs. Liberal.

Politics even influences child removal when they should not ever be removed. If politicians wanted to make a good impact, they'd see to it that decision-makers in these cases were qualified and fit to make the decisions. The CPS caseworkers, judges, police officers, etc., need to have specialized training to work on child abuse and child sexual abuse cases.

Specialized education must be made compulsory for judges and caseworkers. Common sense must be lifted up, too.

There should be no police officer involvement, especially with the children, and most particularly not initially, only properly trained mental health professionals who meet specific training criteria. Legal and law enforcement should only deal with legal and law issues. Police should only be involved if they are investigating a perpetrator, and then they have to meet certain training criteria to be able to do that, especially for child sexual abuse cases. They should have nothing to do with the child victim; it is extremely intimidating for a child and very scary -the entire process. Furthermore, if child rapists can walk around in public, working with people, living relatively 'normal' lives, how does a police officer or a caseworker without very intensive training, especially wisdom from those who have personal experience with them, think they will be able to detect them. They won't, and contrary to police thinking there is no profile that fits a child sexual abuser, most abusers are undetectable when they want to be.

There should exist a Panel of Mothers (protective Fathers as well) who may be screened and, based on their experience with the system, become a part of this panel. There should be one in each state to oversee child welfare issues. They should have direct access to all data that CPS officials have and be consulted regularly on projects, panels, committees, councils, and even court cases if possible. GTPAC does this within MDHHS. What I am suggesting is at a higher, more in-depth level.

We need to advocate for laws and attention devoted to child abuse and child sexual abuse and bring about much-needed awareness on the subject.

Trauma therapy is becoming more mainstream, which is fantastic. However, I think there is a lot of work that still needs to be done. Schools need to be trained and offer trauma-informed therapy, as do preschools. In Michigan, the most dangerous time of a child's life is the time from infancy to one year old. As many places as children frequent, there needs to be at least one trauma-informed therapist.

There are many types of therapy for traumatized and abused children; all of them - that I know of seem to have potential. There is play therapy, drawing, behavioral therapy, cognitive behavioral therapy, and more.

PTSD and complex PTSD can be a result of trauma, abuse, separation from a trusted caregiver, car accidents, fires, and more. This must be addressed as well because PTSD alone causes severe long-term issues.

"There is no evidence that charging the non-abusive parent or removing the child from home benefits the child." (Ewen, Failure to Protect Laws). "Despite exposure to IPV, 83% of the children studied said they were happy with themselves and reported relatively high self-concept scores and low levels of behavioral problems. (Ewen). I understood these children to have had been left with their mother… Federal policy has influenced state policy in this regard as well." (Gainsborough, Scandalous Politics).

148

Because of what has been done to my children by *so many people:* their father, their paternal grandparents, their aunt, custody evaluators, GAL, judges, police officers, acting judges, CPS caseworkers, several mental health workers, etc., I now have hate; hate and anger that I never knew possible for me. Sad to say though, this is what fuels me.

Children seem to be always losing; first, they are abused by someone they are expected to love and trust, then they tell someone they love and trust, then, depending on the scenario, they could be removed from that one someone they loved and trusted and left with the abuser, so now the system has failed them as well, now they are angry and getting in trouble, and they are labeled trouble makers and delinquents, they are getting in trouble at school, outside of school, and are not finding support, empathy or understanding, anywhere they turn. These children are being victimized again and again, over and over. That is criminal, and it is no surprise that our children are turning out angry, sad, and frustrated, youngsters, teenagers and then adults. You wonder why there are school shootings, suicides, crime, gangs, bullying, and all the rest? I don't wonder. Then, those same children/adults are further punished.

I loved listening to my children having fun -when they jumped on the trampoline here, it was glorious! As well as when they were young laughing and playing and running about, especially when we were in Kentucky. Unfortunately, my son's laughter changed; they outgrew that innocence so very early. This book is to give my sons a voice. The voice nobody listened to -if they did, they did not care, believe them, or act on their behalf. They deserved to be heard then and now, as do all children -all of the time.

I still love to hear them laugh and see them smile; it's just not like it was, and it will never be that way again. I didn't have custody of my sons; for almost all of their youth, their abusive father had custody. -I believed what they told me was true - because I saw the behaviors, as did others, and I had lived with their father as well, so I knew what they were saying was true. I could see it in their faces and in the deep sadness in their eyes.

Their eyes show how sad they are and how damaged they feel; their shame and pain are immense. I have pictures of them all over my apartment of the time when I wasn't seeing them very much -mostly school pictures (for the years I was able to get them). They looked so sad, and their eyes showed such an emptiness. I wanted to take them down because of what I could see in their eyes, but it was all I had of them for those time periods.

Where we all play a role in the failure to protect children is all-encompassing. We need to speak out. We need to use our voices. If we, as participants in society, owned up to our part, we could really make a difference for children. Vocalization and action are what it has taken to make any substantial societal change - it's true. We need to demand change for the sake of children.

When children experience cumulative, unspeakable, and heinous trauma at a very young age, and that trauma and abuse are allowed to continue, their 'childhoods' are stolen from them, and their lives and futures become forever altered.

Children are unable to defend themselves against a predator, especially if that predator lives in the same house. Children, generally, are unable to speak for themselves - and if they do speak - they're not listened to. Most children tell us in many ways, through their actions and behaviors, that we have to be educated and alert -we need to open our ears, our hearts, and our eyes and start *doing* for them what they cannot do for themselves. I am in this fight for the long haul, and I hope you will consider joining me.

Castiel recently told me of a coping strategy he developed while over at his father's to help him since he used to cry himself to sleep at night because he missed me. So, he started to get a picture of me in his head and then told himself I didn't love him and I didn't care about him or Gabriel to try to make him not miss me as much. After all, that was what he was being told by the paternal family, so it wouldn't have been that difficult to tell that to himself. Somehow, that helped him go to sleep.

Years of memories taken: bikes, games, laughing, trick or treating, Christmas, birthdays and other holidays, horses, dogs, cats, cooking, going to parks, talking, laughing, playing games, having fun together, a lifetime of experiences taken from us, time and memories that we will never get back.

I fought CPS and the family court system for my sons from 2005 to 2016 – 2017. In those later years, I was just trying to get validation for them, an apology -something. (They have been given the opportunity of having a conversation with an amazing DHHS Director who is heading up the Front-End Re-Design; however, my sons would prefer it come from those who made the devasting decisions. However, they are still on the fence. I hope they take advantage of this opportunity, though). My oldest son first made an "allegation," -if you will, although I didn't exactly realize it at the time, of sexual abuse against his father before he was 3 years old (2004); he is now 22. My sons, one or the other, or both, have given many incredibly detailed descriptions of physical abuse, sexual abuse, emotional, psychological and mental abuse, and neglect inflicted on them by their father, his wife, and the paternal family. Just to clarify, I'm not suggesting all of them sexually abused them, but they told their paternal grandparents, and they laughed at them and told the boys, "He doesn't do that." That's not gaslighting or anything. The paternal family supported, went along with and played a significant role in the abuse of the boys physically, emotionally, and psychologically, and neglecting them.

There were countless sunny days in which I covered the windows, and whether I had a migraine, regular headache, felt sick, or not, I took medication and crawled back into bed. Then I would worry incessantly about my sons, wonder what they were doing, if they were safe, how they were being treated, what they were thinking about, and so on. I would cry and cry some more. My chest and my very heart ached. I wished for terrible things to happen to members of the paternal family. I wondered why God allowed this to happen. I wondered why God didn't strike these awful people down and protect my sons, these innocent little boys. I struggled with my faith. Then, at times, I would pray. I wanted the world to go away. I wanted the end of the world. Then, at least, my sons would no longer be suffering. I found it difficult to go out to the barn to take care of the horses, to groom them, or to spend time with them. This is hard to imagine because while I was growing up, horses and the barn, no matter where we lived, were always my safe place and my first love. Rest assured, our horses never went hungry, as my mom always took excellent care of them, especially when I could not.

Nothing felt safe anymore. There was no joy and no happiness. It's as if the world lost all color. Now, everything was black, white, and gray. Abysmal. Gloom. The only time there was a glimmer of color was when I had a happy memory of my son's flash through my head. It was then that I saw their faces in color.

My mom lost her precious grandchildren as well. She had seen them all the time. Gabriel couldn't say granny, so at that time, she was gingy (ging gee), it was adorable. My mother is from a different generation, one that dealt with loss and grief much differently than I needed to. She tried to pull me from the edge many times, but I just refused to budge.

I am still gut-wrenchingly empty inside. We lost a huge formative and significant part of our lives together at a critical time. In times when monumental changes were happening, powerful memories that would last a lifetime are created to be held and cherished or will haunt forever. I will carry a massive hole inside my soul where the above would have been, but instead, there will reside loss, grief, rage, sadness, and guilt for the rest of my life.

Gabriel disclosed to a psychoanalyst that his dad laughed at him when he screamed; -he screamed when his dad put his penis in his butt, and it hurt; his dad apparently thought that was funny. This was among a plethora of similar disclosures and behaviors to a variety of people in a variety of environments, from both boys for almost 20 years now. How do you get from that to "mother is coaching them to lie"? We've been broken into bits; however, we will continue to try to put ourselves back together.

My sons are incredibly strong and brave young men. To get through the physical and sexual abuse, as well as the degradation, psychological mind-fuckery, emotional warfare, and on and on - -every persecution they suffered, they clearly show stalwartness and courage. They may have felt broken, diminished, and hopeless then. I did as well. But they picked themselves up. Often, they picked each other up, dusted themselves off, and marched on. Over and over and over again, they did this. However, I still wish I could absorb all their pain and atrocious memories so they could go through the rest of their lives without this pain, this burden to bear and work through, and not relive their memories again and again. Unfortunately, I am unable to do that. Still, they go on and work with what they have and through what they can, as they are able. I admire their fortitude. Both of my sons are phenomenal young men, as well as they are my heroes.

Shock
Terror
Broken
Heartbreak
Worry
Emptiness
Loneliness
Despair
Destitute
Dead
Nothingness
Hopelessness
Rage
Guilt
Powerless
Research
Mutiny
Bitterness
Vocalization
Involvement
Acceptance
Contributing
Change

Section Two

General Information Directly from Experts in the Field

Academic and Legitimately Sourced Articles

Definitions

More Personal Experience Mixed in Throughout

Resources

The following information is being delivered to you in a different manner than you'd usually see in other books. There is so much about these subjects that most people are unaware of -including people who need to know it the most. Most of the following has been taken from the source that is listed above, verbatim. The reason I have done this is because I felt I could not do the material justice simply by summing it up, and I wanted you to see it as the author/s of the book or article used it. Most of the material is cited from the source where I initially discovered it; if it was in an article written by Dr. Kathleen Colbourn Faller, I cited her. I didn't always cite all the resources that she used to write her article - one reason for that is I didn't know it. Everything following the source listed is taken from the above-listed source unless otherwise stated.

Some of the information is repetitive -this was not a mistake. It was by choice. For example, I wanted you to really learn the possible behaviors of an abused and traumatized child, and there were some behaviors on one list that were not included on another, yet they were all relevant, especially from my perspective. Lastly, I know the order of words resonates differently to different people and I wanted to do what I could to reach everyone I could. Thank you for your understanding on this point. The information delivered here is only the tip of the iceberg of what is available out there. The hardest part, as has been for this entire book, was what I had to leave out, as there is so much more I wanted to include. Most of my comments and personal experiences are usually in brackets: []. I've included a variety of personal experiences scattered throughout. I hope you find this information as critically useful as I have.

Information for one particular subject, for instance, PTSD, is not only contained in the section for "PTSD," as these subjects intertwine with each other, so you'll find additional topics covered in other sections, and these I did not include in each section they had pertaining information. The topics are listed in no particular order.

My friend, if you are reading this, you are or have gone through severely traumatic times, my heart goes out to you. Look for a support group in your area. There may even be a virtual one you can find that would be helpful. If you are reading this because you work in the justice system and/or are in the field of child welfare, I sincerely thank you for reading this. I hope this helps you in protecting children and understanding protective mothers (it is mostly mothers who have found themselves in this scenario). I hope I have shed some light on these issues and made you aware of situations you previously were unaware of.

Fast Facts and Statistics:

RAINN (Get help 24/7 Call 800-656-HOPE 4673):

Every 68 seconds, an American is sexually assaulted. (not including children under 12 or unreported sexual assaults).

93% of juvenile victims know the perpetrator.

Child sexual abuse is a widespread problem. Every 9 minutes, CPS substantiates or finds evidence for a claim of child sexual abuse. [Add to that; CPS historically, categorically, and regularly has not investigated these cases appropriately and has unsubstantiated cases when they should have been substantiated.]

The effects of child sexual abuse can be long-lasting and affect the victim's mental health.

..4 times more likely to develop symptoms of drug abuse.

..4 times more likely to experience PTSD…

..3 times more likely to experience a major depressive episode as adults.

63,000 [children] were victims of "substantiated or indicated" sexual abuse. [Contrast this number with the massive number of referrals vs. the number of those investigated and the "substantiated" numbers that don't take into account all of the cases that go unreported, not investigated, or unsubstantiated. An estimated 2/3 of cases go unreported.]

Out of the sexual abuse cases reported to CPS in 2013 [and then were investigated and then of those that were substantiated], 47,000 men and 5,000 women were alleged perpetrators.

In 88% of the sexual abuse claims that CPS substantiates or finds supporting evidence of, the perpetrator is male. In 9% of cases, they are female, and 3% are unknown.

Child sexual abuse is a widespread problem.

[As you know, in our case, none of the abhorrent abuse to my sons was substantiated].

Victims of child sexual abuse are often related to the perpetrator.

[Especially for the sexual abuse 'portion' of our case, the same scenario plays out throughout the state of Michigan and every state in our country, exactly the same as ours did. 2/3 of child sexual abuse isn't even reported. There are countless children going through trauma and severe abuse day after day who are not being protected. These are defenseless children, being scarred in ways most will never recover from. I see what it has done to my sons, there are no words to express my feelings of what I have witnessed and what I continue to see and hear. My youngest son (19) is currently going through trauma therapy. I continue to hear new horror stories of what my sons had to endure at their father's house; from X and the paternal family].

Rainn.org/statistics/scope-problem

National Crime Victimization Survey (NCVS)

Top Michigan Child Abuse Statistics 2023:

The number of children examined in homes has increased by 71.8% since 2010, while the number of verified child abuse and neglect victims has increased by 33.7%.

As a result of the Governor's stay-at-home order, calls to the state's child abuse hotline decreased by 50% in a matter of days.

In Michigan, there were more than 147,000 complaints of alleged child maltreatment or neglect in 2020, a 15% decrease from 2019. [Due to COVID-related stay-at-home orders].

Five thousand three hundred sixty-two children were taken from their homes and placed in foster care in 2019, according to MDHHS.

In 2010, Michigan had the 9th highest rate of child abuse and neglect.

According to the MLPP, over 5,000 newborns were verified victims of abuse and neglect in 2011, with 0-1 year of age being the most dangerous year for kids in Michigan.

Child Maltreatment 2022 Report by the Children's Bureau:

… there were 4,276,000 referrals alleging maltreatment that include 7,530,000 children in the United States….. In Michigan, the confirmed victims of abuse and/or neglect ages birth to 17 were 13,000 in 2022. [The number of 'confirmed' cases in Michigan seems to be very low when considering the number of referrals alleging maltreatment that would have been made in the state of Michigan. To me, this only shows there are a lot of true maltreatment cases that are not being confirmed as they should be.]

Child Abuse and Neglect, 2019:

… McInnes (2003) argues the real danger of subscribing to the PAS [Parental Alienation Syndrome] rhetoric is the acceptance of the inaccurate assumption that the majority of CSA [Child Sexual Abuse] allegations made in family court by children but reported by parents are false and result from parental prompting because children lack the capacity to recognize abuse and articulate their experiences. [But on other subjects, they can, and we take them at their word? Just not in these circumstances. Hmmm, that doesn't make any sense to me.] Because allegations of CSA can be difficult to corroborate due to a lack of traditional evidence, they may be deemed false (Faller, 2007). This serves to reinforce the idea that PAS is a common explanation for CSA allegations among those working for or on behalf of the courts, despite empirical research suggesting that, in fact, false allegations of CSA are exceptionally rare (Jenkins, 2003; McInnes, 2003).

The following information has been gathered from a variety of resources online and in books. These are as follows: Safe Kids Thrive, "If I Tell"; Kidsrights, Susan Marcy-Webster and Dr. Emily Phillips; A Mother's Nightmare -Incest, A Practical Legal Guide for Parents and Professionals, John E.B. Myers:

Child Abuse, Child Development, Behavioral Indicators:

Type of Abuse:

Physical:

Someone hurts a child's body or puts them in physical danger. It doesn't matter if the child gets seriously hurt or if it leaves a mark. Any harm is abuse. This includes burning, hits, kicks, bites, holding a child under water (or holding them to anything that causes pain, shakes or throws a child, throwing objects at the child, tying up the child, locking them in a room, closet, or cage, taping a mouth shut, and more.

Possible signs:

Bruises, welts, or other injuries that cannot be explained or do not match the child's story. Bruises in various stages of healing.

Burns, especially from cigarettes, burns that cannot be explained.

Injury marks that have a pattern, such as from a hand, fist, belt, or other objects.

Unexplained fractures, lacerations, or abrasions.

Swollen areas.

Evidence of delayed or inappropriate treatment for injuries.

Injuries at different stages of healing.

Medical or dental issues that go untreated.

Possible Behavioral Signs:

Avoiding any kind of touch or physical contact.

Afraid of going home. Wanting to stay after. Comes to school early and leaves late.

Seem to always be on high alert -hypervigilance.

Wear clothing that does not match the weather conditions -for instance, wearing long sleeves on hot days -to cover up bruises or marks.

Not having friends, not participating in activities.

Self-destructive.

Withdrawn and/or aggressive -behavioral extremes.

Complaints of soreness or moves uncomfortably.

Bizarre explanation of injuries.

Wary of adult contact.

Sexual:

Any kind of sexual activity with a child, not just physical contact. It includes when someone forces a child to take part in pornographic pictures or videos, shows a child pornography, any sexual contact with a child, from kissing in a sexual way to having sex, shows a child their genitals or someone else's genitals, as with "flashing" or the like, tells "dirty" jokes or stories to the child, and more.

Possible Signs:

Bloody, torn, or stained underwear.

Bruising or bleeding around the genitals.

Venereal disease.

Frequent urinary or yeast infection.

Fissures in the genital area or around the anus.

Bleeding when or after having a bowel movement.

Handprint bruising.

Pain, swelling, or itching around the genitals that might cause problems when walking or sitting. -Difficulty walking or sitting.

Itching or pain in and around the anus.

Pregnancy or STDs, especially if the child is under the age of 14.

Refusing to change clothes in front of people.

Running away from home.

Sexual activity or knowledge that people usually have when they are much older.

Searching, looking up and watching pornography at a very young age.

Unexplained bruises, redness, or bleeding of the child's genitals, anus, or mouth.

Pain at the genitals, anus, or mouth.

Sores or milky fluids in the genital area.

Possible Behavioral Signs:

Sexualized activity and play. Excessive seductiveness.

Role reversal, overly concerned for siblings.

Weight changes.

Suicide attempts. Suicidal ideation and plan.

Looking up pornography.

Spacing out -dissociation.

Aggression.

Answers to questions seem rehearsed.

Inappropriate sex play or premature understanding of sex.

Threatened by physical contact, closeness.

Indications of having been threatened.

Nightmares, trouble sleeping, fear of the dark or monsters, or other sleeping problems.

Spacing out.

Loss of appetite, stomach problems, or trouble eating or swallowing.

Sudden mood swings: rage, fear, anger, or withdrawal.

Fear of certain people or places (the child may become quiet or not want to be left alone with a babysitter, a friend, a relative, or some other child or adult.

Sexual activities with toys or other children, such as simulating sex with dolls or asking other children/siblings to behave sexually.

New words for private body parts.

Refusing to talk about a "secret" shared with an adult or older child.

Talking about a new older friend.

Suddenly, having money.

Emotional and Psychological:

A pattern of behaviors that harm a child's emotional well-being and development. This means when someone abuses others while the child is around (such as a parent, brother, sister or pet), fails to show love and affection, name-calling, ignores the child and doesn't give emotional support or guidance, shames, shuns, belittles, criticizes, embarrasses, teases, yells at, threatens, bullies, and more. Group shaming, shunning, humiliation, and gaslighting of a child is also abuse.

Emotional abuse may be name-calling, put-downs, mocking, shunning and/or shaming, terrorization, isolation, humiliation, rejection, corruption, ignoring, yelling at, yelling loudly and closely into a child's ear, gaslighting, etc.

Experts increasingly agree that psychological abuse is the core issue in all forms of child maltreatment. For most Physically abused children, the broken bones and bruises heal with time. For sexually abused children, physical injury is seldom the problem. The body of the physically or sexually abused child usually survives intact. But the child's essential self-worth, his or her inner soul, may be damaged for life by the physical abuse that lies at the heart of physical and sexual abuse. Psychological abuse exists when there is a long-term pattern of negative messages that undermine a child's essential self-worth. (A Mother's Nightmare Incest: A Practical Legal Guide for Parents and Professionals, John E. B. Myers).

Possible Signs:

Speech disorders and delays.

Delayed physical development, failure to thrive.

Substance abuse.

Constant worry about doing something wrong.

Anxiety.

Requiring praise, validation, and approval.

Low self-esteem and depression.

Speech problems.

Delays in learning, delays in cognitive and emotional development.

Doing poorly in school.

Extreme behavior, such as being way too 'obedient' or way too demanding.

Headaches and stomachaches without a clear cause.

Ulcers, asthma, severe allergies.

The child does not seem close to the parent or caregiver.

Showing little interest in friends and activities.

Being left alone or in the care of other young children.

Poor weight gain or growth.

Doesn't get medical, dental, or mental health care (medical neglect).

Missing a lot of school.

Answers to questions seem rehearsed.

Spurning.

Belittling, degrading, and other nonphysical forms of overtly hostile or rejecting treatment.

Shaming or ridiculing the child for showing normal emotions, such as affection, grief, or sorrow.

Consistently singling out one child to criticize and punish, to perform most of the household chores, or to receive fewer rewards.

Public humiliation.

Terrorizing. Includes caregiver behavior that threatens or is likely to physically hurt, kill, abandon, or place the child or the child's loved ones or objects in recognizably dangerous situations. Terrorizing includes placing a child in unpredictable or chaotic circumstances in recognizably dangerous situations. Setting rigid or unrealistic expectations with the threat of loss, harm, and danger if they are not met. Threatening or perpetrating violence against the child. Threatening or perpetrating violence against a child's loved ones or objects.

Exploiting or Corrupting. Including caregiver acts that encourage the child to develop inappropriate behaviors, such as self-destruction, antisocial, criminal, deviant, or other maladaptive behaviors. Modeling, permitting, or encouraging antisocial behavior; prostitution. Performance in pornographic media, initiation of criminal activities, substance abuse, violence to or corruption of others. Modeling, permitting or encouraging developmentally inappropriate behavior; parentification, infantilization, living the parents' unfilled dreams. Encouraging or coercing abandonment of developmentally appropriate autonomy through extreme over-involvement, intrusiveness, or dominance, allowing little or no opportunity or support for the child's views, feelings, and wishes. Micromanaging the child's life. Restricting or interfering with cognitive development.

Denying emotional Responsiveness/Ignoring. Includes caregiver's acts that ignore the child's attempts and need to interact, failing to express affection, caring, and love for the child, and showing no emotion in interactions with the child. Denying emotional responsiveness, such as being detached and uninvolved through either incapacity or lack of motivation. Interacting when only absolutely necessary. Failing to express affection, caring, and love for the child.

Isolating. Includes caregiver acts that consistently deny the child's opportunities to meet needs for interacting or communicating with peers or adults inside or outside the home. Confining the child or placing unreasonable limitations on the child's freedom of movement within his or her environment. Placing unreasonable limitations or restrictions on the child's social interactions with peers or adults in the community.

Possible Behavioral Signs:

Performing poorly in school.

Aggression and outbursts.

Always looking dirty.

Eating more at a meal or saving food for later, stockpiling, hoarding.

Habit disorder (sucking, rocking, biting).

Antisocial, destructive.

Neurotic traits (sleep disorders, inhibition of play).

Passive and aggressive behavioral extremes.

Delinquent behavior.

Developmentally delayed.

Neglect:

When a caregiver doesn't give the child basic care and protection. Such as clothing, food, a home with clean living conditions, heat in cold weather, and more.

Possible Signs:

Abandonment.

Unattended medical needs.

Consistent lack of supervision.

Consistent hunger, inappropriate dress, poor hygiene.

Lice, distended stomach, emaciated.

Inadequate nutrition.

Possible Behavioral Signs:

Regularly displays fatigue or listlessness and falls asleep in class.

Steals food and begs from classmates.

Reports that no caretaker is at home.

Frequently absent or tardy.

Self-destructive.

School dropout.

Extreme loneliness and need for affection.

Need for validation, approval, and praise.

Parental Substance Abuse:

This happens when adults neglect or harm children through the use of drugs or alcohol. Such as when a parent is not able to care for a child because they are high on drugs and alcohol, giving illegal drugs or alcohol to a child, making methamphetamine when a child is around, a pregnant woman's abuse of drugs or alcohol, which exposes her baby to these toxins, and more.

Medical Neglect:

A child is medically neglected when their caregivers don't provide them with needed medical or mental health treatment. Includes unwarranted caregiver acts that ignore, refuse to allow, or fail to provide the necessary treatment for the mental, health, medical, and educational problems or needs of the child. Ignoring the need for or failing or refusing to allow or provide treatment for serious emotional or behavioral problems or needs of the child. Ignoring the need for or failing or refusing to allow or provide treatment for serious physical health problems or needs of the child. Ignoring the needs for or failing or refusing to allow or provide treatment or services for serious educational problems or needs of the child.

Abandonment:

Many states consider this a form of child neglect. It happens when a parent leaves a child with no support or concern for their well-being or when the parent's location is unknown.

Child Trafficking:

This is a type of slavery. Children are trafficked when they're used for prostitution or pornography, or to beg, sell drugs, or work long hours for little pay.

Possible Signs:

Missing school often.

Running away from home.

Sudden changes in style of dress or relationships.

Has an older "girlfriend" or "boyfriend."

They talk about needing to pay off a debt.

They often care for children who are not members of their own family.

Their responses to questions seem rehearsed.

Verbal:

Verbal abuse, also known as emotional abuse, is a range of words or behaviors used to manipulate, intimidate, and maintain power and control over someone. These include insults, humiliation and ridicule, the silent treatment, and attempts to scare, isolate, and control. (Google, Dec. 29, 2022).

Possible Signs:

Isolation and Control

Humiliation, Threatening, and Intimidation

Emotional Manipulation

Gaslighting

(WebMD.com)

Mental:

Mental abuse is the use of threats, verbal insults, and other more subtle tactics to control a person's way of thinking. This form of abuse is especially disturbing because it is tailored to destroy self-esteem and confidence and undermine a personal sense of reality or competence. (How to recognize mental abuse, and why it's not your fault, Maggie Wooll, Nov. 23, 2021).

Possible Signs:

Name Calling

Humiliation

Withholding Affection

Making Threats

Turning Tables

Indifference

(How to recognize mental abuse, and why it's not your fault, Maggie Wooll, Nov. 23, 2021).

Educational:

Educational neglect involves a failure of the parent or caregiver to enroll a child of mandatory school age in school or to provide appropriate homeschooling or needed special educational training… can also involve a failure of the parent or caretakers to exercise care in facilitating school attendance of a child to the extent that the child's education has been impaired or harmed. (What is the difference between educational neglect and truancy?, dorightbykids.org, child-abuse reporting, New York).

Many of these traits could be seen in more than one abuse category.

"Make sure the child feels supported, validated, believed, and knows it is not their fault."

American Academy of Pediatrics, www.aap.org and American Academy of Child and Adolescent Psychiatry, www.aacap.org:

Child Development Chart, Normal Developmental Behaviors:

0-6 Months:

Cognitive

Recognition of mother, no concept of past or future, reaches for familiar people and toys.

Psychological

Attachment to mother/caretaker, totally dependent, totally trusting, learns intimacy.

Motor

Sucking, hands clenched, grip, neck muscles develop, pulls at clothing, laughs and coos.

Moral

None.

Sexual

Erections are possible, and both sexes can be stimulated.

6-12 Months:

Cognitive

Objects can be held in memory, learned through routines and rewards, recognize names, say two to three words besides "mama" and "dada," and imitate familiar words.

Psychological

Separation from the mother, begins to develop a sense of self, learn to get needs met, trusts adults, stretches her arms to be picked up, likes to look at herself in the mirror.

Motor

Rolls over, stands with support, creeps/crawls, walks with help, rolls a ball in imitation of adult, pulls self to standing position and stands unaided, transfers object from one hand to the other, drops and picks up the toy, can feed self a cracker, holds cup with two hands, drinks with assistance, holds out arms and legs while being dressed.

Moral

None.

Sexual

Generalized genital play.

12-18 Months:

Cognitive

Experiments with the physical environment, understanding the word "no," comes when called to, recognizing words as symbols for objects (cat – meows), using 10-20 words, including names, combining two words such as "daddy bye-bye," waves goodbye and plays pat-a-cake, makes the sounds of familiar animals, gives a toy when asked, uses words such as "more" to make wants known, points to his or her toes, eyes, and nose, brings objects from another room when asked.

Psychological

Early social development, egocentric, accepts limits, develops self-esteem (love from family), plays by self.

Motor

Creeps upstairs to get to a standing position alone, walks alone, walks backward, picks up toys from the floor without falling, pulls and pushes toys, seats self in a child-size chair, moves to music, turns pages two or three at a time, scribbles, turns knobs, paints with whole arm movement, shifts hands, makes strokes, uses spoon with little spilling, drinks from cup with one hand unassisted, chews food, unzips large zipper, indicates toilet needs, removes shoes, socks, pants, sweater.

Moral

Fear of authority figures.

Sexual

Continued generalized genital play.

18-36 Months:

Cognitive

Can conduct experiments inside head but limited to experience, rapid language growth, copies adult chores in play, carries on conversation with self and dolls, asks "what's that?" and "Where's my….?," knows 300 words at 2, 900 words at 3, understands a lot more than what they can say, gives first name, holds up fingers to tell age, combines nouns and verbs "mommy go," refers to self as "me," rather than by name, egocentric, assumes you know what he/she knows, likes to hear same story repeated, may say "no" when means "yes."…Use other objects in play that represent real life.

Psychological

Autonomy struggles to learn a system of meeting needs, seeks adult approval, social development increases, points to things he or she wants, joins in play with other children, shares toys, takes turns with assistance, separation anxiety common (look for lack of separation anxiety in children who have endured trauma).

Motor

Can run, throw a ball, play kickball, jump, go upstairs with one hand held by an adult, turn single pages, snip with scissors, and hold crayons with thumb and fingers (not fist) but may ignore adults as they draw since they must concentrate, uses one hand consistently in most activities, rolls, pounds, squeezes, and pulls clay, uses spoon with little spilling, gets drink from fountain or faucet independently, opens door by turning handle, takes off and puts on coat with assistance, washes and dries hands with assistance.

Moral

Knowledge of preferences of authority figures.

Sexual

Continued generalized genital play, early sex-role development, interest in potty behavior, touches and rubs own genitals, disinhibited – no sense of privacy, role-playing to understand what adults are doing, such as playing doctor.

3-5 Years

Cognitive

Wide range of language skills at this age. Can conduct experiments inside the head, cannot sequence, understand some abstract concepts, colors, and numbers (but this does not mean that they can tell you "how many times," they can count tangible objects in a room, like chairs, crayons, etc.), knows shapes, time (not clock time but days before/after, "naptime," "bedtime"), understands family relations (baby/parent), can tell a story, has a sentence length of 4-5 words, has a vocabulary of nearly 1000 words, names at least one color, understands "tonight," "summer," "lunchtime," "yesterday," knows his or her last name, name of the street on which he or she lives, knows several nursery rhymes, uses past tense correctly, can speak of imaginary conditions "I hope," understands basic concept of right and wrong -punishment centered, *at 4 can typically grasp truth vs. lie*, but may confuse the difference between a lie and a mistake.

Psychological

Can cooperate, cannot separate fantasy from reality, has nightmares, models on same-sexed parents, experiences and copes with feelings (sad, jealous, embarrassed), but they are all or nothing, meaning a child can be angry at their parent one minute, but once the parent apologizes feelings shift and all is good again, plays and interacts with other children, dramatic play is closer to reality, *with attention paid to detail, time, and space,* plays dress-up, symbolic representation of self begins (can now use a doll or picture to represent themselves).

Motor

Swings/climbs, uses small scissors, jumps in place, walks on tiptoes, balances on one foot, rides a tricycle, begins to skip, dances, bathes and dresses, runs around obstacles, walks on a line, pushes, pulls, steers wheeled toys, uses slide independently, throws ball overhead, catches a bounced ball, skates, jumps rope, pastes and glues appropriately, skips on alternating feet, buttons and unbuttons, washes hands independently, blows nose when reminded, uses toilet independently, drawing improves and by 4 will trace and draw stick figures.

Moral

Self-esteem is dependent on authority figures, follows peers' fads, negotiates to get needs met, rules are very important, and is protective of parents.

Sexual

Generalized genital play (rubbing genitals until raw is not normal), masturbation to orgasm in females possible, early experimentation, watching/asking about body functions, private parts funny but also serious, gender identity established.

6-9 Years:

Cognitive

Can think using symbols, recognize differences, make comparisons, take another's perspective, define objects by their use, know spatial relationships like "on top," "behind," "far," and "near," know address, identify penny, nickel, dime, knows common opposites like "big/little," asks questions for information, distinguishes left from right, able to separate fantasy from reality, improved sequencing of events. By 8, you should be able to read a face clock.

Psychological

Early close peer relationships, presence of well-developed defenses, develops identity outside of family (school, friends), has likes and dislikes (food, friends, games), chooses own friends, plays simple table games, engages in cooperative play with other children involving group decisions, role assignments, fair play, egocentrism crumbles, suddenly question how others think of them.

Motor

Increasing small muscle motor skills, cutting food with a knife, laces shoes, dressing self completely, tying bow, brushing independently, and crossing streets safely.

Moral

Has a conscience and refinements in moral development.

Sexual

Defenses reduce experimentation, but some continue to play house, wedding, and family role-play games.

10-15 Years:

Cognitive

Can engage in inductive and deductive logic, neurons are present, understands hypothetical situations, conflicts with parents increase.

Psychological

Increased autonomy struggles, increased focus on identity, focus on peer relationships, rebellious, often moody, romantic feelings, feels awkward or strange about his or her body, worries about being normal, frequently changing relationships.

Motor

Greater body competence (e.g., physical coordination), manual dexterity, and growth patterns vary.

Moral

Moral development is legalistic, recognition of principles (e.g., justice), and selection of role models.

Sexual

Puberty, sex organs mature, males ejaculate and have wet dreams, both sexes are able to masturbate to orgasm with fantasies, girls develop physically sooner than boys and may display shyness, blushing, and modesty.

16-21 Years:

Cognitive

Uses formal logic (e.g., opposes racism), debates and can change sides of the debate understands probabilities, uses more flexible abstract thinking, examination of inner experiences, conflict with parents begins to decrease.

Psychological

Interest in relationships solidifies personal identity, becomes goal-directed, sometimes rebellious, increased concern for others, increases concern for the future and places more importance on his or her role in life.

Motor

Heightened physical power, strength, and coordination.

Moral

Identifies with moral principles, rules, limit testing, experimentation with sex and drugs, and examination of inner experiences.

Sexual

Feelings of love and passion, development of more serious relationships, sense of sexual identity established, increased capacity for tender and sensual love.

Child Development ("Normal" for Developmental Level) and Atypical Behaviors That May Be Indicative of Child Abuse:

Committee on Child Abuse and Neglect 2008-2009:

Sexual abuse is a common, but not exclusive, experience among children with sexual behavior problems. Once sexual behavior problems are identified, a careful assessment of family behaviors and the home environment may clarify underlying causes and contributing factors.

Because child abuse and neglect are more common in homes characterized by violence and criminal activity, children who reside in such homes should be carefully assessed for abuse and neglect. Among children with a history of sexual abuse, 52% indicated that they had lived with an adult batterer during their childhood, and 58% of the child sexual offenders who were in-home males also battered their adult female partner. As many as 68% of children with sexual behavior problems have witnessed intimate partner violence among their caregivers. Adult violence in the home is strongly linked to abuse, neglect, and sexual behavior problems in children.

The Child Welfare System Fact Sheet
Children's Rights

The act of separating a child from their family and Community imposes profound trauma on children. The briefest separation can cause emotional harm that can last a lifetime.

After evaluating whether the allegations of child maltreatment met statutory definitions of abuse or neglect, agencies screened out 45.8% of reports and screened 54.2% of reports for further investigation. .... Black children are between 2 and 5 times more likely to have their cases screened in for investigation than white children.

Current estimates indicate that before turning 18, 37.4% of all children, including 53% of black children, in the U.S. will be subjected to a CPS investigation.

...........an estimated 18.4% of black children and 15.8% of Native American [children] will have a substantiated maltreatment case before they turn 18, compared to 11% of white children.

Every 2.5 minutes, a child in the U.S. is separated from their families and placed in foster care, too often with a stranger. In 2020, approximately 64% of all children, including 64% of black children and 65% of native American children, removed from their families experienced family separation because of "neglect." [There are a plethora of resources and services that could be allocated to prevent all of those removals.] Under the current system, "neglect" removals often result from conditions of poverty, including "inadequate housing" or "failure to provide adequate nutrition." Research indicates that black children are 15% more likely than white children to be separated from their families instead of receiving in-home services after an investigation.

… In 2021, a total of [well] over 600,000 children spent time in the U.S. foster care system. On average, children remain in state care for over a year and a half, and 5% of children in foster care languish in the system for 5 or more years.

In 2021, approximately 100,000 children -less than half of youth exiting foster care- were reunified with their families. Native American children are reunited with their families at lower rates than children of any other race.

The harms inflicted by the child welfare system, compounded with existing racial and socioeconomic barriers in American society, produce gross disparities between youth with lived experience in foster care [and the child welfare system] and other young adults.

Because of the trauma of separation, structural inequities, and frequent negative experiences …. Youth with a history in foster care [CPS, any part of the child welfare system] are also significantly more likely to suffer from serious and life-threatening mental health disorders. Individuals with prior involvement…report having attempted suicide within the past year at rates quadruple those of non-foster [etc.] youth without prior system involvement and experience post-traumatic stress disorder at double the rate of U.S. war veterans.

PACEs Connection:

When caring for children with trauma, I believe our first priority is safety and trust, not behavior change.

The following 'lists' come from American Academy of Family Physicians:

Examples of Sexual Behavior Problems in children:

Behaviors that cause emotional distress, anxiety, or physical pain.

Repeated penetration of the vagina or anus with an object or digit.

Behaviors that are persistent, and child becomes angry if distracted.

Behaviors associated with conduct disorders or aggression.

A variety of sexual behaviors displayed frequently or on a daily basis.

Sexual behaviors involving children 4 or more years apart in age.

One child coercing another into participating.

Explicit imitation of sexual intercourse.

Oral-genital contact.

Asking an adult to perform a specific sexual act.

American Academy of Pediatrics Council on Child Abuse and Neglect 2023:

Sexual Behavior Problems: Red Flags:

- Asking a peer or adult to engage in specific sexual acts.
- Inserting objects into genitals.
- Explicit imitation of sexual intercourse.
- Touching animal genitals.
- Sexual behaviors that are frequently disturbing to others.
- Behaviors that persist and are resistant to parental distraction.
- Any sexual behaviors involving children that are 4 or more years apart.
- A variety of sexual behaviors displayed on a daily basis.
- Sexual behavior that results in emotional distress or pain.

- Sexual behaviors are associated with other physically aggressive behaviors.

- Sexual behaviors that involve coercion.

- Behaviors are persistent, and child becomes angry if distracted.

Abusewatch.net and Darkness2light.org

Prevention resources for the community and Professionals:

An overview of statistics:

Sexual abuse touches every life when it leads to loss of trust, decreases in self-esteem, and the development of shame, guilt and depression.

Sexual abuse touches every life when it leads to eating disorders, substance abuse, suicide, promiscuity/prostitution, and other psycho-behavioral issues.

- 1 in 4 girls is sexually abused before the age of 18.

- 1 in 6 boys is sexually abused before the age of 18.

- 1 in 5 children are solicited sexually while on the internet.

- Nearly 70% of all reported sexual assaults (including assaults on adults) occur to children ages 17 and under.

Especially within the walls of their own homes, children are at risk for sexual abuse.

- More than 20% of children are sexually abused before the age of 8.

- Nearly 50% of all victims of forcible sodomy, sexual assault with an object, and forcible fondling are children under 12.

Evidence that a child has been sexually abused is not always obvious, and many children do not report that they have been abused.

- Over 30% of victims never disclose the experience to ANYONE.

- Young victims may not recognize their victimization as sexual abuse.

- Almost 80% initially deny abuse or are tentative in disclosing it.

- Additionally, of those who do disclose, more than 20% eventually recant even though the abuse occurred.

Consequences of child sexual abuse begin affecting children and families immediately. They also affect society in innumerable and negative ways. These effects can continue throughout the life of the survivor, so the impact on society for just one survivor continues over multiple decades.

The way a victim's family responds to abuse plays an important role in how the incident affects the victim.

- Sexually abused children who keep it a secret or who "tell" and are not believed are at greater risk than the general population for psychological, emotional, and physical problems, often lasting into adulthood.

- Children who have been victims of sexual abuse are more likely to experience physical health problems (e.g., headaches).

- Victims of child sexual abuse report more symptoms of PTSD, more sadness, and more school problems than non-victims.

- Victims of child sexual abuse are more likely to experience major depressive disorder as adults.

- Young girls who are sexually abused are more likely to develop eating disorders as adolescents.

- Adolescent victims of violent crime have difficulty in the transition to adulthood, are more likely to suffer financial failure and physical injury and are at risk to fail in other areas due to problem behaviors and outcomes of the victimization.

- Victims of child sexual abuse report more substance abuse problems.

- 70-80% of sexual abuse survivors report excessive drug and alcohol use.

- Young girls who are sexually abused are 3 times more likely to develop psychiatric disorders or alcohol and drug abuse in adulthood than girls who are not sexually abused.

- Among male survivors, more than 70% seek psychological treatment for issues such as substance abuse, suicidal thoughts and attempted suicide. Men who have been sexually abused are more likely to violently victimize others.

- Children who have been victims of sexual abuse exhibit long-term and more frequent behavioral problems, particularly inappropriate sexual behaviors.

- Women who report childhood rape are 3 times more likely to become pregnant before age 18.

- An estimated 60% of teen first pregnancies are preceded by experiences of molestation, rape, or attempted rape.

- The average age of their offenders is 27 years old.

- Victims of child sexual abuse are more likely to be sexually promiscuous.

- More than 75% of teenage prostitutes have been sexually abused.

- Adolescents who suffer violent victimization are at risk of being victims or perpetrators of felony assault, domestic violence, and property offenses as adults.

- Nearly 50% of women in prison state that they were abused as children.

- Over 75% of serial rapists report that they were sexually abused as youngsters.

- Most perpetrators don't molest only one child if they are not reported and stopped.

- Nearly 70% of child sex offenders have between 1 and 9 victims, and at least 20% have 10-40 victims.

- An average serial child molester may have as many as 400 victims in his lifetime. Some have thousands.

Consider reviewing the U.S. History of Child Abuse found also on abusewatch.net

Darkness to Light, Child Abuse Statistics

- Over 90% of child sexual abuse victims know their abuser.

- A small number of juvenile offenders –one out of 8—are younger than age 12. Females constitute 7% of juveniles who commit sex offenses.

Childhood Maltreatment and Antisocial Behavior: Comparison of Self-Reported and Substantiated Maltreatment, American Journal of Orthopsychiatry (Smith, Ireland, Thornberry, and Elwyn):

Accurate Assessment of maltreatment is critical to understanding and interrupting its impact on the life course....Among those with official reports, in young adulthood, about half self-reported maltreatment, whereas 37% of those self-reporting have an official report.

...maltreatment is associated with a higher prevalence of antisocial behavior.

Children's Protective Services (Michigan): Comprehensive Report March 1, 2021

Disposed Cases and Classifications:

Category I (a preponderance is found and involves court intervention)

3,156

Category II (a preponderance is found; the future risk is high)

5,763

Category III (a preponderance is found; future risk is low or moderate)

8,638

Category IV (a preponderance is not found)

54,981

Category V (unable to be located)

573

In FY 2020, 4,972 children were separated from a parent or legal guardian. Five hundred sixty-three had their case closed after either returning home or to another planned living arrangement; 4,409 children had active foster care cases; 203 children's parents had their parental rights terminated.

State-level Data for Understanding Child Welfare in the United States, Child Welfare (Sarah Catherine Williams) Michigan Child Maltreatment (state-level data) FY 2020

Number of referrals made to the child welfare agency:

140,748

Percent of referrals that met criteria for an investigation:

52%

Violence Prevention Centers for Disease Control and Prevention (CDC)

Fast Facts: Preventing Child Abuse and Neglect

Child abuse and neglect are common. At least 1 in 7 children have experienced child abuse or neglect in the past year in the United States. This is likely an underestimate because many cases are unreported. In 2020, 1,750 children died of abuse and neglect in the United States.

Over the long term, children who are abused or neglected are also at increased risk for experiencing future violence victimization and perpetration, substance abuse, sexually transmitted infections, delayed brain development, lower educational attainment, and limited employment opportunities.

Chronic abuse may result in toxic stress, which can change brain development and increase the risk for problems like posttraumatic stress disorder and learning, attention, and memory difficulties.

Child Sexual Abuse and Subsequent Psychopathology: Results From the American Journal of Public Health National Comorbidity Survey (Molnar, Buka, Kes):

Substantial stigmatization is involved in reporting rape or molestation, especially among men. There is little evidence however, that people overreport these experiences and substantial evidence of underreporting, especially among men.

Child Welfare Information Gateway, Children's Bureau Long-Term Consequences of Child Abuse and Neglect:

Childhood maltreatment has been linked to higher risk for a wide range of long-term and/or future health problems, including –but not limited to—the following:

- Diabetes
- Lung Disease
- Malnutrition
- Vision problems
- Functional limitations (i.e., being limited in activities)
- Heart attack
- Arthritis
- Back problems
- High blood pressure
- Brain damage
- Migraine headaches
- Chronic bronchitis/emphysema/chronic obstructive pulmonary disease
- Cancer
- Stroke
- Bowel disease
- Chronic fatigue syndrome

Child abuse and neglect also has been associated with certain regions of the brain failing to form, function, or grow properly. For example, a history of maltreatment may be correlated with reduced volume in overall brain size and may affect the size and/or functioning of the following brain regions:

- The amygdala is key to processing emotions.

- The hippocampus is central to learning and memory.

- The orbitofrontal cortex is responsible for reinforcement-based decision-making and emotional regulation.

- The cerebellum helps coordinate motor behavior and executive functioning.

- The corpus callosum is responsible for left-brain/right-brain communication and other processes (e.g., arousal, emotion, and higher cognitive abilities).

Psychological Consequences:
- Diminished executive functioning and cognitive skills.
- Poor mental and emotional health.
- Attachment and social difficulties.
- Posttraumatic stress.
- Toxic stress.

Michigan Department of Health and Human Services

Fact Sheet March 2023:

For the month of March 2023, the following are pertaining to Children's Protective Services

- Abuse-neglect complaints filed:

  16,543

- Assigned Investigations:

  6,153

- Confirmed cases of abuse and/or neglect:

  1,401

Top Michigan Child Abuse Statistics 2023

- The number of children in examined homes has increased by 71% since 2010, while the number of verified child abuse and neglect victims has increased by 33.7%

- As a result of the governor's stay-at-home order, calls to the state's child abuse hotline decreased by 50% in a matter of days.

Recognizing and Responding to Child Maltreatment, The Lancet (Gilbert, Kemp, Thoburn, Sidebotham, Radford, Glaser)

Professionals in child health, primary care, mental health, schools, social services, and law-enforcement services all contribute to the recognition of and response to child maltreatment. In all sectors, children suspected of being maltreated are under-reported to child protection agencies. Lack of Awareness of the signs of child maltreatment and processes to reporting to child protection agencies and a perception that reporting might do more harm than good are among the reasons for not reporting. Strategies to improve recognition, mainly used in pediatric practice, include training, the use of questionnaires for asking children and parents about maltreatment, and evidence-based guidelines for who should be assessed by child-protection specialists. Internationally, studies suggest that policies emphasizing substantiation of maltreatment without concomitant attention to welfare needs lead to less service provision for maltreated children than do those in areas for which child maltreatment is part of a broad child and family welfare response.

Few maltreated children come to the attention of child-protection agencies, indicating a failure of professionals to recognize maltreatment, failure to report it, and failure of agencies to investigate or substantiate maltreatment. Child deaths related to maltreatment are under-recognized.

Crimes Against Children Research Center, National Children's Alliance Updated Trends in Child Maltreatment (Finkelhor, Jones, Shattuck)

Child welfare authorities ensure the safety of more than 7 million kids. Of those, around 3.9 million children received an investigation or alternative response from child protective services agencies. An estimated 2 million children received prevention services.

It goes without saying (but I'm saying it anyway) that there are millions of children throughout our world and our own nation and state who need the world to not fail them but to provide protection for them and to stop this needless pain and suffering these traumas cause them for the rest of their lives. When abuse happens, and especially when it is allowed to continue, and children are removed from the care of their protector, their lives are derailed and set on a new trajectory. A life trajectory that is full of pain and struggles, one that most never recover from.

[I sincerely hope that with my sons and my story, you will be able to find your own way to participate with the rest of us who are fighting to protect our children. Nobody can tell your story the way you can].

U. N. Convention on the Rights of the Child:

Wikipedia:

The United Nations Convention on the Rights of the Child (CRC or UNCRC) is an international human rights treaty that sets out the civil, political, economic, social, health and cultural rights of children. The convention defines a child as any human being under the age of 18.

Nations that have ratified this convention…are bound by international law. When a state has signed the treaty but not ratified it, it is not yet bound by the treaty's provisions but is …obliged not to act contrary to its purpose.

The UN Committee on the Rights of the Child, composed of 18 independent experts, is responsible for supervising the implementation of the convention by the states that have ratified it. Their governments are required to report to and appear before the UN Committee on the Rights of the Child periodically to be examined on their progress regarding the advancement of the implementation of the convention and the status of child rights in their country.

Individuals can appeal to the Committee on the Rights of the Child if they believe that rights, according to the convention, have been violated.

The UN General Assembly adopted the Convention and opened it for signature on 20 November 1989.…It came into force on 2 September 1990, after it was ratified by the required number of nations. As of 9 June 2023, 196 countries are party to it, including every member of the United Nations except the United States.

The convention deals with child-specific needs and rights. It requires that the "nations that ratify this convention are bound to it by international law." Ratifying states must act in the best interests of the child.

In all jurisdictions, implementing the convention requires compliance with child custody and guardianship laws as every child has basic rights…

The convention obliges states to allow parents to exercise their parental responsibilities. The convention also acknowledges that children have the right to express their opinions and to have those opinions heard and acted upon when appropriate, to be protected from abuse or exploitation, and to have their privacy protected. It requires their lives not to be subject to excessive interference.

[Incidentally, each state of the United States recognizes choices by children at different ages regarding their opinions as to which parent they'd rather live in custody disputes. Some states do not have an age set at all for which the child's voice is recognized for whom they wish to reside; Michigan is one of those states].

The convention forbids capital punishment for children [what a concept]. State parties must "take all appropriate legislative, administrative, social and educational measures to protect the child from all forms of physical or mental violence"…

The United States government played an active role in the drafting of the convention and signed it on 16 February 1995 but has not ratified it. [Do as I say, not as I do]. It has been claimed that the American opposition to the convention stems primarily from political and religious conservatives. For example, The Heritage Foundation considers that "a civil society in which moral authority is exercised by religious congregations, family, and other private associations is fundamental to the American order,"[But, whose morals? Whose religion? And what is the American order?]..the Home School Legal Defense Association (HSLDA) argues that the CRC threatens homeschooling.

During his 2008 campaign for President, Senator Barack Obama described the failure to ratify the convention as "embarrassing" and promised to review the issue, but, as President, he never did. No President of the United States has submitted the treaty to the United States Senate requesting its advice and consent to ratification since the US signed it in 1995. [Parent's rights groups are louder than the voices of children's rights; after all, children are property, isn't that right?]

"We All Have Rights"

In 1989, world leaders made a historic commitment to the world's children by adopting the United Nations Convention on the Rights of the Child – an international agreement on childhood.

It's become the most widely ratified human rights treaty in history and has helped transform children's lives around the world.

But still, not every child gets to enjoy a full childhood [or any childhood at all]. Still, too many childhoods are cut short.

[The CRC] ..has .. enabled more children to have their voices heard and participate in their societies [or at least that is the purpose for it; I'm not certain how effective it is in the many countries who have ratified it].

Contained in this treaty is a profound idea: that children are not just objects who belong to their parents and for whom decisions are made or adults in training. Rather, they are children [and] must be allowed to grow, learn, play, develop, and flourish with dignity.

…[We must]…commit to action to make sure every child has every right.

[Obviously, the American order as my sons and I have experienced was completely void of morals, and especially, rights].

Domestic Violence, Power and Control Wheel: Lundy Bancroft

Child Protection in America: Past, Present, and Future; APSAC Handbook on Child Maltreatment; Evidence in Child Abuse and Neglect; Why Does He Do That? Inside the Minds of Angry and Controlling Men:

Abuse is the product of a mentality that excuses and condones bullying and exploitation, promotes superiority, and casts responsibility onto the oppressed.

For decades, many therapists have been attempting to help abusive men change by guiding them in identifying and expressing feelings. Alas, this well-meaning but misguided approach actually feeds the abuser's selfish focus on himself, which is an important force driving his abusiveness.

…while a small number of abusive men do hate women, the great majority exhibit a more subtle-though often quite pervasive-sense of superiority or contempt toward females….

As I have explained in earlier chapters, abusiveness has little to do with psychological problems and everything to do with values and beliefs. Where do a boy's values about partner relationships come from? The sources are many. The most important ones include the family he grows up in, his neighborhood, the television he watches and the books he reads, the jokes he hears, the messages that he receives from the toys he is given, and his most influential adult role models. His role models are important not just for which behaviors they exhibit to the boy but also for which values they teach him in words and what expectations they instill in him for the future. In sum, a boy's values develop from the full range of his experiences within his culture.

Your abusive partner doesn't have a problem with his anger, he has a problem with your anger. One of the basic human rights he takes away from you is the right to be angry with him. No matter how badly he treats you, he believes that your voice shouldn't rise and your blood shouldn't boil.

Has he ever trapped you in a room and not let you out?

Has he ever raised a fist as if he were going to hit you?

Has he ever thrown an object that hit you or nearly did?

Has he ever held you down or grabbed you to restrain you?

Has he ever threatened to hurt you?

If the answer to any of these questions is yes, then we can stop wondering whether he'll ever be violent; he already has been.

An abuser can seem emotionally needy. You can get caught in a trap of catering to him, trying to fill a bottomless pit. But he's not so much needy as entitled, so no matter how much you give him, it will never be enough. He will just keep coming up with more demands because he believes his needs are your responsibility until you feel drained down to nothing.

One of the obstacles to recognizing chronic mistreatment in relationships is that most abusive men simply don't seem like abusers. They have many good qualities, including times of kindness, warmth, and humor, especially in the early period of the relationship. An abuser's friends may think the world of him. He may have a successful work life and have no problems with drugs or alcohol. He may simply not fit anyone's image of a cruel or intimidating person. So when a woman feels her relationship spinning out of control, it is unlikely to occur to her that her partner is an abuser.

But whether you stay or go, the critical decision you can make is to stop letting your partner distort the lens of your life, always forcing his way into the center of the picture. You deserve to have your life be about you; you are worth it.

Physical aggression by a man toward his partner is abuse, even if it happens only once. If he raises a fist, punches a hole in the wall, throws things at you, blocks your way, restrains you, grabs, pushes, or pokes at you, or threatens to hurt you, that's physical abuse. He is creating fear and using your need for physical freedom and safety as a way to control you.

The scars from mental cruelty can be as deep and long-lasting as wounds from punches or laps but are often not as obvious. In fact, even among women who have experienced violence from a partner, half or more report that the man's emotional abuse is what is causing them the greatest harm.

....Possessiveness is at the core of the abuser's mindset, the spring from which all the other streams spout; on some level, he feels that he owns you and, therefore, has the right to treat you as he sees fit.

Few people are aware of the severe human rights violations committed daily by family court judges across the country. These courts are siding over and over again with proven sexual abusers of children and batterers of women. I wouldn't believe it myself if I hadn't done so much investigating. [Nor would I].

Abuse grows from attitudes and values, not feelings. The roots are ownership, the trunk is entitlement, and the branches are control.

Domestic Violence, Parental Substance Misuse and the Decision to Substantiate Child Maltreatment (Bryan G. Victor, Andrew Grogan-Kaylor, Joseph P. Ryan, Brian E. Perron, Terri Ticknor Gilbert, May 2018):

Families that experience domestic violence and parental substance misuse are disproportionately involved with the child welfare system. Prior research suggests that Child Protective Services (CPS) caseworkers are more likely to substantiate maltreatment allegations when domestic violence and parental substance misuse are identified during the investigation, pointing to one possible mechanism for this disproportionate involvement.... The identification of domestic violence and parental substance misuse during an investigation significantly increased the probability that an allegation would be substantiated. The implication of these findings for child welfare practice is considered in light of the fact that many child welfare agencies do not consider exposure to domestic violence and parental substance misuse in and of themselves to constitute child maltreatment.

Impact of Domestic Violence (Child Welfare Information Gateway, childwelfare.gov):

Domestic violence has a demonstrable, long-term impact on adult victims as well as children who witness violence. Children and youth who are exposed to domestic violence experience emotional, mental, and social damage that can affect their developmental growth. It also has adverse effects on the community at large. To respond to the overwhelming issues associated with domestic violence, child welfare professionals must understand these issues and know how to identify them, as well as assess and respond to those affected by domestic violence.

Domestic Violence and Co-Occurring Issues (Child Welfare Information Gateway, childwelfare.gov):

Research has shown that when domestic violence is present, there is a probability that issues such as poor health, mental health disorders, substance abuse, homelessness, and financial instability are present as well. Service providers should be aware of and know how to address the needs of children, youth, and families who experience multiple issues.

Domestic Violence: A Primer For Child Welfare Professionals (Child Welfare Information Gateway, Children's Bureau, December 2020):

Domestic violence is a devastating social problem that affects every segment of the population, regardless of age, gender, sexuality, or ethnicity. Many families experiencing domestic violence also come to the attention of the child welfare system. Because the overlap in caseloads between domestic violence services (DVS) advocates and child welfare workers is significant, it is important that service providers be viewed as part of one overarching system that works to protect family well-being rather than as belonging to two separate systems dedicated to protecting adults and the other to protecting children.

Domestic violence is defined as a pattern of coercively controlling behaviors used by a person to gain or maintain power and domination over their intimate partner. Some use "intimate partner violence" or simply "partner violence."

Impact of Domestic Violence on Children:

Children and youth who have been exposed to domestic violence are more likely than their peers to experience a range of difficulties. These challenges can include behavioral and emotional struggles that impact their social relationships with children and adults, cognitive problems that interfere with skill development and school performance, and long-term physical and mental health problems. (For more information on the potential negative effects of domestic violence on children, visit the National Child Traumatic Stress Network website.)

Responding to Domestic Violence:

The extensive overlap between domestic violence and child maltreatment requires a specialized and coordinated response in child welfare casework.

Special considerations should be made when gathering information from families experiencing domestic violence, including the importance of making initial contact with the adult who has experienced violence when the offending parent is not present, the necessity of interviewing family members separately and privately, and the caseworker's own safety when interviewing the offending parent.

Following initial assessments, caseworkers should work directly with the nonoffending parent and children when appropriate to put together a safety plan that includes strategies aimed at holding the offending parent accountable for his or her actions.

A child welfare system utilizing a trauma-informed approach routinely screens children and caregivers for trauma, uses evidence-based programs to treat symptoms associated with traumatic stress, and works to increase resilience and strengthen the protective factors of children and caregivers to support the overall family unit.

Institutional and societal changes can begin to eliminate domestic violence only when service providers integrate their expertise, resources, and services into an expansive network.

Overview of Protective Factors for Adult and Child Survivors of Domestic Violence, Practice Tips and Protective Factors, (QIC Domestic Violence in Child Welfare, October 2020):

"When a flower doesn't bloom, you fix the environment in which it grows, not the flower."

-Alexander Den Heijer

As a result of domestic violence (DV), adult and child survivors may become cut off from family and friends, begin to doubt their ability to take care of themselves or their children, and lose hope for a better future. These harmful impacts of domestic violence are exacerbated when survivors are also experiencing poverty, systemic racism, discrimination, food or housing insecurity, and other stressors.

Five Key Protective Factors for Survivors of Domestic Violence:

1. Safer and more stable conditions
2. Social, cultural, and spiritual connections
3. Resilience and a growth mindset
4. Nurturing parent-child interactions
5. Social and emotional abilities

Child Welfare and Domestic Violence The Impact on Children and Families (QIC, Domestic Violence in Child Welfare, September 2018)

Domestic violence remains a serious and potentially deadly problem in the United States, affecting 1 in 3 women and more than 15 million children. (37.3% of women, or approximately 44.9 million women). Approximately 1 in 7 men have experienced severe physical violence from an intimate partner during their lifetime (although men report significantly less).

Lesbian, gay, bisexual, and transgender people experience domestic violence. Data are not always directly comparable; however, bisexual women and men appear to experience domestic violence at slightly higher rates than heterosexual men and women.

1 in 5 children is exposed to family violence in their lifetime, including witnessing violence against a parent or sibling. By age 17, approximately 1/3 of youth have witnessed family violence.

Roughly 7 of every 10 children who witnessed violence saw violence perpetrated by males.

More than 1 in 12 (8.4%) children were exposed to some form of family violence in the past year.

Domestic violence is a significant risk factor for children to experience verbal abuse, physical punishment, physical abuse, [and sexual abuse].

In a national study, more than half (56.8%) of youth who witnessed intimate partner violence had also experienced maltreatment in their lifetime.

A significant percentage of child welfare cases are affected by domestic violence; however, access to services is limited.

Approximately 30 to 60% of men who abuse their partners also abuse their children.

National data on the reporting, response, and treatment of domestic violence is limited.

Data suggest that only about 25% of domestic violence incidents are reported to police. And a national study that surveyed obstacles to seeking help for domestic violence, nearly one in three caregivers reported a fear of police and counselors.

Female victimizations were four times as likely as male victimizations to go unreported due to fear of reprisal from a partner.

A nationally representative study found that children's trauma symptoms were the lowest when perpetrators left the house and highest when the child was forced to move out of the home.

What Are The Power And Control Wheels? (Amanda Kippert, August 16, 2021):

Many survivors of domestic abuse and violence will say that the first time they saw the power and control wheel, what they were going through suddenly made sense. This visual aid, used by advocates, psychologists, educators, health care workers and similar, outlines the common tactics used by abusers.

The Power and Control Wheel was created by the Domestic Abuse Intervention Project (DAIP) in 1984 to both help victims of domestic violence and to educate abusive men. Through focus groups with survivors, they developed a wheel outlining the most common tactics of abusive partners. In contrast with the cycle of violence, the wheel doesn't imply these experiences happen in a certain order but rather, in combination, denote a pattern of power and control, the two facets that hold the wheel together at its center.

Some of the tactics include:

Economic abuse, to deny the survivor access to money

Coercion and threats, like convincing the survivor to do something illegal

Intimidation, to keep the survivor fearful

Emotional abuse, such as degrading the survivor

Isolation is controlling when the survivor can leave the home

Minimizing, denying and blaming, such as gaslighting

Using the children, including threatening to file for custody if the survivor leaves

Male privilege, to define men's and women's roles

"Making the Power and Control Wheel gender-neutral would hide the power imbalances in relationships between men and women that reflect power imbalances in society. By naming the power differences, we can more clearly provide advocacy and support for victims, accountability and opportunities for change for offenders, and system and societal changes that end violence against women."

The Cycle of Abuse

The four-stage cycle starts with a tension-building phase where the "victim becomes fearful and feels the need to placate the abuser." In stage 2, there is an incident, which can include physical, emotional or verbal abuse. There may be anger, blaming, threats and intimidation. After that, Walker theorized that there was often a reconciliation stage where the abuser would try to give excuses for their abusive choices or blame the victim, sometimes downplaying or outright denying the abuse occurred (otherwise known as gaslighting). The final stage is a period of calm where things seemingly go back to "normal." Sometimes, this is referred to as the "honeymoon stage."

But this doesn't last forever, and soon, the cycle starts over again, with tensions building up before another incident.

Some advocate that Walker's diagram oversimplifies abuse.

NCADV, National Coalition Against Domestic Violence (ncadv.org):

Domestic violence is the willful intimidation, physical assault, battery, sexual assault, and/or other abusive behavior as part of a systemic pattern of power and control perpetrated by one intimate partner against another. It includes physical violence, sexual violence, threats, and emotional abuse. The frequency and severity of domestic violence can vary dramatically.

Stop Domestic Violence (Quick Facts About Domestic Violence in the United States, Blog, Planstreet, June 20, 2022):

Children who witnessed domestic violence are at a much greater risk of continuing this cycle of abuse in their lives. It is estimated that a young boy who sees his mother abused is 10 times more likely to abuse his intimate partner.

Young children who witness domestic violence often take the blame for it, which in turn can affect their self-esteem, mental health, and performance at school. They may even experience physical effects associated with anxiety, such as upset stomachs and headaches.

In the long term, children who witnessed domestic violence at a young age are at a much higher risk for health problems when they become adults, including mental health issues, heart disease, diabetes, and obesity.

Domestic violence is pervasive in American Society. Far too many children and adults are victims of this behavior each and every day. The impacts this violence has on both the individual and society as a whole are far-reaching and long-lasting. The first step towards solutions is helping the population as a whole understand just how widespread the problem is. Hopefully, [you are seeing] just how many Americans are victimized by the destructive, selfish, and violent behavior in the home each and every day.

Behind the Façade: The Socially Charming Domestic Abuser, How an Abuse Victim's Attempted Cover-up Might Reveal the Crime (Wendy L. Patrick, J.D., Ph.D. verified by Psychology Today, posted April 12, 2018):

Having spent over 2 decades prosecuting cases of domestic abuse, I've seen that perpetrators can fly under the radar for years because they are able to disarm by charm-clothing themselves with (misplaced) trustworthiness and credibility.

Many domestic violence victims try to conceal their abuse literally and figuratively. Nonetheless, evidence of a turbulent home life often manifests itself through a victim's emotional displays in the workplace, as well as physical signs of abuse, often (unsuccessfully) characterized as frequent "accidents."

Not all abusers leave marks. Some perpetrators can find their abuse to be forms of physical aggression such as pushing and shoving, and sometimes strangulation (potentially fatal), which leaves no marks. Others are even more subtle, controlling their victims through tactics such as domination, intimidation, and humiliation.

Whether physical or emotional, some abusers who mistreat their partners [or children] confine their abuse within their own home, ensuring there is no "evidence" for concerned family, friends or co-workers to observe.

… A Working knowledge of domestic violence risk factors is important to facilitate early detection. In addition, a working knowledge of the resources available to report suspected abuse and to assist victims will better equip family, friends, and coworkers to facilitate an intervention should the opportunity arise.

12 Traits of an Abuser (Laura Petherbridge, CBN.com, Christian Broadcasting Network, 2019):

Often, people–especially churchgoers–assume domestic violence does not happen within committed Christian relationships. But nothing could be further from the truth. After 20 years of observing destructive relationships, I have discovered 12 traits that are most often exhibited by abusers.

[These are:]

Charming

Jealous

Manipulative

Controlling

A victim

Narcissistic

Inconsistent

Critical

Disconnected

Hypersensitive

Vicious and cruel

Insincerely repentant

Why Does He Do That? Inside the Minds of Angry and Controlling Men (Lundy Bancroft, Penguin Random House, LLC., 2002):

Why does abusiveness so often extend to parenting issues?

What are abusive men like as fathers?

At the core of the abusive mindset is the man's view of his partner as a personal possession. And if he sees her as his fiefdom, how likely is he to also see the children as being subject to his ultimate reign? Quite. If he is the children's legal father, he sees them as extensions of himself; otherwise, he tends to see them as extensions of her. Either way, his mentality of ownership is likely to shape his parental actions.

It is next to impossible for the abuser to keep his treatment of the mother a complete secret from their children the way he does with other people because they are almost always around. So he chooses instead to hook them into patterns and dynamics of the abuse, manipulating their perceptions and trying to win their loyalty.

Children are a tempting weapon for an abuser to use against the mother. Nothing inflicts more pain on the caring parent, male or female, than hurting one of his or her children and causing damage to the parent-child relationship. Many abusers sense that they can gain more power by using the children against their partners than by any method other than the most overtly terrorizing assaults or threats. To their destructive mindset, the children are just too tempting a tool of abuse to pass up.

The Abusive Mind-Set: Parenting Implications:

Control

Abusers tend to be authoritarian parents. They may not be involved that much of the time, but when they do step in, it's their way or the highway. The abuser's coerciveness Thus comes into his treatment of the children and his behavior regarding the children, including his bullying of decisions in which the mother should have an equal voice.

Entitlement

Children of abusers often find their father's attention and approval hard to come by. The scarcity has the effect of increasing his value in their eyes, but any attention from him feels special and exciting. Ironically, their mother can come to seem less important to them because they know they can count on her.

Externalization of Responsibility

Children who are exposed to the abuse of their mothers often have trouble paying attention in school, get along poorly with their peers, or act out aggressively. In fact, they have been found to exhibit virtually every symptom that appears in children who are being abused directly. The abuser attributes all of these effects to the mother's poor parenting or to inherent weaknesses in the children.

Manipulativeness

In certain ways, children actually have an easier time living with an abusive parent who is mean all the time. At least then, they know what they're dealing with and who is at fault. But the typical abuser is constantly changing faces, leaving his children confused and ambivalent and increasing the likelihood that they will identify with him in hopes of staying on his good side.

Superiority, disrespect

Children growing up in this atmosphere can gradually come to look down on their mother as a parent, having absorbed the abuser's messages that she is immature, irrational, illogical, and incompetent.

Possessiveness

Not all abusers perceive their children as owned objects, but many do. A man who already considers his partner a possession can find it easy to see his children the same way. But children are not things, and parents who see their children in an objectified way are likely to cause psychological harm because they don't perceive children as having rights.

Public image

It is confusing for children to see people responding to their abusive father as if he were a charming and entertaining person. They're left to assume that his behavior at home is normal, which in turn means that they and their mother must be at fault.

The Abusive Man as Child Abuser

Multiple studies have demonstrated that none who abuse their partners are far more likely than other men to abuse their children. The extent of the risk to children from a particular abuser largely depends on the nature of his pattern of mistreatment toward their mother, although other factors, such as his own childhood, also can play an important role. The increased risks include the following:

Physical Abuse

Sexual Abuse

Psychological Abuse

When Dad Hurts Mom Helping Your Children Heal the Wounds of Witnessing Abuse (Lundy Bancroft, Berkley Books, 2004):

There is no concern as great for an abused mother as her worries about whether her partner will harm her children as he has her. There is a substantial overlap between the particular style of abusiveness a man uses toward his partner and the forms in which he mistreats children; both research studies and my clinical experience indicate that around 40% of abusive men carry their behavior pattern over onto other family members. So, if your partner screams and swears at you, be alert to whether he is verbally abusive to your children as well. If he finds fault with every aspect of your character and barrages you with impossible demands, notice whether he is tearing the children down and making them feel that nothing they do is ever good enough. And if he threatens you, hits you, or shoves you around, check with them periodically to make sure he isn't physically abusing them as well.

[The following are some warning signs]:

Physical Abuse

If he is highly controlling or domineering toward you, and especially if he uses violence, threats, or other physically scary behavior.

If he abuses drugs or alcohol.

If he has rigid attitudes about how children should behave and how strictly or harshly they should be punished.

If he was abused himself growing up.

If he threatens to hurt the children (Which is abuse in itself).

Psychological Abuse

Put-downs.

Name-calling.

Ignoring.

Making and breaking promises.

Sexual Abuse

Men who abuse women have considerably higher rates than other men of violating children's boundaries.

Behavioral Symptoms of Exposure to an Abusive Man:

Bullying, insulting, and physical aggressiveness toward peers.

Withdrawal from social contact, poor peer relationships.

Fear or upset about separation, especially from mom.

Oppositional and defiant behaviors with authority figures, especially mom.

Developmental regression (e.g., bed-wetting or daytime "accidents").

Hyperactivity, anxiety, obsessiveness, or compulsiveness.

Learning and attention problems at school.

Eating problems (e.g., overeating or refusing to eat).

Failure to thrive in infants. [and generally]

Sleeping problems (nightmares, awakening easily, trouble falling asleep).

Violence towards siblings, especially male to female and older child toward younger child.

Running away from home

Primarily in Pre-teens and Teenagers:

Substance abuse.

Poor peer choices.

Violence or verbal abuse toward dating partners and/or perpetrating sexual assault.

Violence or verbal abuse from dating partners and/or sexual victimization.

Violence toward mom.

Physically or verbally intervening to protect mom.

Imitating the abuser's behaviors toward mom.

Emotional Symptoms of Exposure to an Abusive Man

Fear, anxiety, nervousness

Depression, sadness, suicidal desires.

Insecurity.

Guilt, self-blame, shame.

Anger, resentment, bitterness.

Embarrassment or shame toward peers (e.g., reluctance to have friends over to the house).

Feeling responsible to protect mom.

Feeling responsible to protect siblings, especially younger ones.

Worrying about the safety of relatives and friends (generalized anxiety).

Blame and resentment towards siblings.

Blame and resentment toward Mom.

Fantasies of standing up to, assaulting, or killing the abuser.

Desire to have the kind of power the abuser has ("identifying with the aggressor").

Fear of ordinary arguments because of the feeling that they may turn frightening.

Uncertainty about what is real.

Children need their sense of reality validated.

Their father has denied events that they saw or heard.

After severe incidents, your partner and/or you have acted as if nothing happened and have made no further mention of what transpired.

The children have been criticized or ridiculed by the abusive man, by their siblings, or by you for feeling frightened, angry, confused after incidents, or for being afraid of their father.

Police have come to the house and left without taking action or made choices that confuse the children, such as arresting you instead of the abuser.

The Real Perpetrators of Alienation: Abusive Men

Among the most cruel attacks that an abusive man can carry out is a campaign to alienate children from their mothers. The children who are turned against their mothers sometimes appear on the surface to feel triumphant because they got in good with what is known as "identifying with the aggressor"-and escaped their mom's limits and discipline.

But beneath this thin facade are boys and girls who feel frightened, confused, lonely, and self-hating. The loss of their mother means the loss of their one hope for a non-abusive role model and for a source of love and affection that doesn't come with a set of exploitative strings attached. With proper support and intervention, if professionals or the legal system get involved and offer assistance who have been alienated from their mothers by an abuser can find their way back to her.

Childhood Trauma, Abuse, Neglect, and ACE's:

Is it considered child sexual abuse if someone shows a child pornographic pictures but doesn't actually touch the child? (Stop It Now! Last edited August 13th, 2018):

Showing pornographic pictures to a child is considered sexual abuse. Child sexual abuse can include non-touching behaviors.

Purposely exposing a child to adult sexuality is considered a form of child sexual abuse, whether or not a child is touched. Non-touching behaviors can be just as upsetting and emotionally harmful to a child as some touching behaviors. Non-touching behaviors that are considered to be child sexual abuse include:

Showing pornography to a child

Exposing a person's genitals to a child or asking children to expose themselves.

Asking a child to interact sexually with someone else.

Online enticement of a minor for sexual purposes.

Photographing a child in sexual poses.

Exposing a child to sexual acts (including masturbation) either in person or through digital, computer or video images.

Watching a child undress or use the bathroom, often without the child's knowledge (known as voyeurism).

Please note that although there may not be harmful intent, even having adult pornography or sexual toys in the home where a child could come across them has been viewed by authorities as sexual abuse in some circumstances.

Top Michigan Child Abuse Statistics 2023 (January 22, 2024):

The number of children in examined homes has increased by 71.8% since 2010, while the number of verified child abuse and neglect victims has increased by 33.7%.

As a result of the governor's stay-at-home order, calls to the state's child abuse hotline decreased by 50% in a matter of days.

In Michigan, there were more than 147,000 complaints of alleged child maltreatment or neglect in 2020, a 15% decrease from 2019. [Covid impacted everything; child abuse reports were certainly among those that were impacted].

5,362 children were taken from their homes and placed in foster care in 2019, according to MDHHS. [This number does not include those children taken from a primary caregiver or transferred to the care of a relative. This is only the confirmed number of those children who entered the foster care system. Countless more were removed from loving homes].

In 2010, Michigan had the 9th highest rate of child abuse and neglect.

According to the MLPP, over 5,000 newborns were verified victims of abuse and neglect in 2011, with 0-1 year of age being the most dangerous year for kids in Michigan.

What Does Emotional Abuse Look Like? (online):

Rejecting

Parents are caregivers who display rejecting behavior toward a child and will often (purposefully or unconsciously) let a child know, in a variety of ways, that he or she is unwanted. Putting down a child's worth or belittling their needs are some ways this type of emotional abuse may manifest. Other examples can include telling a child to leave, or worse, to get out of your face, calling him names or telling the child that he is worthless, making a child the family scapegoat or blaming him for family/sibling problems. Refusing to talk to or hold a young child as he grows can also be considered abusive behavior.

Harsh criticism, belittling, labeling

Name-calling

Yelling, screaming or swearing at children

Humiliation or demeaning jokes

Teasing about a child's mental capabilities or physical appearance

Refusing love, attention and touch

Physical or emotional abandonment

Shunning the child from the family altogether

Kicking teams out of the home

Locking kids out of the home to discipline or punish

Ignoring

[Parent/s] may show no interest in the child, withhold affection or even fail to recognize the child's presence. Many times, the parent is physically there but emotionally unavailable. Failing to respond to or consistently interact with your child constitutes emotional and psychological abuse.

Inconsistent or no response to a child's invitations to connect

Failure to attend to an infant's physical, social or emotional needs

Refusing to acknowledge a child's interests, activities, schooling, peers, etc.

Abandonment or refusing to acknowledge a child as your own

Denying medical or health care and safe, clean environments

Inability or failure to engage a child emotionally or protect a child from harm

Terrorizing

Parents who use threats, yelling and cursing are doing serious psychological damage to their children. Singling out one child to criticize and punish A and ridiculing her for displaying normal emotions as abusive, threatening a child with harsh words, physical harm, abandonment, or, in extreme cases, death is unacceptable.

Because of teasing, screaming, cursing, raging at a child

Threatening or intimidating behaviors – scaring a child or others in front of a child

Unpredictable, unreasonable or extreme reactions

Verbal threats to harm the child, self or others

Hostility among family members

Inconsistent or unreasonable demands placed on a child

Ridiculing or humiliating a child in front of others [or at all]

Threatening to reveal personal or embarrassing information

Isolating

A parent who abuses a child through isolation may not allow the child to engage in appropriate activities with his or her peers, may keep a baby in his or her room, unexposed to stimulation or may prevent teenagers from participating in extracurricular activities. Requiring a child to stay in his or her room from the time school is out until the next morning,… Or forcing a child to isolation or seclusion by keeping her away from family and friends can be destructive and considered emotional abuse depending on the circumstances and severity.

Leaving a child alone or unattended for long periods of time

Not permitting each child to interact with other children or maintain friendships

Keeping a child from appropriate social any emotional stimulation new line Requiring a child to stay indoors/in their room or away from peers new line Keeping a child from playing with friends and activities, s/he enjoys

Not permitting a child to participate in school activities, parties or group/family events

Harsh and extreme punishment for typical childhood behaviors

Encouraging a child to reject friends or social contact/invitations

Corrupting

Parents who are corrupt may permit children to use drugs or alcohol, engage in cruel behavior toward animals, watch or look at inappropriate sexual contact or witness or participate in criminal activities such as stealing, assault, prostitution, gambling, etc.

Encouraging or rewarding unethical or illegal behavior (drugs, stealing, cheating, lying, bullying)

Promoting or rewarding promiscuity

Giving a child or using the presence a child drugs, alcohol and other illegal substances

Allowing or encouraging children to engage in behavior that is harmful to the self or others.

Exploiting

Exploitation can be considered manipulation or forced activity without regard for a child's need for development. Giving a child responsibilities that are greater than a child of that age can handle or using a child for profit is abusive.

Having expectations beyond the developmental stage of the child

Forcing a child to participate in unwanted activities without just cause Requiring a child to care for a parent or siblings without regard for the child's age or ability

Using blame, shame, judgment or guilt to condemn a child for the behavior of others (parents/peers/siblings)

Unreasonable expectations to perform chores or household duties

Exposing a child to sexually abusive or inappropriate content

Potential Indicators of Child Abuse and/or Neglect (MDHHS) [So, this is directly from the State of Michigan's own Department of Health and Human Services]:

Physical Neglect – Physical Indicators

Unattended medical needs. Lack of supervision.

Regular signs of hunger, inappropriate dress, and poor hygiene.

Distended stomach, emaciated.

Significant weight change.

Physical Neglect-Behavioral Indicators

Regularly displays fatigue or listlessness and falls asleep in class.

Steals/hoards food and begs from classmates.

Reports that no caretaker is at home.

Physical Abuse-Physical Indicators

Unexplained bruises (in various stages of healing), welts, loop marks.

Adult/human bite marks.

Bald spots or missing clumps of hair

Unexplained burns/scalds.

Unexplained fractures, skin lacerations/punctures or abrasions.

Swollen lips/chipped teeth.

Linear/parallel marks on cheeks and temple area

Crescent-shaped bruising.

Puncture wounds.

Bruising behind the ears.

Physical abuse behavioral indicators

Self-destructive/self-mutilation.

Withdrawn and/or aggressive behavior extremes.

Uncomfortable/skittish with physical contact.

Arrives at school late or stays late as if afraid to be at home.

Chronic runaway (adolescents).

Complaints of soreness or moves uncomfortably.

Whereas clothing is inappropriate to weather to cover the body.

Lack of impulse control (e.g., Inappropriate outbursts).

Sexual Abuse-Physical Indicators

Pain or itching in the genital area.

Bruises or bleeding in the genital area.

Sexually transmitted disease.

Frequent urinary or yeast infections.

Extreme or sudden weight change.

Pregnancy under 12 years of age.

Sexual Abuse-Behavioral Indicators

Withdrawal, chronic depression.

Sexual behaviors or references that are unusual for the child's age.

Seductive or promiscuous behavior.

Poor self-esteem, self-devaluation, lack of confidence.

Suicide attempts (especially adolescents).

Hysteria, lack of emotional control.

[I have some observations to make on the above (it's the only reason I included it!). First, there are several abuse types omitted from this 'list,' and the two they have on their list are lacking in many ways. There are many more indicators and behaviors in which one could witness and then extrapolate that abuse might be a possibility in the home for a child. Also, the ones they have here are very specific –too specific, "crescent moon" shaped bruising, linear marks, bruises behind the ear, distended stomach…and so on. How many teachers see the stomachs of children? How many school staff are going to look behind a student's ears? And if there is a bruise, but it's not "crescent" shaped, does it still matter? I want to give MDHHS the benefit of the doubt and think, well they were just trying to give clear examples to people to work, they were *trying*. But we live in a world where the use of, even the mere existence of, common sense seems to be, in fact, a rare gem, especially in governmental agencies and institutions. If they wanted to help people to be able to spot signs of the many different abuse types, they could have done that, and they should have done that. Also, I noticed in the list of neglect behavioral indicators that there is listed self-harm. I found that interesting since years ago, a social worker (that I liked) from the incompetent schools my sons attended (in this particular case, it was the elementary school, which, like the rest in that school system - failed them miserably) called the reporting hotline to report something regarding my oldest son, who was in second grade at the time. Gabriel had been in to see her, and she noticed many cut marks on his arms and she inquired about them. He told her that X and his then-girlfriend had cut him, and those marks were placed there by them. She reported this to CPS. A caseworker called me to inform me there was an investigation. She, just like everybody else who worked on a case involving my children from Washtenaw County CPS, was just as harshly rude to me as she could have been. The boys were at X's house the entire time this all played out; I never saw the marks, I never spoke with the boys, nothing. The caseworker (the same caseworker who would later threaten me she was going to file a motion to terminate my parental rights, as well as the very same caseworker that placed me on Central Registry with absolutely no reason -other than her wanting to because she could), called me several days later and said the case is closed because it was unsubstantiated and she "knew" he was lying and that he didn't get those cuts from them. She laughed as she told me he did that to himself so he could say they did it to him. 1. Are you sure he did it to himself, or was this again more pressure from his father and that family for him to go back on his word as had happened with the sexual abuse allegations? 2. Are you not at all the least bit concerned that a 6-year-old is cutting his own body? If he *did* cut himself, I would think that, in and of itself, would be grounds to investigate. Clearly, there is something not going well in this young child's life for him to think of and follow through with cutting himself. 3. This very specific act is in their department's own list of indicators for neglect. Seriously. And that's funny? For fuck's sake, I was stunn *GTPAC* ed and had no words in which to speak. It's a very concerning action demanding a real reaction from CPS rather than laughter. However, that's how all our cases went with them.

In a similar situation, when Castiel was about the same age as Gabriel had been in the above circumstance, he had many cut marks on his forearm as well. I saw these. I also found the knife he cut himself with; I will never forget that knife. I see it in my head as if I just found it a few minutes ago. Castiel denied cutting himself, but

222

it was clearly obvious that the wounds had been self-inflicted. They were single lines, not at all completely parallel with each other. Some slanted one way, some slanted the other, and some were straight up and down. There were many. Somebody at the school saw these as well - it may have been the librarian. She took her observation to the X suck-up of a principal, and instead of calling CPS right then and there, the idiot principal called X first. (Some mandated reporter, right?) X was then alerted to it and could excuse it away however his pathologically lying mind would see fit, which is exactly what he did. Stupidly, he said and got Castiel to agree, as well as the school staff to agree to the ridiculousness that all those cuts got there from how Castiel was holding a book. Yes, a book. Those were paper cuts. Unbelievable, am I right? If X told that particular principal and many of the school system employees that up was down and down was up, they'd find a way to rationalize that, even in their teeny, tiny, minuscule brains. Our lives even kept getting better because that principal went up to the middle school the same year Castiel did. -I actually liked the former principal of the middle school; she knew something was off for Gabriel, and I was hopeful for her to eventually take action. But only the best staff members always left. They didn't grow up in the backward-looking, redneck town and didn't appear to be the gossipy, back-stabbing type that the others did. I don't blame them for leaving. It just meant everyone that was left was part of the problem rather than any part of a possible solution].

[The only other thing I'd like to say about the above 'list' is that they themselves do not follow it. My sons had all kinds, if not all, of the indicators on that list, but none of it mattered].

Child Abuse Statistics: Michigan and National (Children's Trust Fund 2018):

Michigan, 2018:

In 2018, twenty 7% of investigations resulted in evidence of abuse or neglect.

Of all disposed of investigations in 2018, a total of 25,654 complaints were confirmed, representing 37,738 identified victims.

38% of victims were under the age of 4.

In approximately 65% of all cases, the perpetrator is the parent (biological, adoptive, putative or step-parent).

Nationally, 2016:

During 2016, approximately 77.6% of victims were maltreated by a parent/s, and 22.3% were non-parents.

An estimated 1,700 in 2016 (1,589 children in 2015) died from abuse or neglect.

The Effects of Childhood Trauma (very well mind)

Childhood trauma... Doesn't have to occur directly to the child; for instance, watching a loved one suffer can be extremely traumatic as well. Exposure to violent media can also traumatize children.

Early intervention could prevent your child from experiencing the ongoing effects of the trauma as an adult.

There are many different experiences that can constitute trauma. Physical or sexual abuse, for example, can be clearly traumatic for children.

… Any event can be considered traumatic to a child if:

It happened unexpectedly

It happened repeatedly

Someone was intentionally cruel

The child was unprepared for it

Children with PTSD may re-experience the trauma in their minds over and over again. They may also avoid anything that reminds them of the trauma or they may re-enact their trauma in their play.

Sometimes children believe they missed warning signs predicting the traumatic event. And an effort to prevent future traumas, they become hyper-vigilant in looking for warning signs that something bad is going to happen again.

Children with PTSD may also have problems with:

Fear

depression

anxiety

Anger and aggression

Self-destructive behavior

Feelings of isolation

Poor self-esteem

Difficulty trusting others

Even children who don't develop PTSD may still exhibit emotional and behavioral issues following a traumatic experience. Here are some things to watch out for during the weeks and months after an upsetting event:

Increased thoughts about death or safety

Problems sleeping

Changes in appetite

Anger issues

Attention problems

School refusal

Somatic complaints like headaches and stomachaches

Loss of interest in normal activities

Irritability

Sadness

Development of new fears

A study published in 2015 showed that the more adverse childhood experiences (ACEs) a person has, the higher their risk of health and Wellness problems later in life. Childhood trauma may increase an individual's risk of:

Asthma

Depression

Coronary heart disease

Stroke

Diabetes

A study published in 2016 in Psychiatric Times noted that the prevalence of suicide attempts was significantly higher in adults who experienced trauma, such as physical abuse, sexual abuse, and parental domestic violence, as a child.

A child's relationship with his caregiver–whether his parents, grandparents or otherwise–is vital to his emotional and physical health. This relationship and attachment helps the little one learn to trust others, manage emotions and interact with the world around them.

When a child experiences a trauma that teaches him that he cannot trust or rely on that caregiver, however, he's likely to believe that the world around him is a scary place and all adults are dangerous—and that makes it incredibly difficult to form relationships throughout their childhood, including with peers their own age, and into the adult years.

Long-Term Consequences of Child Abuse and Neglect (Factsheet, April 2019, Child Welfare Information Gateway, Children's Bureau):

Aside from the immediate physical injuries children can experience through maltreatment, a child's reactions to abuse or neglect can have lifelong and even intergenerational impacts. Childhood maltreatment can be linked to later physical, psychological, and behavioral consequences as well as costs to society as a whole. These consequences may be independent of each other, but they also may be interrelated. For example, abuse or neglect may start the physical development of the child's brain and lead to psychological problems, such as low self-esteem, Which could later lead to high-risk behaviors, such as substance use. The outcomes for each child may vary widely and are affected by a combination of factors, including the child's age and developmental status when the maltreatment occurred, the type, frequency, duration, and severity of the maltreatment, and the relationship between the child and the perpetrator. Additionally, children who experience maltreatment often are affected by other adverse experiences (e.g., parental substance use, domestic violence, poverty), which can make it difficult to separate the unique effects of maltreatment (Rosen, Handley, Cicchetti, & Rogosch, 2018).

Physical Health Consequences

Some long-term physical effects of abuse or neglect may occur immediately (e.g., brain damage caused by head trauma), and others can take months or years to emerge or be detectable. There is a straightforward link between physical abuse and physical health, but it is also important to recognize that maltreatment of any type can cause long-term physical consequences.

Childhood maltreatment has been linked to a higher risk for a wide range of long-term and/or future health problems, including but not limited to the following (Widom, Czaja, Bentley, & Johnson, 2012; Monnat & Chandler, 2015; Afifi et al., 2016):

Diabetes

Lung disease

Malnutrition

Vision problems

Functional limitations (i.e., being limited in activities)

Heart attack

Arthritis

Back problems

High blood pressure

Brain damage

Migraine headaches

Chronic bronchitis/emphysema/chronic obstructive pulmonary disease

Cancer

Stroke

Bowel disease

Chronic fatigue syndrome

Child abuse and neglect also has been associated with certain regions of the brain failing to form, function, or grow properly. For example, a history of maltreatment may be correlated with reduced volume and overall brain size and may affect the size and/or functioning of the following brain regions (Bick & Nelson, 2016):

The amygdala, which is key to processing emotions

The hippocampus, which is central to learning and memory

the orbitofrontal cortex, which is responsible for reinforcement-based decision-making and emotion regulation

The cerebellum, which helps to coordinate motor behavior and executive functioning

The corpus callosum, which is responsible for left brain/right brain communication and other processes (e.g., arousal, emotion karma, higher cognitive abilities)

Child abuse and neglect can cause a variety of psychological problems. Maltreatment can cause victims to feel isolation, fear, and distrust, which can translate into lifelong psychological consequences that can manifest as educational difficulties, low self-esteem, depression, and trouble forming and maintaining relationships. Researchers have identified links between child abuse and neglect and the following psychological outcomes.

Diminished executive functioning and cognitive skills

Poor mental and emotional health

Attachment and social difficulties

Posttraumatic stress

Victims of child abuse and intellect often exhibit behavioral difficulties even after the maltreatment ends. The following are examples of how maltreatment can affect individuals' behaviors as adolescents and adults.

Unhealthy sexual practices

Juvenile delinquency leading to adult criminality

Alcohol and other drug use

Future perpetration of maltreatment

Strong, frequent, or prolonged activation of a person's stress response system, often referred to as toxic stress, can have long-lasting damaging effects on an individual's health, behavior, and ability to learn (National Scientific Council on the Developmental Child, 2014). Toxic stress can be caused by experiencing ACEs, Including child maltreatment. It can change an individual's brain architecture, which can cause the person's stress response system to be triggered more frequently and for longer periods of time and place him or her at an increased risk for a variety of physical and mental health problems, including cardiovascular disease, depression, ending anxiety (National Scientific Council on the Developing Child, 2014). Trauma-informed approaches, however, can help improve outcomes for individuals affected by toxic stress, and there is evidence that social and emotional support (e.g., consistent parenting practices and community supports) can alleviate its effects (U.S. Department of Health and Human Services (HHS), Administration for children and families (ACF), 2017).

Incest

Understanding and Treating Survivors of Incest (Counseling Today, a Publication of the American Counseling Association, David M. Lawson, March 6, 2018):

Child abuse of any kind by a parent is a particularly negative experience that often affects survivors to varying degrees throughout their lives. However, child sexual abuse committed by a parent or other relative, that is, incest, is associated with particularly severe psychological symptoms and physical injuries from many survivors. For example, survivors of father-daughter incest are more likely to report feeling depressed, damaged and psychologically injured than survivors of other types of child abuse. They are also more likely to report being estranged from one or both parents and having been shamed by others when they tried to share their experiences. Additional symptoms include low self-esteem, self-loathing, somatization, low self-efficacy, pervasive interpersonal difficulties and feelings of contamination, worthlessness, shame and helplessness.

Greater symptom severity for incest survivors is associated with:

Longer duration of abuse

Frequent abuse episodes

Penetration

The high degree of force, coercion and intimidation

Transgenerational incest

A male perpetrator

The closeness of the relationship

Passive or willing participation

Having an erotic response

Self-blame and shame

Observed or reported incest that continues

Parental blame and negative judgment

Failed institutional responses shaming, blaming, ineffectual effort

Early childhood onset

Incest that begins at a young age and continues for protracted periods-.... Often results in avoidance-based coping skills (for example, avoidance of relationships and various dissociative phenomena). These trauma-forged coping skills form the foundation for present and future interpersonal interactions and often become first-line responses to all or most levels of distress-producing circumstances.

More than any other type of child abuse, incest is associated with secrecy, betrayal, powerlessness, guilt, conflicted loyalty, fear of reprisal, and self-blame/shame. It is of little surprise, then, that only 30% of incest cases are reported by survivors.

Betrayal trauma theory is often associated with incest. Psychologist Jennifer Freyd introduced the concept to explain the effects of trauma perpetrated by someone on whom a child depends. Freyd holds that betrayal trauma theory posits that under certain conditions, betrayals necessitate a 'betrayal blindness' in which the betrayed person does not have conscious awareness or memory of the betrayal. Freyd wrote in her book Betrayal Trauma: The Logic of Forgetting Childhood Abuse.

Betrayal trauma theory is based on attachment theory and is consistent with the view that it is adaptive to block from awareness most or all information about abuse (particularly incest) committed by a caregiver. Otherwise, total awareness of the abuse would acknowledge betrayal information that could endanger the attachment relationship. This "betrayal blindness" can be viewed as an evolutionary and non-pathological adaptive reaction to a threat to the attachment relationship with the abuser that thus explains the underlying dissociative amnesia and survivors of incest. Under these circumstances, survivors often are unaware that they are being abused, or they will justify or even blame themselves for the abuse. In severe cases, victims often have little or no memory of the abuse or complete betrayal blindness. Under such conditions, dissociation is functional for the victim, at least for a time.

Approximately 95 to 97% of individuals with dissociative identity disorder report experiencing severe childhood sexual and physical abuse.

Incest, betrayal trauma and dissociative disorders are often features of a larger diagnostic categorization-complex trauma.

Incest survivors rarely experience a single incident of sexual abuse or only sexual abuse. It is more likely that they experience chronic, multiple types of abuse, including sexual, physical, emotional and psychological, within the caregiving system by adults who are expected to provide security and nurturance.

Among the criteria highlighted for complex trauma are:

Disturbances in emotions: affect dysregulation, heightened emotional reactivity, violent outbursts, impulsive and reckless behavior, and dissociation.

Disturbances in self: defeated/diminished self, marked by feeling diminished, defeated and worthless and having feelings of shame, guilt or despair (extends despair).

Disturbances in relationships: interpersonal problems marked by difficulties in feeling close to others and having little interest in relationships or social engagement more generally.

There may be occasional relationships, but the person has great difficulty maintaining them.

Early onset of incest, along with chronic exposure to complex trauma contexts, interrupts typical neurological development, often leading to a shift from learning brain (prefrontal cortex) to survival brain(brainstem) functioning. As explained by Christine Courtois and Julian Ford, survivors experience greater activation of the primitive brain, resulting in a survival mode rather than activation of brain structures that function to make complex adjustments to the current environment. As a result, survivors often exhibit an inclination toward threat avoidance rather than being curious and open to experiences. Complex trauma undermines survivors' ability to fully integrate sensory, emotional and cognitive data into an organized, coherent whole. This lack of a consistent and coherent sense of self and one's surroundings can create a near ever-present sense of confusion and disconnection from self and others.

Or intermittent complex trauma exposure creates an almost continual state of anxiety and hypervigilance and the intrinsic expectation of danger. Incest survivors are at an increased risk for multiple impairments, revictimization and loss of support.

The relational engagement component is particularly critical because, for many survivors, to be attached often has meant to be abused.

Trauma: Incest is a highly damaging form of abuse that most often results in PTSD. (Susanne Babbel MFT, PhD, Somatic Psychology, February 7, 2013, Verified by Psychology Today):

PTSD as a result of incest can result in a variety of coping mechanisms, including self-injury.

The first thing anyone can do to help a victim of incest is to believe them.

Incest is a type of sexual abuse that can (but does not always) include sexual intercourse, sexually inappropriate acts, are the abuse of power based on sexual activity between blood relatives. The important thing to remember is that incest is a form of sexual abuse. As a form of abuse, it is highly damaging to a child's psyche and most often results in prolonged post-traumatic stress disorder (PTSD).

Incest is a reprehensible form of abuse not just because it is cloaked in shame and stigma but because this type of sexual abuse, in particular, affects young victims by implicating and damaging their primary support system. This can be very confusing for children who have been taught to be wary of strangers but to trust family. Because they are in the beginning stages of developing their value systems and trust models, the betrayal of incest can be utterly confusing, if not permanently damaging, to a child's delicate psyche.

How Incest PTSD Manifests

PTSD as a result of incest can result in a variety of coping mechanisms, including:

Self-injury

Substance abuse

Eating disorders

Issues with disassociation

Promiscuity

A Mother's Nightmare -Incest: A Practical Legal Guide for Parents and Professionals, John E. B. Myers:

Most offenders plan their abuse by grooming their victims. Warner-Kearney (1987) found that 90% of incestuous fathers admitted that they deliberately tried to build trust with their intended victims. 73% of the offenders felt that trust was "important" in that it decreased the chance of exposure. To further reduce the risk of exposure, many offenders follow a slow progression in which most of the time is spent gaining the child's and family's trust.

Approximately 2% to 5% of men who sexually abuse children and adults are sadists who derive pleasure from inflicting pain. For sadists, the primary goal is causing suffering. Sexual gratification is secondary.

Sex offenders routinely blame sexual offenses on stress, impulse, happenstance, marital problems, alcohol, or even the victim.

Can a child who thinks Santa is real be trusted? When it comes to some of the finer points of differentiating fantasy from real life, young children are not as accomplished as older children and adults. In the main, however, young children can reliably distinguish fact from fiction. Moreover, the fact that a young child believes in Santa Claus does not mean that the child confuses fact with fantasy. After all, children believe in Santa Claus because their parents tell them he's real!

Many believe that children are highly suggestible, especially when questioned by adults. Psychological research discloses, however, that children are not as suggestible as many adults think. By the time children are 9 or 10, they appear to be no more suggestible than adults. Although children [can be] suggestible, adults are too, and children are not so suggestible that their descriptions of abuse should be disregarded. In case after case, children's descriptions of sexual abuse have an undeniable ring of veracity.

....There is the unfortunate fact that a woman's natural and appropriate emotions can be used against her.

Overvaluing the evidence of sexual abuse is a trap you simply must avoid. I've talked to many mothers who fell into this deadly snare and paid the ultimate price. They lost their child to the man they believe is a molester. It breaks my heart when this happens. Don't let it happen to you. How can you avoid it? ....Most important, put your case in the hands of attorneys and mental health professionals who are experts on child sexual abuse. They are the ones who know how to gather and evaluate the evidence to build a strong case.

[I am guilty of 'overvaluing' the evidence, there was so much in my sons' case. There was a plethora of credible and compelling notes, reports, and behavioral and emotional symptoms; I thought this evidence mattered. It was undeniable. Initially, I was naïve and believed in the justice system and thought my sons were safe. Wow, I've never been so wrong].

Conspiracy of Silence The Trauma of Incest, Sandra Butler:

The first public recognition of ....'s problem took place at her school. Logically, that was the point at which sensitive intervention might have been offered to her. Why wasn't it?

We assume we have provided for our schoolchildren's needs: we hire visiting nurses to make sure students are in good health, require immunizations to be certain children are protected from certain diseases and pay for hot lunch programs and staff of guidance counselors. Teachers hold periodic parent conferences, formulate careful lesson plans and maintain tidy records of students' attendance, citizenship and scholastic achievements.

Indeed, we like to think we are caring for the whole child. However, seldom do any of our educational efforts speak to the issue of sexually victimized children. There are special sex-education classes in schools to deal with the biological facts of reproduction but not the more complex nature of sexuality-nothing that speaks to the feelings or anxieties our children experience concerning their bodies and sexual responses. Educators are as uncomfortable with such matters as the rest of society, so the more emotionally awkward issues of sexual ethics and morality, rather than stern lectures about venereal disease as a consequence of sexual activity - seldom are openly discussed. As a result of the educational void, children are left to share a wealth of misinformation with each other or remain uninformed.

In school, to whom can children go for advice and support concerning sexual abuse, ignorance, or anxiety? Are children to be held accountable for keeping sexual secrets when the adults in our schools have made it clear that they do not want to hear about them?

[This brings very specific events to the forefront of my mind. The very first contact with Washtenaw County CPS in the State of Michigan; a very young caseworker came out to our home. I would eventually learn that most caseworkers I came in contact with over the many years clearly hated their jobs. I felt they just wanted to close out the case with the least amount of effort in the shortest amount of time. That being said, that particular case worker not only straight up lied in her report, but she used leading assumptions that made it appear I was planning something nefarious and that I was a bad mom. My sons were 3 and 1 at that time. The complaint was regarding my oldest son making the statement/question when I changed his diaper, "Finger up the butt?" "Thumb up the butt?" "Daddy do." And then he turned over and raised his bottom up in the air. The second thing was that he had gotten dolls in his Happy Meal that he was playing with later in the car. I could see what he was doing in my rearview mirror. He was placing the dolls in sexual positions (missionary, 'from behind,' held at the genital area, and dolls kissing each other); I remember one statement he made while he was doing that very clearly. He said "It's ok if you're family." Since this cold stranger did not get any kind of disclosure from my two-year-old son, her [wise] suggestion for me was to "wait until they were in school and he says something to a teacher, and then the teacher reports something. Really? I was astounded by that. Because, sure, that makes a lot of sense. Kindergarten is a mere three years away, and I'm certain on the first day, he will enter a new building full of entirely new people and a new classroom, ask to talk to his wonderful teacher right there on the spot and tell her exactly what has been happening to him and his brother for the past several years. Right.

The very next thing I think of is after the boys, and I had moved to Kentucky and my oldest son was enrolled in Headstart. The children were having lunch, and one child said something about his father, and then Gabriel said his dad made him eat poop and drink pee. The teacher scolded him and said they were not to talk about such things in school. She minimized him, threatened, and humiliated him. He was reaching out for help, and guess what? He was in school. Sadly, this incident foreshadowed all the following years of his school experience.]

Darkness to Light, Child Abuse Statistics:

- Over 90% of child sexual abuse victims know their abuser.

- A small number of juvenile offenders –one out of 8—are younger than age 12. Females constitute 7% of juveniles who commit sex offenses.

Treating the Effects of Childhood Trauma (Amy Morin, LCSW, very well mind, updated October 14, 2019):

Although adults often say things like, "he was so young when that happened. He won't even remember it as an adult," childhood trauma can have a lifelong effect. And while kids are resilient, they're not made of stone.

Children with PTSD may re-experience the trauma in their minds over and over again. They may also avoid anything that reminds them of their trauma, or they may reenact their trauma in their play.

Children with PTSD may also have problems with:

Fear

Depression

Anxiety

Anger and aggression

Self-destructive behavior

Feelings of isolation

Poor self-esteem

Difficulty trusting others

What is child abuse or neglect? What is the definition of child abuse and neglect? (HHS.gov, U.S. Department of Health and Human Services, Child Welfare Information Gateway, childwelfare.gov, 10/15/2019):

Every year, more than 3 million reports of child abuse are made in the United States. It's a terrible epidemic that we at Child Help are dedicated to putting an end to. To do this, we need to 1st increase awareness of the issue itself.

Child abuse is one a parent or caregiver, whether through action or failing to act, causes injury, death, emotional harm, or risk of serious harm to a child. There are many forms of child maltreatment, including neglect, physical abuse, sexual abuse, exploitation and emotional abuse.

Physical abuse of a child is when a parent or caregiver causes any non-accidental physical injury to a child. There are many signs of physical abuse.

28.3% of adults report being physically abused as a child.

Sexual abuse occurs when an adult uses a child for sexual purposes or involves a child in sexual acts. It also includes when a child is older or more powerful and uses another child for sexual gratification or excitement.

20.7% of adults report being sexually abused as a child.

When a parent or caregiver harms a child's mental and social development or causes severe emotional harm, it is considered emotional abuse. While a single incident may be abuse, most often, emotional abuse is a pattern of behavior that causes damage over time.

10.6% of adults report being emotionally abused as a child.

Child neglect is when a parent or caregiver does not give the care, supervision, affection and support needed for a child's health, safety and well-being.

MOSAIC (Mothers of Sexually Abused Children), Stop it Now - Stop Abuse Campaign:

…..[well over] 500,000 children are sexually abused each year….However, this does not include the majority of cases that are never reported to authorities...Assuming that only 30% of cases (Finkelhor) are reported to authorities, the real number could be... [at least] 650,000 cases.

- 93% of victims knew the offender.

- 30% of the victims were between ages 4-7.

- Four children die every day because of child abuse, and 75% of these are under 4 years old.

- A report of child abuse is made every 10 seconds.

- Abuse occurs at every economic, social, and cultural level.

- 80% of adults who have been abused as children develop psychiatric disorders such as depression, eating disorders, and PTSD.

- Children with a prior history of sexual abuse are extremely likely to be revictimized, with an estimate of increased risk of over 1000%

- Most mental health and child protection professionals agree that child sexual abuse is not uncommon and is a serious problem.

Jinich and Litrownik developed an acronym to help mothers support children when they disclose. This acronym, BRAVE, stands for:

- Believe the report of the child.

- Reach out and comfort the child, providing emotional support.

- Assure the child that it is not his/her responsibility to the offender.

- Validate the feelings of the child, assuring him/her that these are understandable emotions.

- Encourage the child to talk as much as possible about the abuse.

Updated Understanding Children's Sexual Behaviors, What's Natural and Healthy, Toni Cavanaugh Johnson PhD.:

The following characteristics can be used to assess whether a child is engaging in sexual behaviors that may require a professional evaluation. (These are summarized from the original text).

1. The children engaged in sexual behaviors do not have an ongoing mutual play relationship.

2. Sexual behaviors are engaged in by children of different ages or developmental levels.

3. Sexual behaviors are out of balance with other aspects of the child's life and interests.

4. Children who seem to have too much knowledge about sexuality and behave in ways more consistent with adult sexual expression.

5. Sexual behaviors are significantly different than those of other same-age children.

6. Sexual behaviors continue in spite of consistent and clear requests to stop.

7. Children appear unable to stop themselves from engaging in sexual activities.

8. Children's sexual behaviors elicit complaints from other children and/or adversely affect other children.

9. Children's sexual behaviors are directed at adults who feel uncomfortable receiving them.

10. Children (4 years and older) do not understand their rights or the rights of others in relation to sexual contact.

11. Sexual behaviors progress in frequency, intensity, or intrusiveness over time.

12. Fear, anxiety, deep shame, or intense guilt are associated with sexual behaviors.

13. Children engage in extensive, persistent, mutually agreed upon adult-type sexual behaviors with other children.

14. Children manually stimulate or have oral or genital contact with animal/s.

15. Children sexualize nonsexual things, interactions with others, or relationships.

16. Sexual behaviors cause physical or emotional pain or discomfort to self or others.

17. Children use sex to hurt others.

18. Verbal and/or physical expressions of anger precede, follow, or accompany the sexual behavior.

19. Children use distorted logic to justify their sexual actions. ("She didn't say no.")

20. Coercion, force, bribery, manipulation or threats are associated with sexual behaviors.

Abused Boys The Neglected Victims of Sexual Abuse, Mic Hunter, endorsed by Daniel Sexton, Childhelp, U.S.A.:

Thinking About the Factors as a Continuum

Using the factors I have discussed earlier as a guide for imagining a continuum, the sexual abuse pattern that would probably have the least negative impact on a victim's life would be this one: a single, nonviolent encounter at a later stage of childhood, with a complete stranger, combined with a family and a society that noticed that something undesirable had been done to the child, believed the victim, and provided him with support and guidance. At the other end of the continuum would be a pattern of ongoing, frequent, violent abuse that started at a young age and was perpetrated by numerous close family members, combined with a hostile attitude toward the child from society when he attempted to gain assistance.

The Sexual Abuse of Boys, Edison Court:

Sexual abuse flourishes in the darkness of secret-keeping. We believe that one of the best ways to create change is to make it safe to openly discuss sexual abuse…

Even though the public dialogue about sexual abuse seems to focus on girls who are perpetrated against by men, boys are all too frequently victims of sexual abuse…

..boys and men can be especially unlikely to disclose…Sadly, when boys don't disclose, many don't receive the help and support needed to heal.

…In particular, men often feel like their gender identity has been compromised by sexual abuse. One male survivor put it simply" "…..sexual abuse to a man is abuse against his manhood as well."

Many male survivors express that in the years following the abuse, they felt like they needed to conform to masculine norms that included appearing strong and independent. This gender conformity can become a barrier to accessing healing resources.

ACE's Resource Packet: Adverse Childhood Experiences (ACEs) Basics (CAHMI -The Child & Adolescent Health Measurement Initiative, Johns Hopkins Bloomberg School of Public Health, AcademyHealth):

The term adverse childhood experiences (ACEs) refers to a range of events that a child can experience that lead to stress and can result in trauma and chronic stress responses. Multiple, chronic or persistent stress can impact a child's developing brain and has been linked in numerous studies to a variety of high-risk behaviors, chronic diseases and negative health outcomes in adulthood, such as smoking, diabetes and heart disease. For example, having an ACE score of 4 increases a person's risk of emphysema or chronic bronchitis by 400% and suicide by 1200%.

ACEs have been measured in research, program and policy planning contexts. For example, the 2011/12 National Survey of Children's Health included 9 ACE items adopted from their original ACE study. Additionally, tools to assess ACEs in clinical settings are available in the original ACE study. Researchers measured 10 ACEs. Counting each ACE as one, individuals were reported as having an ACE score of 0 to 10. Measures included:

Physical, emotional and sexual abuse

Physical and emotional neglect

Households with mental illness, domestic violence, parental divorce or separation, substance abuse, or incarceration

You can calculate your own ACE score here: acestoohigh.com/got-your-ace-score/

The original ACEs study found a relationship between the number of ACEs and a number of high-risk behaviors and negative health outcomes across the lifespan. As the number of ACEs a person has increases, so does the risk for outcomes such as heart disease, depression, cancer, smoking and obesity.

Evidence from the field of neuroscience clearly demonstrates that ongoing exposure to traumatic events in childhood (also commonly referred to as ACEs) –such as physical or emotional abuse or neglect, witnessing or experiencing violence in the home or community, substance abuse or mental illness in the home, the absence of a parent due to divorce or incarceration, severe economic hardship, or discrimination–disrupts brain development, leads to functional differences in learning, behaviors and health and is associated with both immediate and long-term impacts on health.

...the first 3 years of life -which is a crucial period of child development.

Trauma-informed care encompasses 3 levels of focus from a systems level: addressing policy and procedures, creating approaches for organizing and delivering services and providing specific programs or interventions for families.

Trauma-informed trainings are designed to provide a set of critical skills and competencies for staff that also result in new skills for families. Trauma-informed staff training should build skills and competencies, including the following:

Understanding the neurobiology of trauma can assist with a subsequent shift away from "shame and blame" to a more compassionate understanding of what happened, or is happening, to them;

A focus on interpersonal interactions-the ability to create trust, respect and connection with others;

Creating safe, stable, nurturing physical and social environments that can support trauma healing;

Deep and compassionate listening to self and others;

Self-reflection to develop the ability to shift perception and attitudes, release fear and promote choice and empowerment;

Understanding the historical trauma associated with race, culture and gender and the need for ongoing self-reflection of cultural biases;

Self-management of difficult emotions and behaviors; and,

Activation of self-care.

Lifestyle changes can .. help you cope with and work through your trauma. Consider adding meditation, breathing exercises, and physical activity and exercise. Journaling is another wonderful tool that can help you unpack your feelings.

[For me, exercise, such as weight-lifting or resistance training, and just plain exercise has always helped me enormously. I listened to 'angry' music a lot when I was enjoying my rage-fueled workouts. Music -all types of genres served to medicate me as well. Whether I was working out or not, I never watched TV or movies because I couldn't, as that was something my sons and I used to do together, and I didn't want to watch anything without them. But I listened to a lot of music and worked out. I still need my daily dose of exercise!]

If you are recovering from a trauma like abuse, abandonment, growing up with mentally ill parents, or parents who abused alcohol or drugs, you may want to join a support group specific to that experience. Speaking with … others who experienced similar ACEs as you did can be invaluable to your recovery.

Childhood traumas can live in our psyches and our bodies for years…, and it's common to feel triggered easily at their mere mention.

Definitions of Child Abuse and Neglect (Child Welfare Information Gateway, Children's Bureau -an Office of the Administration for Children and Families, childwelfare.gov):

At the Federal level, the Child Abuse Prevention and Treatment Act (CAPTA) has defined child abuse and neglect as "any recent act or failure to act on the part of a parent or caregiver that results in death, serious physical or emotional harm, sexual abuse, or exploitation, or an act of failure to act that presents an imminent risk of serious harm.

What is Child Abuse and Neglect?

Recognizing the Signs and Symptoms (Child Welfare Information Gateway, Children's Bureau, April 2019):

The first step in helping children who have been abused or neglected is learning to recognize the signs of maltreatment.

The following signs are of general maltreatment and can help determine whether a child needs help:

Child

Shows sudden changes in behavior or school performance

Has not received help for physical or medical problems brought to the parent's attention

Has learning problems or difficulty concentrating that cannot be attributed to specific physical or psychological causes

Is always watchful, as though preparing for something bad to happen

Lacks adult supervision

Is overly compliant, passive, or withdrawn

Comes to school or other activities early, stays late, and does not want to go home

Is reluctant to be around a particular person

Discloses maltreatment

Parent

Denies the existence of–or blames the child for–the child's problems in school or at home

Asks teachers or other caregivers to use harsh physical discipline if the child misbehaves

Sees the child as entirely bad, worthless, or burdensome

Demands a level of physical or academic performance the child cannot achieve

Looks primarily to the child for care, attention, and satisfaction of the parent's emotional needs

Shows little concern for the child

Parent and child

Touch or look at each other rarely

Consider their relationship entirely negative

State consistently they do not like each other

Sexual Abuse Incest Victims and Their Families (Jean M. Goodwin, 2nd Edition, Year Book Medical Publishers, 1989):

Childhood sexual abuse is the category of abuse with the longest and most fascinating history of disbelief. Victim credibility has been the central issue in such cases since the Inquisition. As he began working with female patients who reported childhood seductions, Sigmund Freud came to realize that 16th-century inquisitors had been processing similar narratives. "Why are their confessions under torture so like the communications made by my patients in psychological treatment?" He wrote of the accused witches. The inquisitors interpreted the sexual accusations of those they interrogated as evidence that the devil had assumed the guise of a male relative in order to consummate intercourse with the woman who was, therefore, obviously a witch.

Breaking the Bonds of Child Abuse:

A Guide to Political Action (Jeffrey P. Bennett with Francine Philips, published by The Free Press, 1995):

Child abuse is not new. In fact, it's one of the oldest, most widely practiced immoral behaviors in the world. From the ancient time of child sacrifices, child slavery and child marriages (very often the same thing) to our 20th-century abuses of chimney sweeps, sweatshops and coal mining, the basic premise has never changed. Children are property. And not very valuable property at that.

Waiting for "them" to take care of child abuse and its after-effects is not working. Because in every county in every state in the United States, "they" are a mixed bag of social workers, police, judges, probation officers, adoption agencies and foster parents who are all too often working against each other and more often than not working against the best interests of the children.

Grooming:

What is familial Sexual Grooming? Understand how perpetrators manipulate families to gain access to children (Elizabeth L. Jeglic Ph.D., posted December 5, 2023, verified by Psychology Today):

Perpetrators of child sexual abuse may not only sexually groom the child but also their family.

Familial grooming involves the selection of a child due to family vulnerability and the development of trust.

Family grooming may be more common when the victim is a child as opposed to a teenager.

About 2/3 of all cases of child sexual abuse may involve familial sexual grooming.

Child sexual abuse (CSA) is a serious global problem. However, most CSA go undisclosed and undetected. One reason for this is that the perpetrator may use sexual grooming behaviors.

Grooming: Know the Warning Signs (RAINN Rape, Abuse, and Incest National Network, 800-656-4673 or HOPE July 10, 2020):

One tool common to those who sexually abuse kids is grooming: manipulative behaviors that the abuser uses to gain access to a potential victim, coerce them to agree to the abuse and reduce the risk of being caught. While these tactics are used most often against younger kids, teens and vulnerable adults are also at risk.

Grooming can take place online or in person. It's usually employed by a family member or someone else in the victim's circle of trust, such as a coach, teacher, youth group leader or others who naturally have some interaction with the victim.

Grooming behaviors are not only used to gain a victim's trust but often are used to create a trustworthy image and relationship with their family and community. Child and teen sexual abusers are often charming, kind, and helpful--exactly the type of behavior we value in friends and acquaintances.

Though grooming can take many different forms, it often follows a similar pattern.

Victim selection: abusers often observe possible victims and select them based on ease of access to them or their perceived vulnerability.

Gaining access and isolating the victim: abusers will attempt to physically or emotionally separate a victim from those protecting them and often seek out positions in which they have contact with minors.

Trust development and keeping secrets: abusers attempt to gain the trust of a potential victim through gifts, attention, sharing "secrets," and other means to make them feel that they have a caring relationship and to train them to keep their relationship secret.

Desensitization to touch and discussion of sexual topics: abusers will often start to touch a victim in ways that appear harmless, such as hugging, wrestling and tickling, and later escalate to increasingly more sexual contact, such as massages and showering together. Abusers may also show the victim pornography or discuss sexual topics with them to introduce the idea of sexual contact.

The attempt by abusers to make their behavior seem natural to avoid raising suspicions. For teens, who may be closer in age to the abuser, it can be particularly hard to recognize tactics used in grooming. Be alert for signs that your teen has a relationship with an adult that includes secrecy, undue influence or control, or pushes personal boundaries.

Also, know that there is no profile of who may be a sex offender. Thus, just because someone seems like a nice guy, is a pillar of the community, is a woman, or a minor does not mean that they cannot be engaging in CSA. Make sure to look at their behavior and your child's reactions to them independently of their characteristics and relationship with your family.

Coaching:

Coaching Children about Sexual Abuse: A Pilot Study of Professionals' Perceptions (Child Abuse & Neglect Volume 31, Issue 9, September 2007, Pages 947-959; Kathleen Coulborn Faller):

.....sexual abuse cases are particularly controversial because evidence is often limited to the child's account. A hypothesis that might explain away a child's account of abuse is that the child has been coached. This explanation has been strongly endorsed by those accused (e.g., Butler, Fukari, Dimitrius, & Krooth, 2001; Freyd, 1993; Goldstein, 1992; Wakefield & Underwager, 1988)... Despite declarations that coaching must be routinely considered when child abuse is alleged, there is scant research to support coaching as a viable explanation for children's accounts of abuse. Although relevant studies do not always directly address the coaching of children, they support the conclusion that coached statements and other types of false abuse allegations by children are uncommon.

There is other support for fathers being at greater risk of making false allegations than mothers. ...... fathers were 16 times more likely to make false reports done mothers (Bala & Schuman, 2000)..... Children are the least likely to affirm falsely a negative participatory event (falling off a tricycle and needing stitches) and most likely to affirm a neutral, non-participatory event (seeing someone standing at a bus stop) (Ceci, Huffman et al., 1994).

.... Children's failure to report actual touching of their bodies during [a] medical exam occurs at much higher frequencies than false reports of touching (Goodman et al., 1994; Goodman et al., 1997; Saywitz, Goodman, Nicholas, & Moan, 1991; Steward et al., 1996).

Research on adults regarding their sexual abuse during childhood indicates that failure to disclose sexual abuse occurs at very high rates, again suggesting false negatives are a greater problem than false positives.

Thus, on balance, research findings from studies of sexual abuse cases, from analog research, from high certainty sexual abuse cases, from adult survivors of sexual abuse, and from national child protection data said just that children falsely claiming abuse are being coached to state they have been abused, when they have not, should not be a primary preoccupation of child abuse professionals.

Despite their research that false allegations and indeed coached allegations of abuse occur at low rates, there are no studies of professionals' perceptions of coaching children.

Of the 192 respondents to the survey, 189 provided responses to the statement, "I have worked on a case where I thought a child was coached." Of these, 79.7% responded yes, 7.3% no, and 11.5 were unsure (three respondents, 1.5%, left this question blank).

The findings provide support for the view that most professionals who participated in this study believe that they have worked on child abuse cases in which the child was coached. [In direct conflict with research regarding the real number of possible coached cases -very rare.] Almost 80% of respondents indicated they had worked on such a case. For most, the number of coached cases was small, five or fewer, but more than a fourth of respondents who answered this question indicated they had worked on a score or more of cases involving a coached child, and four respondents reported 100 or more. [These numbers in this relatively small study of those who claim to be "professionals" make me physically ill. How many children were traumatized by disclosing and not being believed, and how many of these children were returned to their perpetrator, who now has the license to further abuse without the protection of a knowing caregiver?]

When child abuse professionals must address a child's allegation of abuse, they should appreciate that it is [incredibly] uncommon for the allegation to derive from coaching. Although this study indicates that most respondents believe they have worked on a small number of coached cases, the vast majority of respondents...think that mothers are the most likely to coach and that they do his coaching in the context of divorce/custody disputes [all are] beliefs that can be challenged empirically.

254

…McInnes (2003) argues the real danger of subscribing to the PAS [Parental Alienation Syndrome] rhetoric is the acceptance of the inaccurate assumption that the majority of CSA allegations made in family courts by children but reported by parents are false and result from parental prompting because children lack the capacity to recognize abuse and articulate their experiences. Because allegations of CSA can be difficult to corroborate due to a lack of traditional evidence, they may be deemed false (Faller, 2007). This serves to reinforce the idea that PAS is a common explanation for CSA allegations among those working for or on behalf of the courts, despite empirical research suggesting that, in fact, false allegations of CSA are exceptionally rare (Jenkins, 2003; McInnes, 2003). [Children lack the capacity to recognize abuse? Do they lack the capacity to articulate their experiences? Hogwash. They are not little robots that still need programming, although I'm sure there are some who believe that -I sure as hell do not. Even when they've grown up being abused, they know in their bodies and in the pits of their stomachs that there's something wrong with it. They may block themselves from expressing many emotions about it - that happens a lot. Children do not lack the capacity to 'recognize' abuse, nor to articulate it, in whatever way their stage of development will allow them to. I would know if somebody was sticking something up my butt. That's no different for a child. Furthermore, can we resort to common sense once again? Just for a second? I do not for a heartbeat believe that a young child could say things such as "Thumb up butt?" "finger up the butt?" "dada showed me icky stuff on his 'puter," "Daddy stuck a stick up my butt," "Dad peed in my mouth," "Dad peed on my back…..on my butt," "Dad stuck his penis in my butt"… (I tried to put these in age progression, there are many, many more examples) without them being true. Seriously, do you really think someone could "coach" a child to say such things, with details to go along with these statements, over and over, spontaneously? It's unfathomable to me for anyone to think that especially child 'protective' services.]

Child Witness Law and Practice, 1990 Cumulative Supplement (John E. B. Myers, Wiley Law Publications, 1990):

A child's reaction to being subject to sexual assault of any form may include responses most adults, unfamiliar with the subject, find peculiar. A child may, for example, fail to disclose the defendant's criminal sexual acts immediately and may also oscillate between admitting the abuse and denying it. Expert witness testimony merely aids the jurors and assessing a child's credibility under such abusive circumstances and in no way impinges upon the jury's obligation to decide ultimately the victim's credibility.

The "coached" or "programmed" child may be one who has no more than a few words to describe something of which he has no real knowledge. When a verbal child is encouraged to provide details, the details usually either validate the experience or evolve into imaginative descriptions that give away his lack of understanding of what is being said. The developmental inability of preschoolers to fabricate much factual content about sexual acts with adults should be kept in mind. Similarly, as anyone who has ever tried to coach or prepare a child to perform a nursery-school play has learned, preschoolers, unless they are professionally trained actors, have difficulty retaining consistent presentations of things that have little meaning to them in real life.

Young children who have been coached into providing false allegations of abuse often describe abuse in a unidimensional way that lacks convincing detail and depth. Young children often remember events in a random, scattered way.

The specialized skill and knowledge required for competent evaluation of suspected child sexual abuse is beyond the ken of most physicians and mental health professionals. It's clear that lay jurors are in no position to evaluate suspected abuse. Properly qualified experts can assist jurors in sifting through the mountain of complex and sometimes conflicting and counter-intuitive information presented in many child sexual abuse cases.

Coaching Children About Sexual Abuse: A Pilot Study of Professionals' Perceptions: (Kathleen Coulborn Faller):

……..studies generally conclude that children's failure to report actual touching of their bodies during the medical exam occurs at much higher frequencies than false reports of touching.

When child abuse professionals must address a child's allegation of abuse, they should appreciate that it is uncommon for the allegation to derive from coaching. … Although this study indicates that most respondents believe they have worked on a small number of coached cases, the vast majority of respondents nevertheless think that mothers are the most likely to coach and that they do this coaching in the context of divorce/custody disputes, beliefs that can be challenged empirically.

Despite declarations that coaching must be routinely considered when child abuse is alleged, there is scant research to support coaching as a viable explanation for children's accounts of abuse. Although relevant studies do not always directly address the coaching of children, they support the conclusion that coached statements and other types of false abuse allegations by children are uncommon.

Research on adults regarding their sexual abuse during childhood indicates that failure to disclose sexual abuse occurs at very high rates, again suggesting false negatives are a greater problem than false positives.

Oates et al. (2000) conducted a replication of the Jones and McGraw study, with minor methodological differences. They reviewed all sexual abuse cases … and found only 2.5% involved "erroneous accounts by children." They further examined these erroneous accounts and found 3 cases (.5%) that involved adult-child collaborative false cases, which **might** entail coaching. [Emphasis added].

The US Department of Health and Human Services collects data from all states regarding reports of child maltreatment made to Child Protective Service Agencies. 8 states (16%) recently added intentional false allegations to their categories of disposition. In 2004, a total of 917 intentional false allegations were designated out of approximately 3 million reports involving 5.5 million children, or 0%, according to the report (US DHHS, 2006). These statistics include all types of maltreatment and do not designate the source or dynamics of false reports.

Thus, on balance, research findings from studies of sexual abuse cases, from analog research, from high certainty sexual abuse cases, from adult survivors of sexual abuse, and from national child protection data suggest that children falsely claiming abuse or being coached to state they have been abused, when they have not, should not be a primary preoccupation of child abuse professionals.

…which suggests that false allegations of sexual abuse by children, caused by coaching or other dynamics, are uncommon (Jones & McGraw, 1987; Oates et al., 2000; Trocme & Bala, 2005). The perception that mothers are the parents who coach, however, is not supported by existing research (Bala & Schuman, 2000; Thoennes & Tjadan, 1990; Trocme & Bala, 2005).

McGraw & Smith (1992) demonstrated a predisposition by child protective service workers to consider custody cases false, even when there was evidence of abuse.

The perceptions that mothers are responsible for coaching, that custody cases are at greatest risk of false allegations, and that the false allegations derive from collusion between the mother and the child are central components of the Parental Alienation Syndrome (PAS), a theory formulated by Richard Gardner (Gardner, 1987, 1989, 1992, 1995). Gardner believed that, although most reports of incest were true, the vast majority of incest cases when parents are divorced or divorced were false. He asserted that mothers in divorce/custody cases were vindictive and calculating, engaging in a series of exclusionary maneuvers to prevent hapless fathers from having access to their children. He stated that falsely claiming sexual abuse and securing the child's collusion in this false allegation is the "ultimate weapon" in this exclusionary process.

Although Gardner's theory of PAS has been questioned because he provides no supporting data (Faller, 1998; Myers, 1997), and PAS is inconsistent with other research findings (e.g., Johnston, 2003; Johnston & Kelly, 2004; Neustein & Goetting, 1999). [It is also ridiculous to categorically deny allegations during separations, divorces, custody battles and so on because once children feel safe -as in they are residing with the parent who is not abusing them, there is a far greater chance that child will disclose that abuse at that time when they haven't before].

The findings…. suggest that children alleging abuse, perhaps particularly sexual abuse, when there is also marital dissolution may be in jeopardy of being labeled coached children.

Psychological Testing used in Custodial Evaluations:

The Cult of Personality: How Personality Tests are Leading Us to Miseducate Our Children, Mismanage, Our Companies, and Misunderstand Ourselves, Annie Murphy Paul:

Wood and his coauthors' numerous criticisms of the Comprehensive System come down to three very serious charges. First, many of its scores have "essentially zero validity"—that is, when the Rorschach reports that the test taker is depressive, narcissistic, or overly dependent, that person is quite likely not to exhibit those traits at all. In part, that's because Rorschach makes claims about a large number of human qualities, often based on scant evidence. For example, under the Comprehensive System, if a test taker reports seeing just one "Reflection"—a mirrored image in what are, after all, symmetrical blots—he or she is deemed egocentric, with "a marked tendency to overvalue personal worth." If the test taker discerns a single item of food, that individual "can be expected to manifest many more dependency behaviors than usually expected," according to Exnor. Only a handful of the more than one hundred variables in the Comprehensive System, says Wood, have stood up under investigation. (His contention is supported by a study published in the *Journal of Clinical Psychology*, which found that only 20 percent of Comprehensive System scales examined by the article authors could identify a statistically significant difference between groups of normal people and groups of people with serious mental illness.)

The second of the group's criticisms concerns the "norms" provided by the Comprehensive System, or the standards of normality against which test takers are judged. The Rorschach routinely "over pathologizes" healthy people, Wood and the others maintain, making them seem much more dysfunctional than they really are. "If Rorschach scores for a normal adult are interpreted according to Exner's norms," they write, that person will appear "self-focused and narcissistic," "unconventional with impaired judgment and distorted perceptions of reality," "depressed, anxious, tense and constrained in emotional expression," "insecure and fearful of involvement," "vacillating and inefficient," with "low empathy," "a tendency to withdraw from emotions," and "poor emotional control." The Comprehensive System's model of normality, they say, doesn't actually represent normal people.

Today, the Rorschach inkblot test is used in a great variety of ways: to diagnose the mentally ill, to evaluate troubled children, to select candidates for high-risk jobs, and even to check out professional athletes and Catholic priests........one of its most common, and most controversial, uses it as evidence in criminal and civil legal cases........ in criminal forensic evaluations,......test results also contribute to decisions about sentencing and parole....Jeffrey Dahmer's [results] "were normal to the point of being mundane."

[These tests are given in custody evaluations to decide the voracity of child abuse allegations and discover who the 'better parent' is.]

.....the Rorschach is "seriously flawed and should not be used in court or the consulting room."

What's Wrong with the Rorschach? James M. Wood, M. Teresa Nezworski, Scott O. Lillienfeld, Howard N. Garb:

In surveys, the Rorschach typically ranks as the second most widely used personality test among clinical psychologists. (Number one is the Minnesota Multiphasic Personality Inventory, usually called the MMPI, a yes-no questionnaire that is used to identify psychological symptoms and disorders.)

31% of psychologists who evaluate parents in custody evaluations use the Rorschach.

35% of psychologists who evaluate children for abuse or neglect use the Rorschach.

The Rorschach is not merely a psychological test. It's also a social and scientific phenomenon......we tell the extraordinary story of how this creaky, flawed assessment technique, invented over 80 years ago, has become one of clinical psychology's most widely used tools, paradoxically still popular in an era when space stations are orbiting the earth, and biologists are unlocking the secrets of the human genome.......we've alerted our fellow psychologists to the problems of the Comprehensive System for Rorschach.....[we hope to address] professionals whose work can benefit from the knowledge of the Rorschach's flaws......lawyers, judges, psychiatrists, social workers, counselors, disability evaluators, medical administrators, and health planners.....as well as members of the general public....[as well as custody evaluators].

In the 1950s and 1960s, such prominent critics [of the Rorschach] as Lee J. Cronbach, Arthur Jensen, and Hans Eysenck had concluded that the validity of Rorschach scores is generally either poor or nonexistent. Eysenck denied that any Rorschach score had well-demonstrated validity. Cronbach, Jensen, and other critics expressed a more moderate view, concluding that the validity of a few Rorschach scores was above zero but too weak to be useful in clinical work.

In the 1950s, psychologists' tendency to over-diagnose psychopathology on the basis of the Rorschach was well-documented.......By the 1990s, however, Rorschach's tendency to over-pathologize normal people was virtually forgotten.

Overall, psychologists using the Comprehensive System diagnosed more than 75% of apparently normal individuals as disturbed.

One of the oldest and most serious problems with the Rorschach is its tendency to over-pathologize, that is, to make normal people appear sick........research evidence suggests that more than 25% of normal individuals are identified as "narcissistic" by the Comprehensive System. More than 50% are identified as having "poor reality testing" or "distorted thinking."

ACEs and PCEs (PACEs):

The National Child Traumatic Stress Network (NCTSN):

Children who come to the attention of the juvenile justice system are a challenging and underserved population with high rates of exposure to trauma. The NCTSN has developed resources to help juvenile justice professionals (including judges, attorneys, law enforcement, probation officers, frontline residential staff, and mental health personnel) understand and provide trauma-focused services to these youth, creating trauma-informed juvenile justice systems that are effective, and ensure the safety of the youth, family members, staff, and community.

More than 80% of juvenile justice-involved youth report experiencing trauma, with many having experienced multiple, chronic, and pervasive interpersonal traumas.

Beyond the ACE core: Examining relationships between timing of developmental adversity, relational health and developmental outcomes in children. (Hambrick, Brawner, Perry, Brandt, Hofmeister, and Collins). Archives of Psychiatric Nursing.

The association between developmental adversity and children's functioning is complex, particularly given the multifaceted nature of adverse experiences. The association between the timing of experience and outcomes is under-researched and clinically under-appreciated.

Findings expand the understanding of the association between the timing of adversity and relationally impoverished experiences and children's functioning. Although early life experiences are significantly impactful, relationally enriched environments may buffer these effects.

ACEs and Juvenile Justice (Jamieson), Center for Child Counseling:

The effect of sudden loss on a child can be potentially devastating…

85% of all juveniles who interface with the juvenile court system are functionally low literate. These are likely youngsters who have been struggling at school…..juvenile incarceration reduces the probability of high school completion and increases the probability of incarceration later in life, and you can see that early negative indicators like poor social skills and self-regulatory difficulties (often identified as early as kindergarten) are reliable on tracking poor future outcomes. It's our job to intervene and disrupt the pipeline of despair that moves children from childhood adversity to contact with the juvenile justice system to adult incarceration. We need to help children before they fall apart through prevention and intervention services and improved education for those working in the juvenile justice system.

Adverse Childhood Experiences (ACEs) Child Welfare Information Gateway.

Children thrive in environments where they feel safe...... Unfortunately, children who are in contact with the child welfare system have experienced negative and often traumatic situations that can have a lasting impact.

ACEs are traumatic events that occur before a child reaches the age of 18. ACEs include all types of abuse and neglect, such as parental substance use, incarceration, and domestic violence...A landmark study in the 1990s found a significant relationship between the number of ACEs a person experienced and a variety of negative outcomes in adulthood, including poor physical and mental health, substance use, and risky behaviors.

ACEs and associated social determinants of health, such as living in under-resourced or racially segregated neighborhoods, frequently moving, and experiencing food insecurity can cause toxic stress (extended or prolonged stress). Toxic stress from ACEs can negatively affect children's brain development, immune systems, and stress-response systems. These changes can affect children's attention, decision-making, and learning.

Children growing up with toxic stress may have difficulty forming healthy and stable relationships. They may also have unstable work histories as adults and struggle with finances, jobs, and depression throughout life. These effects can also be passed on to their own children. Some children may face further exposure to toxic stress from historical and ongoing traumas due to systemic racism or the impacts of poverty resulting from limited educational and economic opportunities.

YouTube video: Dr. Nadine Burke Harris, Ted Talks, on ACE's, it's a little over 15 minutes. I strongly recommend you watch this. She has other videos on YouTube about trauma as well.

Child Separation:

The Child Welfare System Fact Sheet (Children's Rights, January 2023):

The act of separating a child from their family and community imposes profound trauma on children–even the briefest separation can cause emotional harm that can last a lifetime. Once in foster care, many children are separated from their siblings, bounced between foster care placements, and further abused in their out-of-home placements. Youth with a history of involvement in the foster care system experience poor outcomes long after they exit care, including greater involvement with the criminal legal system, less educational achievement, and less long-term financial success than their peers without system involvement.

Because of the trauma of separation, structural inequities, and frequent negative experiences in care, youth with a history in foster care are also significantly more likely to suffer from serious and life-threatening mental health disorders. Individuals with prior involvement in care report having attempted suicide within the past year at rates that quadruple those of non-foster youth without prior system involvement and experience post-traumatic stress disorder at double the rate of US war veterans.

[I believe that separation and removal from loving primary caregivers into foster care, institutions, other relatives, and especially abusive relatives, all create severe trauma and culture shock to a child, whether they have siblings or not. Even if they are placed in the care of kind family members, the abrupt and sudden change will be traumatic. This, to me, only requires common sense to know actions such as these would be harmful and further abusive to a child. Humanity -what we who still have it are required to spread to those who have abandoned it. With it, we can do better for all children, especially abused and neglected children. They deserve better, more thoughtful, and empathetic decisions].

Effects of Separation on Young Children: Implications for Family Court Decision Makers (Peter Ernest Haiman Ph.D. peterhaiman.com):

Recently, I watched helplessly as the court made a decision I knew what exacerbate, if not cause, child abuse and additional trauma to a 2-year-old child. The mother was the primary caregiver, and it was to the mother that the child turned for comfort into stress. The father was emotionally unstable, which he took out on his wife and his daughter. Yet the judge supported placing the girl with her father on a trip to Canada for four weeks. This was much too long a separation from the primary caregiver. Yet the mother's attorney did not object. Nor did this attorney advocate in court for an expert witness to provide information about attachment research and the effects of visitation schedules on young children, as the mother had requested.

Children who grow up feeling secure in their primary relationship will undergo normal emotional development. They will be equipped to handle constructively most traumas that may occur, either during childhood or later in life.

On the other hand, children who are subjected to disruptive separation at an early age lack this secure foundation. This lack interferes with the development of the right side of the brain you might wonder if they will simply outgrow any damage that might have occurred. Unfortunately, that is usually not the case. Research has shown that children who do not develop secure attachments with the primary caregiver during the first years of life later are unable to calm themselves down; they're more likely than secured children to overreact to stimuli. Insecure children have less impulse control and less ability to tolerate stress, coming up unless ability to tolerate frustration than do individuals who have experienced a more secure childhood (Toth & Cicchetti, 1998). They also are more at risk for anxiety, depression, aggression, violence, suicide, and substance abuse. In my opinion, one of the most socially significant effects of insecure attachment is the fact that these individuals lack the ability to empathize.

When undue separation is imposed on an infant or toddler, in that child's eyes, this need for verbal self-expression is overpowered by feelings of loss and fear. This is how the child experiences undue separation. The child can feel forcibly silenced as a result. The child feels a powerful need to say something but at the same time feels this need must be forcibly repressed.

When an infant or youngster has been away from a primary attachment figure, such as the mother, he or she yearns to have the mother back. The child naturally rejoices when the mother returns. If, however, the child feels that the mother has been gone too long or has been away too frequently, the child's reaction will be mixed.

In each case the youngster's behavior is saying the same thing: "I am totally dependent by nature. I am attached emotionally to you. It is from you that I learned I can trust to get my love and to get all my needs met when I need to have them met. I feel you are doing what a good parent is supposed to do: be there consistently and reliably for me so I can learn to trust in you. I won't be able to trust myself unless I learn to trust in you first. But then something bad happened.

You were gone when I needed you. You were away when I needed to be held. You were gone when I needed to hear the sound just of your voice. You were not there when I needed someone to comfort me. The time grew longer and longer without you. You were gone. I started to cry. I couldn't stop crying. You should have been there to protect me. You were not there to look at. I felt so weak. I could not eat."

Decisions made in family court that affect the life of a young child but that are not based on well-researched theories of psychosocial development, such as attachment theory, hurt the very validity of the court. These decisions too often result in short- and even long-term psychological damage to the individual.

Every child should have the right to have his or her developmental needs fully described in court.

When evaluating a parenting plan, toddlers and preschoolers will show a well-trained observer how well the plan is working. Even nonverbal infants can express how well their needs have been met. Advocates are essential at this stage, as well, to let the court know if the plan is working. When will this vital process become standard in the family court system? It seems we have a long road to travel.

Early Mother-Child Separation, Parenting, and Child Well-Being in Early Head Start Families (Kimberly Howard, Anne Martin, Lisa J. Berlin, & Jeanne Brooks-Gunn, Columbia University, Duke University, January 13, 2011):

Multiple regression models revealed that controlling for baseline family maternal characteristics and indicators of family instability, the occurrence of a mother-child separation of a week or longer within the first two years of life was related to higher levels of child negativity (at age 3) and aggression (at ages 3 and 5). The effect of separation on child aggression at age 5 was mediated by aggression at age 3, suggesting that the effects of separation on children's aggressive behavior are early and persistent.

A central component of attachment theory is the notion that caregivers must be present and accessible in order for their children to become attached to them….. Separations as brief as one week in duration can negatively impact the quality of the relationship between mother and child (Bowlby, 1969/1982).

The effects of foster care have shown that maltreated children who are placed in foster care often exhibit higher levels of problem behaviors than children who were not removed from the care of their parents, particularly if the foster caregivers are unfamiliar to the child. The most commonly held explanation for these findings is that disruptions to the parent-child attachment are so unsettling to children, even those who were maltreated by their parents, that they result in negative social-emotional outcomes ranging from mild to quite severe (Lawrence, Carlson, & Egeland, 2006).

Early separation has also been explicitly linked to insecure/disorganized attachment and subsequent mental health problems.

While it is known that traumatic or extended separations can negatively impact children's development, the present study suggests that even relatively minor separations of a week or more that occur within the first two years of life are not entirely without adverse consequences for children's development. Although more information is certainly required about the physical and emotional contexts that might buffer the effects of separations on children's development, it is clear that a mother's physical accessibility during the first years of life has important implications for supporting positive child development.

The Dangers of Separating Children From Parents, What History & Attachment Research Tell Us About the Consequences of Separation, Lisa Firestone Ph.D., Compassion Matters, posted June 26, 2018, verified by Psychology Today:

As the California Psychological Association stated, "The harm caused by this abuse and trauma has been done. Our profession's scientific literature has documented that separating children from their parents can lead to anxiety, depression, attachment difficulties, trauma, and long-term emotional and intellectual damage." The American Psychological Association similarly wrote, "decades of psychological research show that children separated from their parents can suffer severe psychological distress, resulting in anxiety, loss of appetite, sleep disturbances, withdrawal, aggressive behavior and decline in educational achievement. The longer the parent and child are separated, the greater the child's symptoms of anxiety and depression become."

Separation and isolation from one's family increase the risk of suicide.

PTSD:

Trauma and Stressor-Related Disorders in Children (Children's Hospital of Philadelphia, 2022):

Post-traumatic stress disorder (PTSD).

Children and adolescents with PTSD have symptoms such as persistent, frightening thoughts and memories or flashbacks of a traumatic event or events. Other symptoms may include jumpiness, sleep problems, problems in school, avoidance of certain places or situations, depression, headaches or stomach pains.

Acute stress disorder (ASD).

The symptoms of ASD are similar to PTSD but occur within the first month after exposure to trauma. Prompt treatment and appropriate social support can reduce the risk of ASD developing into PTSD.

Adjustment disorders.

Adjustment disorders are unhealthy or unhelpful reactions to stressful events or changes in a child's life. These reactions can be emotional, such as depressed mood or nervousness, or behavioral, such as misconduct or violating the rights of others.

Reactive attachment disorder (RAD).

Children with RAD show limited emotional responses in situations where those are ordinarily expected. This might show in a lack of remorse after bad behavior or a lack of response to positive or negative emotional triggers. Children with RAD may not appear to want or need comfort from caregivers. They may not seem to care when a toy is taken away from them.

Disinhibited social engagement disorder DSED.

Children with DSED are unusually open to interactions with strangers. They can be over-eager to form attachments with others, walking up to and even hugging strangers. They may wander off with strangers without checking with their parents or caregivers.

Unclassified and unspecified trauma disorders.

Some emotional and behavioral reactions to trauma do not fit in the diagnostic categories above. This category is used for those cases.

Post-Traumatic Stress Disorder (PTSD) (Newsletter: Mayo Clinic Health Letter):

[PTSD] Symptoms cause significant problems in social or work [or school] situations and in relationships. They can also interfere with your ability to go about your normal tasks.

Symptoms:

Intrusive Memories

Recurrent, unwanted, distressing memories of the traumatic event

Reliving the traumatic event as if it were happening again (flashbacks)

upsetting dreams or nightmares about the traumatic event

Severe emotional distress or physical reactions to something that reminds you of the traumatic event

Avoidance

Trying to avoid thinking or talking about the traumatic event

Avoiding places, activities or people that remind you of the traumatic event

Negative Changes in Thinking and Mood

Negative thoughts about yourself, other people or the world

Hopelessness about the future

Memory problems, including not remembering important aspects of the traumatic event

Difficulty maintaining close relationships

Feeling detached from family and friends

Loss of interest in activities you once enjoyed

Difficulty experiencing positive emotions

Feeling emotionally numb

Changes in Physical and Emotional Reactions

Being easily startled or frightened

Always being on guard for danger

Self-destructive behavior, such as drinking too much or driving too fast

Trouble Sleeping

Trouble concentrating

Irritability, angry outbursts or aggressive behavior

Overwhelming guilt or shame

For children 6 years old and younger, signs and symptoms may also include:

Re-enacting the traumatic event or aspects of the traumatic event through play

Frightening dreams that may or may not include aspects of the traumatic event

If you have suicidal thoughts:

Reach out to a close friend or loved one.

Contact a minister, a spiritual leader or someone in your faith community.

Call a suicide hotline number – in the United States, call the National Suicide Prevention Lifeline at 1-800-273-TALK (1-800-273-8255) to reach a trained counselor.

Make an appointment with your doctor or a mental health professional.

[More that affects the chance of getting PTSD and/or the severity of it:]

The way your brain regulates the chemicals and hormones your body releases in response to stress.

PTSD (David Geffen School of Medicine):

PTSD isn't automatically considered a disability, but it can be treated as a disabling condition if an individual's symptoms impede critical daily functions, such as getting out of bed, leaving the house, or completing work duties. These individuals often need extra support and may qualify to receive disability benefits.

CPTSD stems from exposure to recurring or prolonged traumas or trauma types that lead to additional, often compounding, symptoms and complications.

Several evidence-based interventions have been shown to reduce PTSD symptoms. They include:

Trauma-Focused Cognitive Behavioral Therapy (TF-CBT)

Cognitive Processing Therapy (CPT)

Prolonged Exposure (PE)

Eye Movement Desensitization and Reprocessing (EMDR)

Narrative Exposure Therapy (NET)

"The idea behind the majority of trauma-focused interventions is helping people process the traumatic event," Dr. Blanca Orellana explains.

Using the word "heal" is important … It underscores that a condition as complex as PTSD leaves lasting changes on an individual.

"Individuals can expect things to resurface as they go through various developmental stages," Dr. Orellana says. "For example, if a child experienced sexual abuse, symptoms and memories may resurface when they begin dating again and when they have their first sexual encounter."

When people can identify and label their emotional states, they can better use appropriate coping strategies for different feelings.

People can help others going through PTSD by focusing on behaviors within their control, such as how they react to the person they're hoping to support. "In terms of providing trauma-informed care, we encourage people to try thinking in terms of 'what happened to you?' rather than 'what's wrong with you?'"

Dr. Orellana says that even just shifting that mindset can help someone be more supportive, empathetic, and accepting of someone's reactivity or symptom presentation.

She compares the psychological wounds of PTSD to physical wounds. Ignore them, and they may get worse, becoming contaminated and infected.

"You have to clean out the wound. You use some alcohol or hydrogen peroxide, and it hurts, but it's momentary. The cleaning process helps the wound heal. After that, you might still have a little scar, but that's all it is, just a little scar."

PTSD can affect anyone.

PTSD is not easily resolved and not resolved in the same time frame or in the same way by any two people, even those who experienced the exact same trauma. It's not something people can just "get over."

The best hope for healing from PTSD comes from working with a mental health professional experienced in trauma.

"Instead of asking if they work with trauma, say, 'What are the specific interventions you use for treating trauma?'" She says. "Ask them to talk about their approach in working with patients who have experienced trauma."

Treatment, – Symptoms,- and Complex-Post-Traumatic Stress Disorder (NHS, nhs.uk/)

PTSD develops in about 1 in 3 people who experience severe trauma.

[However, I'm not certain how they came up with this statistic, as between my sons and I, we are 3 for 3. We all have CPTSD. Maybe it is a biological component for us?]:

Symptoms of CPTSD

Feelings of shame or guilt

Difficulty controlling your emotions

Periods of losing attention and concentration (dissociation)

Physical symptoms, such as headaches, dizziness, chest pains and stomach aches

Cutting yourself off from friends and family

Relationship difficulties

Destructive or risky behavior, such as self-harm

Suicidal

People with complex PTSD often find it difficult to trust other people. You may be offered more therapy sessions than usual, so you have time to build a trusting relationship with your therapist.

You should be offered ongoing support after your treatment ends.

CPTSDfoundation.org

The Long-Term Harmful Effects of Childhood Sexual Abuse (Shirley Davis):

A victim of childhood sexual abuse experiences anger, shame, and despair that often is directed inward, causing huge problems such as impulsiveness, aggression, delinquency, hyperactivity, and substance abuse.

When children are sexually molested, their bodies circulate stress hormones in response to fear and uncertainty. These hormonal changes ready their bodies for the flight/fight/freeze response. Unfortunately, because childhood sexual abuse is a chronic problem, meaning it occurs often, the stress hormones do not have a chance to return to baseline, causing damage to vital regions of the brain.

The developing brains of children form many abnormalities, including limbic irritability and underdeveloped and lack of differentiation of the left hemisphere of the brain, as seen by insufficiencies in the cerebral cortex and hippocampus that affect the way memories are stored and retrieved.

Other abnormalities include deficient left to right hemisphere integration meaning there is a marked change during memory recall because of underdevelopment of the middle portion of the corpus callosum (the pathway connecting the two hemispheres of the brain).

There is also abnormal activity in the middle strip between the two hemispheres of the brain, the cerebellar vermis. This brain region plays an important role in emotional and attentional balances plus regulates electrical activity inside the limbic system.

Child sexual abuse is an epidemic that is a scourge upon humanity, with so many children having their childhoods cut short.

Victims of CSA have no responsibility for what happened to them as they are innocent children who do not understand what was being done to them.

There are some major damages done to the developing brains of children who experience CSA, including mental, physical, and brain changes. Some of these changes are permanent and affect the children [into adulthood].

[All of the damage to the brain and body that is referenced throughout this information is applicable to all forms of child abuse, not 'just' CSA (child sexual abuse)].

The Body Keeps The Score Brain, Mind, and Body In The Healing of Trauma Bessel Van Der Kolk, M.D.:

Having been exposed to family violence as a child often makes it difficult to establish stable, trusting relationships as an adult. Trauma, by definition, is unbearable and intolerable. Most rape victims, combat soldiers, and children who have been molested become so upset when they think about what they experienced that they try to push it out of their minds, trying to act as if nothing happened and move on. It takes tremendous energy to keep functioning while carrying the memory of terror and the shame of utter weakness and vulnerability.

Long after a traumatic experience is over, it may be reactivated at the slightest hint of danger, mobilize disturbed brain circuits and secrete massive amounts of stress hormones. This precipitates unpleasant emotions, intense physical sensations, and impulsive and aggressive actions. These posttraumatic reactions feel incomprehensible and overwhelming. Feeling out of control, survivors of trauma often begin to fear that they are damaged to the core and beyond redemption.

…The birth of three new branches of science has led to an explosion of knowledge about the effects of psychological trauma, abuse, and neglect. Those new disciplines are neuroscience, the study of how the brain supports mental processes; developmental psychopathology, the study of the impact of adverse experiences on the development of mind and brain; and interpersonal neurobiology, the study of how our behavior influences emotions, biology, and mindsets of those around us.

….trauma produces actual physiological changes, including a recalibration of the brain's alarm system. An increase in stress hormone activity and alterations in the system that filter relevant information from irrelevant. We now know that trauma compromises the brain area that communicates the physical, embodied feeling of being alive. These changes explain why traumatized individuals become hypervigilant to threats at the expense of spontaneously engaging in their day-to-day lives. They also help us understand why traumatized people so often keep repeating the same problems and have such trouble learning from experience. We now know that their behaviors are not the result of moral failings or signs of lack of willpower or bad character—they are caused by actual changes in the brain.

….The mere opportunity to escape does not necessarily make traumatized animals or people take the road to freedom…..many traumatized people simply give up. Rather than risk experimenting with new options, they stay stuck in the fear they know……They, too, had been exposed to somebody (or something) who had inflicted terrible harm on them---harm they had no way of escaping…..Their fight/flight response had been thwarted, and the result was either extreme agitation or collapse.

Scared animals return home, regardless of whether a home is safe or frightening. Are traumatized people condemned to seek refuge in what is familiar? If so, why, and is it possible to help them become attached to places and activities that are safe and pleasurable?

In PTSD, the critical balance between the amygdala (smoke detector) and the MPFC (watchtower) [parts of the brain] shifts radically, which makes it much harder to control emotions and impulses.

279

As long as the trauma is not resolved, the stress hormones that the body secretes to protect itself keep circulating, and the defensive movements and emotional response keep getting replayed.

The trauma that started "out there" is now played out on the battlefield of their own bodies, usually without a conscious connection between what happened back then and what is going on right now inside.

Children have no choice but to organize themselves to survive within the families they have. Unlike adults, they have no other authorities to turn to for help—their parents *are* the authorities.

…… "Traumatic experiences are often lost in time and concealed by shame, secrecy, and social taboo," but the study revealed that the impact of trauma pervaded these patients' adult lives…..high ACE scores turned out to correlate with higher workplace absenteeism, financial problems, and lower lifetime income. [As well as lower life expectancies].

As the ACE score rises, chronic depression in adulthood also rises dramatically. For those with an ACE score of four or more, its prevalence is 66% in women and 35% in men, compared with an overall rate of 12% in those with an ACE score of zero.

Self-acknowledged suicide attempts rise exponentially with ACE scores. From a score of zero to a score of six, there is about a 5,000% increase in the likelihood of suicide attempts.

If you've been hurt, you need to acknowledge and name what happened to you……As long as you keep secrets and suppress information, you are fundamentally at war with yourself.

Symptoms of PTSD often include statements like "I feel dead inside." [A direct personal quote from each of my sons at different times].

The ACE study showed how early abuse devastates health and social functioning…

Brain Development and Abuse:

Structural and Functional Brain Abnormalities Associated With Exposure to Different Childhood Trauma Subtypes: A Systemic Review of Neuroimaging Findings (Laura L. M. Cassiers, Bernard G. C Sabbe, Lianne Schmaal, Dick J. Veltman, Brenda W. J. H. Penninx, & Filip Van Den Eede, Frontiers in Psychiatry, published online August 3, 2018):

Childhood trauma subtypes, sexual abuse, physical abuse, emotional maltreatment, and neglect may have differential effects on the brain that persist into adulthood.

Sexual abuse was associated with structural deficits in the reward circuit and genitosensory cortex and amygdala hyperreactivity during sad autobiography memory recall. Emotional maltreatment correlated with abnormalities in fronto-limbic socioemotional networks. In neglected individuals, white matter integrity and connectivity were disturbed in several brain networks involved in a variety of functions. Other abnormalities, such as reduced frontal cortical volume, were common to all maltreatment types.

[The following trauma subtypes have some different nuances than what we've previously seen, so I'm including them. These are the definitions used to conduct the study above].

Sexual Abuse: Any sexual act with a minor, including sexual penetration, molestation with genital contact, attempted sexual abuse with physical contact, child prostitution or pornography and exposure to sexually explicit material or voyeurism.

Physical Abuse: Hitting a child with hands or an object, kicking, punching, throwing, deliberately dropping, shaking, grabbing, dragging, pushing or pulling, or otherwise causing actual or threatened physical harm.

Physical Neglect   Refusal of custody or the deliberate failure to provide or seek needed care, supervision, nutrition, clothing, shelter, personal hygiene or other disregard of a child's physical needs and safety.

Emotional Abuse   Verbal assaults or other abuse, threats, terrorization, administration of unprescribed substances or close confinement.

Emotional Neglect   Inadequate nurturing and affection, deliberate failure to provide or seek needed care for emotional-behavioral problems, allowing substance abuse or maladaptive behavior, overprotectiveness, inappropriately advanced expectations, inadequate structure and exposure to maladaptive behaviors and environments or domestic violence.

The Biological Effects of Childhood Trauma (Michael D. De Bellis, MD, MPH, & Abigail Zisk A. B., Duke University, published online February 16, 2014):

Trauma in childhood is a grave psychosocial, medical, and public policy problem that has serious consequences for its victims and for society. Chronic interpersonal violence in children is common worldwide. Developmental traumatology, the systemic investigation of the psychiatric and psychobiological effects of chronic overwhelming stress on the developing child, provides a framework and principles when empirically examining the neurobiological effects of pediatric trauma.

The Effects of Child Abuse on the Developing Brain (KeepKidsSafe Stop Childhood Sexual Abuse, keepkidssafe.org:

While the impact of sexual abuse can take many forms–emotional, social, and also physiological–often victims are simply told to seek professional counseling without learning what damage may actually have been done. With a lack of understanding come victims of child sexual abuse, and their families often think they can simply "get over it" after a period of time. But when left untreated, the effects of child abuse can lead to unchecked developmental difficulties that can actually be measured by looking at abuse survivors' brains.

The human brain is the central hub of the nervous system. In a normally "balanced" nervous system, your stress response and arousal to danger act to keep you safe. You feel fear or panic in situations where you should feel fear and panic.

Abuse causes stress to the brain. Children with a history of sexual abuse often suffer the consequences of what science calls "body dysregulation." This means that children and adult survivors respond to stimuli in their everyday lives to an exaggerated degree. Many survivors are hypersensitive to sounds, smells, tastes, and touches that are otherwise safe or don't deserve such a dramatic response.

This degree of nervous response can take its toll. An overactive stress response inhibits many everyday life functions and can lead to trouble socializing normally with other people. Stress can also lead to self-medicating and substance abuse as "outlets" to curb anxiety. You may even pass up positive events or life-changing encounters thanks to an over-inflated sense of fear.

Some survivors' nervous systems may also "numb" them camera a condition scientists call "analgesia." This means the child or adult has chronic trouble evaluating their own internal physical sensations. If they hurt themselves, they may not realize it until their condition becomes dangerous. The opposite can also be true: many adult survivors of mistreatment complain about chronic physical problems where no true cause exists.

Neuroscientists such as Dr. Martin Teicher of Harvard and Dr. Bruce Perry of the Child Trauma Academy in Houston have shown direct connections between childhood abuse and abnormal brain development.

Brain structures alone aren't the only targets of abuse. Chemicals inside the brain are crucial for development and are also at risk. The hormone cortisol channel, for example, is responsible for our stress response. In the mind of an abused child or adult survivor, cortisol is produced more than in the brains of people with no history of abuse. Other chemicals specific to the brain (neurotransmitters), such as serotonin, epinephrine, and dopamine, help regulate our good moods and sense of accomplishment. Abused brains tend to make less of these chemicals, which can lead to bouts of depression or "impulsive aggression" later in life.

What's more, very high levels of stress chemicals change a child's brain circuitry. The more pronounced the stress and abuse, the more "toxic" chemicals such as cortisol are to the system. Research also shows that victims who were abused by close family members must cope with more negative brain development outcomes than other victims of abuse.

Everything we've covered, brain structures and long-term conditions are all intimately connected. The amygdala produces cortisol; stress and abuse increase cortisol inside the brain; prolonged stress can make children and adult survivors "hypersensitive" to stimuli and stress, and stress that goes unchecked is a main ingredient of many depressive and aggression disorders.

Critical brain structures grow, and crucial connections happen during the first three years of a child's life. Neuroplasticity, or the brain's ability to "rewire" itself, is an ongoing power of the mind. This being said, the scars and long-term effects of childhood sexual abuse are never fully healed.

How Emotional Abuse in Childhood Changes the Brain (Leonard Holmes, PhD, Updated on November 15, 2021):

Childhood emotional abuse and neglect can result in permanent changes to the developing human brain. These changes in brain structure appear to be significant enough to potentially cause psychological and emotional problems in adulthood, such as psychological disorders and substance misuse.

Emotional Neglect can include failing to:

Believe in the child

Create a close-knit family [but not 'overly-close,' -not intrusive, or invasive, or of course not incestuous

Make the child feel special or important

Provide support

Want the child to be successful

Negative experiences can disrupt those developmental periods, leading to changes in the brain later on.

… The timing and duration of childhood abuse can impact the way it affects those children later in life. Abuse that occurs early in childhood for a prolonged period of time, … can lead to particularly negative outcomes.

[After using MRI technology]… There and clear differences in nine brain regions between those who had experienced childhood trauma and those who had not. The most obvious changes were in the brain regions that help balance emotions and impulses, as well as self-aware thinking.

Childhood abuse and neglect can have several negative effects on how the brain develops. Some of these are:

Decreased size of the hippocampus, which is important in learning and memory.

Dysfunction at different levels of the hypothalamic-pituitary-adrenal (HPA) axis, which is involved in the stress response.

Less volume in the prefrontal cortex, which affects behavior, emotional balance, and perception

Overactivity in the amygdala, which is responsible for processing emotions and determining reactions to potentially stressful or dangerous situations

Reduced volume of the cerebellum, which can affect motor skills and coordination

The Body Keeps The Score Brain, Mind, And Body in the Healing Trauma (Bessel van Der Kolk, M.D., Penguin Books, 2014):

Mapping the Electrical Circuits of the Brain

["Normal" brain waves vs. PTSD brain waves when shown the same group of images, 3 similar images and one image that has no relevance to the other 3].

Patterns of Attention. Milliseconds after the brain is presented with input. It starts organizing the meaning of the incoming information. Normally, all regions of the brain collaborate in a synchronized pattern, while the brainwaves in PTSD are less coordinated; the brain has trouble filtering out irrelevant information and has problems attending to the stimulus at hand.

Shunning and Shaming:

Shunning: The Trauma of Being Cut Off, Destructive cults control members through fear of ex-communication, (Steven A. Hassan PhD, Freedom of Mind, September 20, 2021, verified by Psychology Today):

Shunning is a dangerous practice used by cults.

Unless it has happened to you, it is impossible to describe the pain, confusion, and suffering a person endures when they are excommunicated.

Shaming Children is Emotionally Abusive. Children respect those who respect them. (Karyl McBride, PhD., The Legacy of Distorted Love, September 10, 2012, verified by Psychology Today).

Shaming and humiliating a child can have long-term devastating effects.

Adult children raised by narcissistic parents frequently tell similar childhood stories of shame and humiliation. Often, these shaming acts take place in front of other people.

Is it any wonder that young people in these situations grow into adults with self-doubt, depression, and anxiety?

Shaming and humiliating children is emotionally abusive. It is not OK to smack children physically or with words. Young people deserve and are entitled to reach out, attach and bond with their caretakers. It is an expectation that the parent will provide safety, protection, acceptance, understanding, and empathy.

When children are emotionally or psychologically abused, they grow up feeling unloved, unwanted, and fearful. Normal development is interrupted and it sends the wounded child into exile. This is when negative internal messages are developed.

Shaming and humiliation cause fear in children. This fear does not go away when they grow up. It becomes a barrier to a healthy emotional life and is difficult to eradicate. If these same children become parents, the possibility also exists that the fear and negativity can be unwittingly passed through the generations.

When children are shamed, humiliated and then silenced, it represses the harm that may re-surface later in life. If this happens, it can be in the form of self-destruction or cruelty to others.

Make the commitment to never shame a child.

Why Is Shame the Most Damaging Aspect of Child Sexual Abuse? Childhood Sexual Abuse creates the most shame of any childhood abuse. (Beverly Engel L.M.F.T., The Compassion Chronicles, December 14, 2022, verified by Psychology Today):

Connecting childhood sexual abuse and the negative behaviors you practice can be the first step toward healing shame.

Shame is not one feeling or experience but a cluster of feelings, experiences and beliefs.

The cluster of shameful feelings includes humiliation, helplessness, and self-doubt.

Shame is the most disturbing experience an individual will ever have about themselves; No other emotion feels more deeply disturbing…

If you were sexually abused as a child, you probably know that the abuse has negatively affected you in multiple ways. But what you might not know is that shame, and the consequences of shame are among the most destructive and debilitating of the many negative effects of child sexual abuse.

Victims often suffer from the following as a result of the shame they experience after having been sexually abused:

Self-loathing

Self-destructiveness (engaging in dangerous activities such as unprotected sex and reckless driving)

Self-harm

Disgust and hatred of the body or certain parts of the body

Neglect of the body

Self-sabotaging behavior

Extreme fear of criticism, judgment

Isolating and withdrawing behavior

Addictions, including alcoholism, drug addiction, food addiction, and sexual addiction

Defenses, such as putting up walls, need to be in control

Perfectionism

Rage and abusive behavior (emotional, physical, or sexual)

Relationship problems, including negative patterns, difficulties with intimacy

Sexual dysfunction, sexual anorexia, compulsive sexual behavior, and fantasies

Suicide ideation

Shame is a painful, self-conscious emotion typically associated with a negative evaluation of self. It is the desire to withdraw or isolate oneself, and feelings of distress...

A significant aspect of shame is an intense fear of exposure-of having one's badness or inadequacy seen by others. This fear of exposure prevents the person from feeling "a part" of life and creates a deep sense of loneliness and isolation. Many former victims live in the fear of "being found out" – of those around them finding out about this sexual abuse. The secretive nature of child sexual abuse and the likelihood that many former victims have kept the abuse a secret only adds to their shame.

... the analytical, problem-solving area of the brain is still in development. The child may not be able to recognize that they carry no responsibility for the abuse. As the child tries to fill in the gaps on their own to understand why someone would abuse them, they may come up with reasons like, "I did something wrong," or "I asked for this." And while none of these thoughts reflect reality, the accompanying shame can be powerful enough to convince a former victim they are true.

If you were sexually abused as a child or adolescent, you undoubtedly suffer from shame. Your shame may come from the fact that the things that were done to you or the things you were forced to do made you feel dirty, contaminated, or damaged. Your shame may come from the fact that you blame yourself for the abuse. It may come from the fact that you felt some physical pleasure…

There are many reasons why former victims of child sexual abuse (CSA) are often overwhelmed with shame and, in fact, haunted by shame. One major reason is the way that victims are perceived and treated in our culture. Being perceived as a victim is synonymous with being seen as weak or a loser, and we tend to despise weakness in any form. This is especially true for male victims. In our culture (and virtually every culture in the world), we blame victims for their own victimization.

There is an implied (and often verbalized) belief that no one is a complete victim-that they must have played a role in their own victimization.

In our culture, we are supposed to "get over" adversity and "move on," many people don't have much tolerance or patience for those who don't.

The truth is it takes time to recover from adversity, especially one such as childhood sexual abuse.

It takes many years for most former victims to heal from the multitude of effects of childhood sexual abuse. They aren't malingering; they aren't just trying to get attention, and they shouldn't be shamed because they are still suffering.

What You're Saying When You Give Someone the Silent Treatment. (Daryl Austin, The Atlantic, 3/26/21):

The silent treatment goes by many names: shunning, social isolation, stonewalling, ghosting…. They are all essentially forms of ostracism.

"Every new method of connection can be used as a form of disconnection" (Williams).

"Because we humans require social contact for our mental health, the ramifications of isolation can be severe," Joel Cooper, a psychology professor at Princeton, told me. "In the short term, the silent treatment causes stress. In the long term, the stress can be considered abuse.

Silent treatment is a particularly insidious form of abuse because it might force the victim to reconcile with the perpetrator in an effort to end the behavior, even if the victim doesn't know why they're apologizing. "It's especially controlling because it deprives both sides of weighing in," Williams said. "One person does it to another person, and that person can't do anything about it."

The silent treatment might be employed by passive personality types to avoid conflict and confrontation, while strong personality types use it to punish or control.

One study found that social rejection provoked a response in its victims similar to that of victims of physical abuse; the anterior cingulate cortex area of the brain -the area thought to interpret emotion and pain -was active in both instances. "Exclusion and rejection literally hurt," John Bargh, a psychology professor at Yale, told me.

[I included both types of shaming in this section. The shame that one feels from particular abuse types and the abusive shunning and shaming inflicted on a person/child.]

Animal Abuse and its Correlation to Child Abuse:

Understanding the Link between Animal Cruelty and Family Violence: The Bioecological Systems Model (International

Journal of Environmental Research and Public Health, May 17, 2020, Jegatheesan, Enders-Slegers, Ormerod, & Boyden):

Violence towards animals and violence towards people are often interconnected problems…

… professionals addressing and/or treating an animal or a human being who has been subjected to abuse are uniquely situated to act in the role of 'first responders' when they suspect or recognize animal abuse, human abuse, and family violence.

… Researchers worldwide… Found correlations between the abuse directed toward partners, children, and companion animals.

"Where there are poor states of human welfare, there commonly exists poor states of animal welfare…" (Jordan & Lem).

Often, companion animals can become victims during family violence or used as pawns by the perpetrators to instill and enforce fear and control over their partner and children, creating interlocking systems of companion animal abuse, child abuse, and family violence.

In 1981, Hutton, a social worker in England, highlighted that animal abuse could be used as a diagnostic indicator for family violence. His study found that 82% of families known to the Royal Society for the Prevention of Cruelty to Animals (RSPCA) for animal abuse or neglect were also known to Social Services as having children at risk or having signs of physical abuse or neglect.

….A survey of pet-owning families and the US with substantiated child abuse and neglect… found that animals were abused in 88% of homes in which children have been physically abused. In the majority of these cases, the abuse of the animals was perpetrated by a parent…. Numerous studies in the millennium to date have documented the co-occurrence of family violence and animal abuse internationally.

Companion animals are often considered cherished family members and can also be subjected to abuse as a form of intimidation and retaliation to have/maintain control and power by the perpetrator. Although all cases of family violence can have a negative effect on children, frequency, length, and severity of the violent act well influence its effect. Children who are frequently exposed to severe forms of family violence are found to be more likely to abuse animals than our children who are regularly exposed to animal abuse. Five key areas of child development are documented as having a significant traumatic impact on our physical or biological functioning, behavioral, emotional development, social adaptation, and cognitive development.

Your family violence shelters accept companion animals, even though it is now well recognized. This is why victims with animals delay fleeing and thus remain in jeopardy. To address this problem, some countries have introduced pet fostering services. The UK has a number of pet fostering services...... A pet fostering service has recently been established in the Netherlands.

Cruelty and Human Abuse (Jason Bales, ladyfreethinker. org, January 6, 2021):

[Histories of diabolical animal abuse (I will spare you the details) occur in many notorious killers profiles: Ted Bundy, Jeffrey Dahmer, John Wayne Gacy, The Boston Strangler, Albert DeSalvo, Dennis Rader, Eric Harris and Dylan Klebold, Kip Kinkel, Luke Woodham, and many more].

Animal cruelty is linked to all forms of human abuse, from domestic violence to sexual assault.

Despite clear evidence suggesting the connection between animal abuse and future criminal behavior, authorities have failed to treat cases of animal cruelty with the same severity as violence against humans.

Arming people is statistically more likely when animal cruelty is involved. And animal cruelty must be taken seriously.

Household pets are often used as a way to control or further harm victims.

Domestic violence survivors have reported in studies… that their abusers threatened to kill, torture, or otherwise harm their companion animals–or actually followed through on the threats–to prevent them from leaving their abusive situations.

Abusers also use animal abuse or threats against survivors' beloved animals to isolate victims and children, to eliminate competition for attention, and to force the family to keep violence a secret…

This cruel behavior is commonplace for domestic violence victims, with more than 85% of women entering shelters discussing incidents of pet abuse in their families.

Another study published in Violence Against Women… found that women and domestic abuse shelters were 10 times more likely to report their partner had hurt or killed their pet compared to a group of women who had not experienced intimate violence.

In households prone to family violence, animals are often the first victims of abuse, followed by children, according to Cynthia Hodges.

88% of families surveyed that had incidents of child abuse also had incidents of animal abuse.

63% of children entering shelters admitted to incidents of pet abuse in their families.

… witnessing animal abuse can have a severe psychological impact on children.

Animal cruelty must be taken more seriously if this vicious cycle of abuse is ever going to end.

Officials Raise Awareness of the Correlation Between Animal Cruelty, Child Abuse, and Other Forms of Interpersonal Violence (Connecticut Department of Agriculture, 4/29/2022):

Officials from across the state today discussed the correlation between animal cruelty, child maltreatment and other forms of interpersonal violence.

"The connection between animal cruelty and child abuse has been well-documented and serves as a reminder of the importance of our cross-reporting requirements between the Department of Children and Families and the Department of Agriculture on a regular if not daily basis," said the agriculture commissioner Brian P. Hurlburt.

"Royalty to animals is a heinous crime, and often a serious warning sign of additional potentially involving children and domestic partners," stated Attorney General William Tong.

The barbaric individuals who abuse people and animals must be held accountable for their callous cruelty and inhumanity," stated Senator Richard Blumenthal.

Animal Abuse and Human Abuse: Partners in Crime (PeTa, People for the Ethical Treatment of Animals):

Acts of cruelty to animals are not mere indications of a minor personality flaw in the abuser; they are symptomatic of a deep mental disturbance. Research in psychology and criminology shows that people who commit acts of cruelty to animals don't stop there-many of them move on to their fellow humans.

Goals: parents, communities, and courts are beginning to realize that shrugging off cruelty to animals as a "minor" crime is like ignoring a ticking time bomb.

Take children seriously if they report that animals are being neglected or mistreated. Some children won't talk about their own suffering but will talk about animals.

Intentional cruelty to animals is strongly correlated with other crimes, including violence against people.

Family Courts and Child Abuse:
Lundy Bancroft:

Few people are aware of the severe human rights violations committed daily by family court judges across the country. These courts are siding over and over again with proven sexual abusers of children and batterers of women. I wouldn't believe it myself if I hadn't done so much investigating.

We hear from time to time about horrible human rights atrocities happening around the globe. Our government claims that it stands in favor of human rights, and our leaders are in the news demanding consequences for other countries that are abusing their populations. But there is a huge denial about how widespread and common these kinds of atrocities are in the United States and that we are not nearly as different from other countries as we would like to believe we are.

Women Are Routinely Discredited: How Courts Fail Mothers and Children Who Have Survived Abuse, Jessica Klein, August 14, 2021. This piece was published in partnership between the Guardian and The Fuller Project:

Burdened by the high cost of legal help and penalized by courts that favor fathers, women risk losing children to abusive partners.

When women accuse former partners of abusing their children, they risk uphill legal battles. Navigating a criminal justice system that tends to favor those who have the most resources to make their case can become a nightmare, as women seeking justice from their alleged abusers learn how far they must go to be taken seriously. [Typically, they can never go far enough, or the farther they go, the more they are seen as hysterical or delusional.]

Mothers who accuse their partners of abuse can be seen as the "less cooperative" parent in custody and visitation cases, say, lawyers and domestic violence experts because they're not facilitating a relationship between father and child, a relationship the court sees as important for the child's development. Opposing counsel can portray them as combative and intransigent, making their clients appear to be better custodial parents. [Furthermore, they will take custody away from mothers, what about the relationship between the children and their mothers in development?]

As a result, mothers often find themselves on the defensive, says Joan Meier, a clinical law professor and the director of the National Family Violence Law Center at the George Washington University Law School.

"That's like the ticket to death," she says. "If you're a mom and you raise [allegations of] child sexual abuse [by the father], the odds are you lose custody."

In 2019, Meier looked at 200 cases in which mothers alleged child sexual abuse by fathers and found that courts sided with the mothers in just 15% of the cases. In the same study, she found that, of 1,137 cases where mothers alleged domestic violence, courts credited the claims in just 517 cases. (In general, mothers tend to be custodial parents, usually as a result of out-of-court settlements, says Meier. 80% of mothers have primary custody of their children, compared with approximately 20% of fathers, according to 2015 census data.)

Accusing your partner of child abuse can be a lengthy, unpredictable process for mothers seeking justice in US family courts; historically, the process has pushed women to take drastic measures to protect their children from allegedly abusive guardians.

Wariness of child sexual abuse allegations also has roots in Child Protective Service workers' training. According to Meier, CPS workers are taught to scrutinize child sexual abuse claims more closely when families are going through custody litigation and flagging claims they believe are fishy. "In such cases, I call it taxpayer-funded child abuse," says Meier, "because they are basically helping abusive fathers keep custody."

"The biggest problem I have isn't the fact that I have an abusive ex-husband; it's the fact that the courts have not only not done anything, but they've penalized me and my children." "Stephanie."

"I think that there is confusion and disbelief about what the real outcomes are in family court. Generally, women are still not believed. They are routinely discredited. They are routinely deemed hysterical." Says Kasser.

Disparities at Adjudication in the Juvenile Justice System: An Examination of Race, Gender, and Age (U of M Child and Adolescent Data Lab, Michael Evangelist, Joseph P. Ryan, Bryan G. Victor, Andrew Moore, Brian E. Perron, November 2017):

Black and male youth are overrepresented at every stage of juvenile justice processing. …. Findings indicate that being black, male, and in the middle of the juvenile court age jurisdiction were associated with an increase in the probability of receiving a formal adjudication after controlling for prior referrals and the type and severity of the underlying offense. The magnitude of racial and gender disparities differed across ages and was greatest for the least serious offenses.

The National Child Traumatic Stress Network Resources (NCTSN):

Children who come to the attention of the juvenile justice system are a challenging and underserved population with higher rates of exposure to trauma. The National Child Traumatic Stress Network has developed resources to help juvenile justice professionals (including judges, attorneys, law enforcement, probation officers, frontline residential staff, and mental health personnel) understand

and provide trauma-focused services to these youth, family members, staff, and the community.

More than 80% of juvenile justice-involved youth report experiencing trauma, with many having experienced multiple, chronic, and pervasive interpersonal traumas.

Protecting Your Child from Sexual Abuse in Custody Cases Custody Court Crisis (Stop Abuse Campaign, Arlaine Rockey, Attorney at Law 2003-2019):

Why aren't the children protected?

Most people think that making allegations of sexual abuse is a sure way for the protective parent to win the custody case. Nothing could be further from the truth.

There is a backlash in full force in our legal system against protective parents. "Protective parents" are those acting to protect their children from abuse, be a child physical or sexual abuse or domestic violence in the home. Protective parents are, much more often than not, mothers. The Father's Rights Movement has been built on the myth that evil mothers have lodged false allegations of sexual or physical abuse or domestic violence against millions of fathers just to deprive and alienate them from their children.

If there is a custody case (or domestic violence protective order case) ongoing, it is customary for CPS to be highly skeptical of sexual (or physical) abuse (or domestic violence) allegations. Perhaps worried about being pawns, CPS generally just doesn't want to get involved. This aversion, unless there is clear medical evidence of sexual abuse… which is extremely rare, or the child's clear disclosure of sexual abuse, often manifests itself in the allegations being unsubstantiated, which makes the CPS investigator a nice witness for the abuser.

Hundreds of thousands, if not millions, of dollars, have been paid to psychologists all over this country who perform court-ordered custody evaluations. [Generally, these are not helpful, if not extremely damaging, to the protective mothers for the reasons I have previously stated].

[The custody evaluations will come back with a variety of common 'diagnoses' for mothers]…Borderline Personality Disorder… Munchausen's Syndrome (factitious disorder)…or a Delusional Disorder (…where the protective parent is delusional that the child has been abused and has "induced" the same delusion in the child victim). These custody evaluations and their recommendations are used to force protective parents into unfavorable custody settlements or to fully divest them of custody, doing the unthinkable, giving custody to the abuser [which is exactly what happened in our case; I was labeled "delusional," and supposedly the boys believed they were abused because of my "delusions" (how preposterous, how could any sane person have rationalized that?). Furthermore, as I've also previously stated, "Delusional" is not a formal mental health diagnosis in the DSM IV, which is what Dr. Miso Gynist used for his evaluation. X "is a man's man," and I was "delusional."In this scenario, it's pretty clear to me who's having delusions].

Mislead are desperate protective parents too often consent to the court appointment of a Guardian ad litem ("GAL"), often an attorney, for the children. It sounds like a great idea. Give the children their own attorney who will investigate the case and advocate for the children's best interests. However, all too frequently, these attorneys, often well-meaning volunteers, are not experienced in handling cases involving child abuse or domestic violence. When faced with abusers who are well-spoken and financially secure wearers of suits and ties, GALs, much like judges, find it hard to believe that these professionals could possibly be abusers. Too many mothers, in their desperation to protect their Children Act a little crazy. They generally make a lot less money than their ex-husbands, which also apparently means they offer less security for their children. If the GALs do not believe the abuse allegations, these protective parents are at risk of having the GAL recommend that the fathers get custody. Like the custody evaluations, GAL recommendations are also used to force protective parents into unfavorable custody settlements or to fully divest them of custody, again doing the unthinkable: giving custody to the abuser.

…Maybe It is because sexual abuse is so despicable that people just do not want to believe it really happens. Whatever the reasons, protective parents fighting to protect their children are now stuck with this reality, and the best thing they can do is try to find an attorney highly experienced with these issues and navigate the minefield.

Gathering evidence [for the court], write the following down:

Sexual acting out with a sibling or another child or adult

Use of a toy or object in a sexual manner

Repeated irritation around private parts

Disclosures (child telling you or someone else about the abuse)

Complaints of pain while urinating or using the bathroom

Enuresis or encopresis after being potty trained

Self-mutilation (cutting, hair pulling, etc.)

Blood or tears around the vagina or anus

Night terrors

Saying or doing things that show a more advanced knowledge of sex

Masturbation (although most masturbating in children is normal behavior)

abuser shows child favoritism, gives child gifts

Child's drawings or writings

Also, write down other relevant information such as:

List of all people who have access to the child (possible abusers)

List all witnesses who might have heard or have seen the child say or do something unusual, all caretakers, and those witnesses who you told about things that happened soon after or while they happened, with their names, addresses and telephone numbers.

Make a chronological history of any physical abuse of your child, siblings, or yourself from the abuser.

Write about the abuser's history, including any history of being abused, of any other people in his family who were abused or abusers, any criminal record history of alcohol or drug abuse, and names and addresses of former spouses or girlfriends.

Use of child pornography by the abuser

[I think writing as many of these things that you witness down on paper is a great idea. My advice, though, is to keep it in one notepad, make sure the notepad cannot be found, keep a pen with it, and write down only the facts: what you saw and/or heard, date, time, where, and the names of any other people around who heard and saw if you can. My attorney suggested I write these facts down, and I ended up writing a whole bunch of things, mainly things I did not understand at the time that I thought meant something -I didn't want to forget it because I wanted to get other people's thoughts on them. Sadly, those things took precedence in the eyes of the custodial evaluator and the judge, and they ignored all the very pertinent information].

[I found no matter how great your attorney is -as mine was investigative, dedicated, very hard-working, research-oriented, and simply put, quite great! -I couldn't have had a better attorney. However, it depends more on the judge or referee you are stuck with. The referee had her mind made up right from the beginning, and she was not going to be moved, no matter what the evidence or arguments were. My heart breaks for any protective mother of a child who has been abused, who has had or will have a case in front of her. Most likely, the vast majority of judges see these cases through the very same lenses she saw them through disbelief, bias, hatred for the protective parent (because they assume the allegations are untrue - which is extremely rare), ignorant of these issues, God-complex, controlling, and remiss of empathy and compassion. It is enraging and depressing at the same time].

If the child tells you something that makes you think that the child has been sexually abused… it is critical that you take your child to a doctor or a therapist soon after the child tells you or another person anything about the sexual abuse so that you (or the other person) will later be able to testify to what the child said at trial.

… There is a hearsay exception for statements in aid of treatment. The child's statements that prompted you to take the child to the ER or doctor can also come into evidence under the same hearsay exception. [I wish I would have known this then].

Your attorney should give CPS information that might tend to prove that the sexual abuse has occurred but do not count on CPS substantiating the sexual abuse.

Even if CPS is unsubstantiates, the CPS records and investigators can still be helpful to prove that the sexual abuse actually occurred.

It is not unusual for sexual abuse to occur in the context of a battering relationship where the abuser might sexually and even physically abuse the child and also physically and sometimes sexually abuse the mother, who is the protective parent in the custody case.

.. My advice to you is not to ask for or agree to the appointment of a guardian ad litem to represent your child in the custody case. The basic reason for this advice is that a GAL just creates one more variable that you cannot control in your case. All too often, GALs, besides usually not having training in sexual abuse cases, also seem to gravitate toward the parent who appears more stable financially and emotionally in a sexual abuse custody case that usually turns out to be the abuser.

Quite often, judges rubber stamp the custody evaluation recommendations, so custody evaluations are very important and should be requested and consented to only with extreme caution. Choosing a psychologist is critical. Find a psychologist,…. Who has experience in sexual abuse, either an evaluation and treatment of victims or perpetrators? You should also investigate to make sure the potential psychologists are not aligned with the Father's Rights Movement… you need to try your best to get a sexual abuse expert to do the custody evaluation.

Be warned that most custody evaluators recommend a form of shared parenting or joint custody, with one parent having primary custody and the other having secondary custody.

… Make sure your attorney reviews everything you write before you submit it to the psychologist.

After the customer evaluation is finished, you and your attorney need to review it 1st to see if the psychologist got the facts straight. If there is a glaring problem, your attorney can write a letter to the psychologist setting out the discrepancies. Your attorney also should take a deposition of the custody evaluator if the outcome is not favorable to your position. Your attorney should investigate the custody evaluator's background, including his or her resume, books or articles, written conferences at which he or she presented, and any affiliations with any certain groups that would show a bias, such as father's rights groups. Your attorney should subpoena the custody evaluator's complete file and review its contents, preferably prior to or at the deposition.

If the psychologist who did the custody evaluation did not adequately address the issue of sexual abuse or found that there was no sexual abuse, depending on their recommendations in the custody of valuation, you might want to hire a different psychologist who is an expert in child sexual abuse to critique the custody evaluation and to do another evaluation solely on the issue of sexual abuse.

If there is actual medical evidence of sexual abuse, for example, tears caused by a sexually transmitted disease, you may need to have the doctor testify and explain how that medical evidence would tend to show that sexual abuse occurred.

You should not forget that you also have to present basic evidence that you are a fit parent and that it is in that child's best interest to be in your custody.

…mothers are viewed all the more skeptically by the Court.

… outlined [above are] some possible reasons why sexually abused children are not protected by the Courts.

If you are unable to protect your child by way of your custody case, you can consider any criminal charges that might be able to be brought against the abuser, even for other things the abuser has done wrong.

If you run with your child against any court order or law, you will most likely be committing a felony. When your child is found, then the abuser will stand a good chance of gaining permanent custody of your child, and you may well end up in prison.

Mother Seeks Courtroom Reform for Sexually Abused Children and Protective Parents (Claire Chiamulera, June 1, 2013, Americanbar.org):

[This is another case like mine where the mother was the protective parent who knew her daughter was being sexually abused by her ex-husband. She faced barriers at every turn, and her ex-husband ultimately won custody].

I wanted to make a difference for those working in the fields of domestic violence, child abuse, or child trauma so that such maltreatment would not continue. I wanted to open the eyes of the legal system to mothers "trapped" in similar situations. I also wanted to make the public aware of the tragedy taking place in our courts and to make a difference in saving other children and protective mothers.

After experiencing the system failure time and time again despite evidence of abuse, hearing my daughter's cries for help hearing after hearing, enduring year after year of the abuse not being heard, and finally becoming financially depleted, I began to realize a main problem was lack of education and training among professionals handling these cases.

There are thousands of cases in our courts in every state with the same outcome as mine and my daughter's.

The failure of various systems when child sexual abuse is reported and how these cases are turned against the protective parent in family court illustrates a Catch-22 situation. Mothers who report sexual abuse nearly always lose custody. Research shows children are placed in full or partial custody of their identified sexual abuser 90% of the time. Unfortunately, many judges, attorneys, and mental health professionals do not understand the overlap of domestic violence and child abuse.

When the child resists going with the abuser and the mother asks for protection from the family (divorce), the mother is labeled dangerous and considered to be alienating the child from the father. The "Parental Alienation Syndrome" is relied on heavily, although it isn't approved by the American Medical Association or the American Psychological Association, and is considered "junk science" that should not be allowed in courts. In my experience, judges ignore or minimize I've had hands of sexual abuse and do not allow abuse findings in court.

Research shows that in family courts, false allegations of child sexual abuse remain rare. Family court judges may not understand the evidence that is essential to correct decision-making. Incorrect family court decisions will have damaging effects, either by subjecting the child to continue to abuse and/or by depriving the child of a relationship with a non-abusive parent.

No child should be placed in unsupervised contact with a domestic violence abuser against the child's will. Children need safe homes and need to have their constitutional rights protected. Giving an abuser control over the mother and the child is the ultimate act of re-victimization. The mother is treated as a criminal with the loss of the children she tried to protect. She is often ordered to receive minimal, supervised visits, sometimes lasting for years (even though she is not the abusive parent), jailed, given gag orders, depleted financially, and ordered to pay child support. Finally, she may experience a de facto termination of her parental rights when the court disallows visits.

New measures must be taken. Most important are to: 1. Not be so quick to ignore abuse allegations and assume it is a vindictive ex-wife; 2. Listen to the children; and 3. Educate and understand these cases as domestic violence and child abuse cases, not "high conflict" cases.

Never ever give up. It is crucial to stay in your child's life no matter how you may be prevented from seeing your child. Your child needs to know you are fighting for him or her. If you can't see your child because of court orders, speak out and seek changes in practice, policies, and legislation. Get help finding a pro bono attorney or educating yourself so you can advocate for yourself in court. It is sad that most mothers are destitute after a few years, paying for attorneys, evaluators, litigation, and therapy for themselves and their children.

Judges must be trained by child sexual abuse and domestic violence experts, not by other judges.

Develop a system to more easily remove incompetent, poorly trained professionals.

[I've long held onto ideas that I think could fix this massive court problem or at least make the problem much less prevalent in our country. However, it will take a lot of work, a lot of policy, and a lot of change. So, there are family courts that deal with marriage dissolution and property division. Let's let them deal with those cases - especially if they are not contested, and there are no children involved. There are juvenile courts that deal with juvenile crime. While I believe these need an overhaul and a reminder that they are making decisions that will affect children's entire lives, I think these issues should remain in this separate court system. However, I believe the actors within this system need to be appropriately trained and look at a child's history and take their history into account when making penalty decisions. Perhaps an intensive, inpatient therapeutic treatment center would make more sense than locking them away in prison or juvenile delinquency centers - wherein they will not have the opportunity to recover or better themselves for their futures. Placing anyone, particularly children, into a prison-juvenile detention-type environment only sets them up for future recidivism. Let's give them a chance instead. So, what I think should exist is a children's court devoted only to cases regarding the past, present, and future of children. Be it custody, education, or, of course, abuse. The judges and actors in this court system would be extensively trained and knowledgeable of child development, normal expectations vs. what may possibly be seen if abuse exists, all forms of child abuse, physical, emotional, sexual, etc., and/or behavioral indicators, domestic violence and its impact on children, substance use disorder and its impact on children, etc. The focus would be on prevention, in-home services, and keeping the children with their protective parent, moving away from foster care and adoption services, and far away from the termination of parental rights. The focus would be on the child and the unpressured wishes of the child].

Biased Family Court System Hurts Mothers (Garland Waller, Women's eNews, womensenews.org, September 5, 2001):

Studies show that in approximately 70% of challenged cases, battering parents have been able to convince authorities during custody battles that their victim is unfit or undeserving of sole custody, according to a recent report published by the American Judges Foundation.

…I read that a family court judge has awarded custody of a 3-year-old girl to the father who has violently beaten her mother. I do not even lift an eyebrow when a 2-year-old boy who comes home from unsupervised visitation with his dad has a diaper filled with his own rectal blood, and that same child is later turned over to his father on a full-time basis. And when a mother is thrown into jail, denied the right to ever see her children again because she brought up the issue of child abuse in a family court, I'm sickened but not shocked.

These injustices are commonplace today in the closed-door family court system. These courts often claim to operate in a manner consistent with the "best interests of the child." In practice this often means that a judge, often a male judge, biased and imperious, defines that phrase. These judges decide, time and time again, winning woman raises the allegation of sexual abuse in a custody dispute that it is she who will lose her children forever.

… thousands of women are losing custody of their children to men with histories of violence and sexual abuse. Sure, these cases are complicated, but it doesn't take a legal genius to figure out that it's not good for kids to watch daddy break mommy's jaw. Research shows a high correlation between domestic violence and child sexual abuse.

Open the courtrooms to the public and make judges accountable for their rulings.

Get rid of the "best interests of the child" as the standard for custody and replace it with a new concept called the "approximation standard." That means that the judge should try to approximate the same setup for the children that existed before the divorce. If mom was with the kids 70% of the time before the divorce, she would be with them seven 8% of the time after the divorce. In non-contested custody cases, the mother and father generally agree to this on their own.

Most significantly, the allegation of child abuse in a custody battle must be considered a rebuttable presumption. That is, the sworn testimony of a parent or child claiming abuse is presumed to be true unless and until the accused sufficiently challenges its veracity.

We have created a system that purports to be gatekeeper-keeping victims from victimizers-but the system is really the welcome mat for victimizers to have access to the victims," says Richard Ducote, a nationally recognized child advocate and attorney. He adds that there has been virtually no change in the process during the past two decades.

In fact, a pilot study in the early 1990s by the California Protective Parent Association and Mothers of Lost Children found that 91% of fathers who are identified by their children as perpetrators of sexual abuse received full or partial unsupervised custody of the children and that in 54% of cases, the non-abusing mother was placed on unsupervised visitation.

In essentially every case in which courts place children with abusers, despite substantial evidence of sexual abuse or domestic violence and no evidence of fabrication on the protecting parent's part, it is the parental alienation syndrome that is used by the judge, the evaluator or the child's lawyer to ignore and discount the abuse evidence and to wrongfully construe all of the child's symptoms as evidence of alienation.

Framing Contests In Child Custody Disputes: Parental Alienation Syndrome, Child Abuse, Gender, and Father's Rights (Michele A. Adams, Family Law Quarterly, Vol.40, No.2, Summer 2006):

Signs of major trauma, i.e., lacerations to the anal office, are very rarely observed. Minor injuries may sometimes be seen and typically include anal erythema, abrasions, or fissures. In the vast majority of cases, there are no visible signs of trauma to the anal area.

[When I took my sons to the ER because I was instructed to do so by a CPS caseworker -knowing that it had been several days since the incident my sons told me about, and I figured there would be no 'evidence' found. However, on the anus of my oldest son, who was about 8 at that time, a fissure (at least one) was found. At a separate ER visit, there was a fissure found on the anus of my youngest son. Although "fissures" cannot be used as determinants of child sexual abuse, I'm not sure how else a young child is going to obtain tears around the anus].

Childhood, It Should Not Hurt, Claire Reeves, C.C.D.C., LTI Publishing, 2003:

The only people who can break this unending cycle are the judges, social workers, police and other government officials who preside over the individual situations. The only answers to help them recognize and understand generational cycles of abuse are intervention, education and ever-vigilance.

… The judge usually orders a psychological evaluation of both parties to determine each parent's mental health and overall character. Here's what those reports often find: the non-offending parent, horrified at the harm done to the child and the betrayal of his/her lifetime partner, appears distraught, frightened, anxious, angry and out of control. The perpetrator, adept at putting up a front and manipulating everyone and everything around him/her, appears cool, personally injured by the accusation and in full control.

Fathers seek custody to avoid new child support and protection laws. Under gender-neutral laws, men could bring bogus custody challenges to intimidate their wives into settling for less, but now there is evidence that men are seeking custody and obtaining custody for a related reason. There is agreement that men are challenging their wives for custody of the children precisely because it is cheaper to keep them than to pay child support. This growing trend corresponds to new laws that require the non-custodial parent to pay for child support. Men are now being taught by their lawyers to avoid child support. They should obtain custody to force their ex-wives into paying child support instead.

Family Court is where divorce cases are heard, where custody and visitation issues are resolved, alimony and child support settlements are made, and property is divided between divorcing partners. [Unfortunately, many officials, professionals, and parents consider children under 18 to be "property"].

Family court is not the appropriate court to hear issues of child sexual abuse. Nevertheless, many of the cases I've seen over the years have begun and ended in family court rather than being moved to dependency/juvenile courts because child sexual abuse allegations raised during divorce come under the authority of the family court handling the custody part of that divorce. Consequently, those allegations are automatically suspected by the judge, social workers, law enforcement, etc., as an attempt to gain an advantage. Yet, if you were to find out your mate was sexually abusing your child, your first thought of recourse or defense would probably be divorce!

Thus, the protective partner is faced with the ultimate conundrum: you cannot let the child remain living with the abuser, yet you cannot get the child away from the abuser by divorcing him/ her. Dealing with this dilemma at a time when emotions are running at their highest is the hardest thing a person can face. ....

What's more, the child sexual abuse issue is not commonly raised as the reason for the divorce. If it were, it usually appears during the divorce proceedings **when the child victim finally feels safe enough to disclose to the non-offending parent.** ....

The only people who can break this unending cycle are the judges, social workers, police, and other government officials who preside over individual situations. The only answers to helping them recognize and understand generational cycles of abuse are intervention, education and ever-vigilance.

From Madness to Mutiny: Why Mothers Are Running from the Family Courts -and What Can be Done About it, Amy Neustein and Michael Lesher:

Americans believe they are safe from arbitrary abuse of governmental power. Child protective services, "law guardians," and family court judges can cast aside the norms of due process when suppressing an allegation of sexual abuse.

Americans believe that constitutional protections follow them everywhere—but family courts are an exception, at least for protective parents; as one family court judge put it, "There is no First Amendment in my court." Americans believe that sexist stereotypes have been soundly expelled from American political life—yet family courts still stigmatize mothers who make abuse allegations as "hysterical," "vindictive," and "hostile," as if, in family courts, the appearance of an angry woman still scandalizes. We see no point in trying to minimize the injustice of such phenomena.

…family court judges can sacrifice objectivity when they feel their authority threatened by a protective mother.

Law guardians [or Guardian ad Litem] reflect the priorities and attitudes of the system of which they are a part. Just as family court judges may scrutinize a parent accusing the other of child abuse more closely than the abuse allegation itself……. Just as the judicial system can ignore procedural rules and safeguards while it pursues a protective parent, law guardians may also behave like outlaws.

…law guardians have committed acts including lying to the family court and to higher courts, suppressing evidence of sexual abuse, and communicating false or incomplete information to state prosecutors and child protective service caseworkers who were trying to investigate claims of sexual abuse.

Since law guardians theoretically speak for the children, they are in a uniquely powerful position to cripple an accusation of child abuse simply by refusing to credit it. By the same token, they can quickly become the objects of outrage and parental mutiny when protective mothers believe they are failing to observe their legal duties to protect the children.

[A break for reflection…. The Guardian ad Litem assigned to our case for our sons failed them miserably. GAL Slymee was an unscrupulous attorney, much like the attorney for the plaintiff. He would have preferred being at a bar getting drunk than 'dealing' with our case. Initially, I naively thought that he 'got it,' that he may have actually understood the sinister workings of our case. It wasn't until late in the case that I discovered the truth of the matter. The attorneys were downstate to take the deposition of a crucially important witness in our case: Dr. Dee Fender, whose clinic completed assessments on my sons, and they joined other professionals in believing my sons had, in fact, been abused in many ways, including sexually. It was a very clear and detailed testimony of the evidence they had that led them to believe the boys had been sexually abused, physically abused, and emotionally abused by X. Her deposition took up most of a summer day in Ann Arbor, MI. She gave an incredibly undisputable testimony, which I don't believe the judge in our case in Northern Michigan ever viewed or read. –She couldn't have possibly made the decision she did had she done that. My attorney, Mr. Tru Lee Valyent, the GAL, and I had walked to the parking structure together. The Gal asked the two of us if we wanted to continue our conversation about the testimony and my sons at a different location. Mr. Tru Lee Valyent had to head back up to Northern Michigan, where he lived. Apparently, GAL Slymee was not in a hurry to get back up north where he lived. I was, always have been, and will forever remain eager to discuss my sons, their case, and their experiences with anyone who will listen. He wanted to be near his hotel, so we went to one of the chain restaurants next to the hotel he was staying at. I don't recall either of us getting anything to eat, although it was "happy hour," so free appetizers were provided. I had most of one drink (I am not a drinker), and I am not sure how many drinks he had. I tried to keep the conversation on my son and the deposition. I should have noticed that he kept taking it adrift. Since I felt that we were not having a productive conversation, and I needed to get home to take care of our horses, I stated I needed to get home to do just that. He kept asking if I wanted another drink, ordered himself another, and I kept trying to break free. I was getting irritated, and we soon left the bar. We had parked next to each other in the parking lot of his hotel, so we walked back towards the vehicles together. Admittedly, there had been times in our conversation when I felt uncomfortable with his comments, but he was old enough to be my father, if not my grandfather, so I had thought nothing of it. As I was trying to leave, he invited me to go up to his hotel room to have more drinks and continue our conversation there. Finally, I knew his objective. Of course, I declined that invitation. As I was trying to go, I turned my face towards my car, at which point he put one hand on my lower back and tried to kiss me on my mouth. Since I had turned my face away, he got my cheek. I wasn't rude because I always had to consider how any action I took towards anybody could affect my sons, but I was short with him. He kept one hand on my lower back, and now had one on my arm, and attempted to kiss me again. This time, I think he finally got the picture because I don't remember him trying to kiss me another time. At this point, I was rushing to get out of there. I was still polite and told him I'd see him later. I joked and said our horses are going to be coming through the fence. However, I often wonder what his written final argument would have said had I gone up to his room. I am a woman of integrity, so that thought never crossed my mind at that moment. But, in retrospect, I would have done absolutely anything to change the course of history for my sons and spare them any of the horror they've had to live through -which would have included going up to that hotel room if it would have made a difference. In hindsight, I frequently wonder what the contents of the GAL's final argument would have been and then, consequently, what the judge's decision would have been had I gone up there.

The judge requested all final arguments to be written. (Mr. Tru Lee Valyent provided an undeniable account of the facts and backed it up with documentation and research), as I would later learn GAL Slymee's final argument after all these years with so much having happened was one page. The judge provided her written conclusion shortly thereafter. We all know her conclusion.

Wait a minute, man,

You mispronounced my name,

You didn't wait for all the information

Before you turned me away,

Wait a minute, Sir,

You kinda hurt my feelings,

You took me for a joke. You took me for a child,

You took a long hard look at my ass and then
played golf for a while,

You took me out to wine dine 69 me,

But didn't hear a damn word I said,

I see right through you,

Hello Mister Man,

You didn't think I'd come back,

You didn't think I'd show up with my army,

and this ammunition on my back.

(excerpts from Alanis Morissette's Right
Through You)

When children are removed from the custody of protective mothers, the *mothers* find their visits under the same CPS supervision usually enforced against alleged offenders.

[This] gives the agency unfettered discretion to make visits torture for parents and children.

CPS malfunction stems from its very nature. Of particular concern are its wide-ranging powers and the secrecy within which it operates………..attitude among CPS officials is that they alone should control the decisions and behavior of families they deal with. They have absconded God-like powers that should not be theirs for the taking. [contributes to the malfunction].

Agencies mistakenly act as if they have been given total control over the daily life and future of the child and, without parental involvement or consent, arrange for evaluations, services, and the sharing of information.

Spurious Neglect Petitions: ….The District of Columbia's definition of "psychological abuse" is typical: it requires a showing that a mother suffers from an actual, definable mental illness and, *in addition,* proof that this mental health condition poses a real threat to the well-being of the child.

…CPS has sought—and obtained—the removal of young children from their mother's homes.

The Hostage Child, Sex Abuse Allegations in Custody Disputes, Leora N. Rosen and Michelle Etlin, Indiana University Press, 1996:

The county attorney, not the prosecutor, usually decides whether an alleged molester will be charged with child abuse, child neglect, or something called "endangerment" in a civil proceeding. The county attorney also represents another powerful client, the social service agency. In an abuse hearing, the standard before a family court judge -not a jury-is "clear and convincing evidence" that abuse did occur at a particular time, in a particular way. A judge may call the evidence "not convincing" merely because he is not convinced. [A Judge in Florida] stated on TV that he was upset by being asked to rule against a father who was a professor of political science at Miami University. He characterized his problem as being asked to "say that somebody put his penis…. In somebody else's tush!" For that, he said, "The evidence has to be conclusive, and I looked at it, and it was not conclusive." The evidence that he "looked at" included the boy's disclosure that his father had molested him; a police officer who believed the boy had been sexually assaulted; the children's services division, which believed the boy had been sexually assaulted; and the opinion of the medical director of the Miami rape treatment center, who had examined a tear to the child's anus and concluded that the boy had been sodomized. [But the judge] was not convinced. Obviously, there is no definition of what constitutes "clear and convincing" evidence.

After a case has been examined by social services, bounced around through county government, examined by professionals, subjected to the vagaries of prosecutors and courts and handled and mishandled by lawyers, it is almost impossible to pinpoint where in the system things went wrong. Even narrating and documenting such a case becomes nearly insurmountable because, at any juncture, there can be half a dozen twists. It would take a person of enormous strength to get through this maze and still remain calm and in control at all times, especially if her child is at risk or, worse yet, still being abused. As a result, "mistakes" pile up that are later charged against the protective parent: she should not have said this, she should not have done that, she should have gone to a different doctor, hired a different lawyer, made sure a certain subpoena was issued, made a particular call, not made that call, etc., etc., ad nauseum.

319

At the end of this travail, most victimized mothers and their advocates mistakenly identify one piece of the puzzle as "the problem," often picking the moment when they were the most shocked or astounded. One mother insists that interviews should be videotaped because children are often intimidated; another thinks that medical examinations should always be done with colposcopes so photographs can record the results; another wants judges hearing custody cases to be required to consider certain kinds of evidence; another believes that prosecutors should be legally required to issue whatever subpoenas the complaining witness demand. Although all these arguments can lead to attempts to change the law or pass new ones designed to make the system work, the impassioned and fragmented responses of victims and their bedraggled advocates have never changed the big picture.

We argue that the system is, in fact, working -in the way it has chosen to work. No matter which adjustment we support, it will continue to do what it chooses in response. The political and practical reality is that the goal of this system is to perpetuate itself and the policies, written and unwritten, by which it has already chosen to operate.

The system, as we have outlined it, appears capricious at best and unreliable at worst. This does not mean, however, that children are never protected from sexual abuse. It is important to remember that our overview is applicable primarily to incest cases or cases of intra-familial sexual abuse. A somewhat different set of principles applies in cases involving stranger molesters. Some steps in the system are the same for both kinds of cases, but others differ, depending on the identity and legal rights of the named perpetrators. Strangers do not have inalienable rights over a child and cannot sue for custody. Even in criminal court, different procedures are used, and these, in turn, affect civil proceedings. For example, a biological father accused of molesting his own child is usually given an exculpatory polygraph by the prosecutor's office. If he doesn't want to submit to the test, or if he takes it and fails, that is not used against him since the test is not admissible as evidence. However, if he passes the test, the charges against him are usually dismissed immediately. Strangers accused of molesting children are not given this same courtesy.

The bottom line is that a child is more likely to be protected by the system from a stranger-molester (from whom his own parents can protect him) than from an incest perpetrator.

What steps lead to the agency finding? There is no standard answer to this question. Usually, the child is interviewed by agency personnel. The child's own therapist, mother, doctor, and other trusted significant adults may be completely ignored; the child is usually expected to repeat her disclosure to a stranger interviewing her on behalf of the agency. The interviewer does not need to follow any particular procedure. Social workers are subjected to rigorous cross-examination about their conclusions only if they do, in fact, believe a child and go to court to support the allegations. If, however, they disbelieve the allegations-regardless of the reason conclusion is automatically accepted as the basis for an unfounded case, and their rationale is not challenged. Some children have been subjected to as many as 14 interviews [or more]. As long as they continue to disclose, they stay on the treadmill, but the first time they fail to disclose, the case is marked as recent and considered unfounded. If, after a recant, a child returns to the original story, the disclosure is considered "inconsistent" and thus unfounded. In the face of multiple interviews, most molested children will recant at some point because the sheer volume of interrogation leads them to feel that their disclosures are not being believed. Molested children, who are especially insecure, are very vulnerable to such tactics, and they may recant at some point because they feel threatened in general. [Others believe recantation is part of the process, that after a child discloses - the time will vary, but due to pressure from an outsider or pressure they've put on themselves, they recant and generally come back to their original disclosure if given the opportunity].

Child Witness Law and Practice 1990 Cumulative Supplement, John E. B. Myers:

A child's reaction to being subject to sexual assault of any form may include responses most adults, unfamiliar with the subject, find peculiar. A child may, for example, fail to disclose the defendant's criminal sexual acts immediately and may also oscillate between admitting the abuse and denying it. An expert witness's testimony merely aids the jurors in assessing the child's credibility under such abusive circumstances but in no way impinges upon the jury's obligation to decide ultimately the victim's credibility.

Child Welfare System:

The Child Welfare System Fact Sheet Children's Rights:

The act of separating a child from their family and Community imposes profound trauma on children. The briefest separation can cause emotional harm that can last a lifetime.

After evaluating whether the allegations of child maltreatment met statutory definitions of abuse or neglect, agencies screened out 45.8% of reports and screened 54.2% of reports for further investigation. ………… Black children are between 2 and 5 times more likely to have their cases screened in for investigation than white children.

Current estimates indicate that before turning 18, 37.4% of all children, including 53% of black children, in the U.S. will be subjected to a CPS investigation.

………..an estimated 18.4% of black children and 15.8% of Native American [children] will have a substantiated maltreatment case before they turn 18, compared to 11% of white children.

Every 2.5 minutes, a child in the U.S. is separated from their families and placed in foster care, too often with a stranger. In 2020, approximately 64% of all children, including 64% of black children and 65% of native American children, removed from their families experienced family separation because of "neglect." [There are a plethora of resources and services that could be allocated to prevent all of those removals.] Under the current system, "neglect" removals often result from conditions of poverty, including "inadequate housing" or "failure to provide adequate nutrition." Research indicates that black children are 15% more likely than white children to be separated from their families instead of receiving in-home services after an investigation.

… In 2021, a total of [well] over 600,000 children spent time in the U.S. foster care system. On average, children remain in state care for over a year and a half, and 5% of children in foster care languish in the system for 5 or more years.

In 2021, approximately 100,000 children -less than half of youth exiting foster care- were reunified with their families. Native American children are reunited with their families at lower rates than children of any other race.

The harms inflicted by the child welfare system, compounded with existing racial and socioeconomic barriers in American society, produce gross disparities between youth with lived experience in foster care [and the child welfare system] and other young adults.

Because of the trauma of separation, structural inequities, and frequent negative experiences …. Youth with a history in foster care [CPS, any part of the child welfare system] are also significantly more likely to suffer from serious and life-threatening mental health disorders. Individuals with prior involvement…report having attempted suicide within the past year at rates quadruple those of non-foster [etc.] youth without prior system involvement and experience post-traumatic stress disorder at double the rate of U.S. war veterans.

The Child Welfare System Fact Sheet (Children's Rights January 2023):

Under the current system, government agencies receive reports with claims of child maltreatment, investigate those claims [maybe], determine if they believe abuse or neglect occurred [incorrectly or correctly], and often remove children from their homes and place them into the physical and/or legal custody of the state.

The "front end" of the child welfare system is a series of decision points between an initial report of suspected child abuse or neglect and a child's removal from their home.

In 2020, U. S. child welfare agencies received a total of 3.9 million reports involving 7.1 million children. An overwhelming 65.7% of these reports came from law enforcement personnel and "helping professionals," including educational, medical, social services, and mental health personnel. At this stage, black children are reported twice as often as white people.

After evaluating whether the allegations of child maltreatment met statutory definitions of abuse or neglect in 2020, agencies screened out 45.8% of reports and screened 54.2% of reports for further investigation. At the screening stage, black children are between two and five times more likely to have their cases screened for investigation than white children.

During investigations, Child Protective Services ("CPS") and/or law enforcement conduct interviews, assessments, home visits, and various background checks to determine whether allegations of child maltreatment are substantiated. Current estimates indicate that before turning 18, 37.4% of all children, including 53% of black children, in the U.S. will be subjected to a CPS investigation.

Despite the common misconception that most maltreatment cases involve abuse, 76.1% of substantiated maltreatment reports in 2020 involved allegations of "neglect." In contrast, physical abuse constituted 16.5%, sexual abuse constituted 9.4%, and sex trafficking constituted 0.2% of substantiated maltreatment reports. Importantly, an estimated 18.4% of black children and 15.8% of Native American children will have a substantiated maltreatment case before they turn 18 compared to 11% of white children.

Every 2.5 minutes, a child in the US is separated from their families and placed in foster care, too often with a stranger. In 2020, approximately 64% of all children, including 64% of black children and 65% of Native American children, removed from their families experienced family separation because of "neglect." Under the current system, "neglect" removals often result from conditions of poverty, including "inadequate housing" or "failure to provide adequate nutrition." Research indicates that black children are 15% more likely than white children to be separated from their families instead of receiving in-home services after an investigation.

While most children in foster care live in family settings, 9% (approximately 35,300 children) live in institutions or group homes. Black and Native American children are more likely than children of any other race to experience three or more placements during their time in foster care. If children remain in foster care for 15 of the most recent 22 months, federal law allows states to legally terminate their parents' rights. One in 100 American children will experience termination of parental rights ('TPR") by the age of 18. For children removed from their families, 20% will experience TPR, including 18% of black children and 16% of Native American children. And 2021, more than 52,000 children who were rendered "legal orphans" by the state through TPR were awaiting adoption. Many of these children remain without guardians until they ultimately turn 18 and "age out" of the foster care system.

The harms inflicted by the child welfare system, compounded with existing racial and socioeconomic barriers in American Society, produce gross disparities between youth with lived experience…and other young adults.

Because of the trauma of separation, structural inequities, and frequent negative experiences,… youth with a history [of child welfare]… are also significantly more likely to suffer from serious and life-threatening mental health disorders. Individuals with prior involvement… report having attempted suicide within the past year at rates quadruple those …youth without prior system involvement and experience post-traumatic stress disorder at double the rate of U.S. war veterans.

American Psychological Association Improving Decision Making (Herman):

……a number of empirical studies have demonstrated that additional training alone does not result in any significant, sustained improvement in forensic interviewing skills, even when such training is intensive……….Only when intensive training is combined with subsequent ongoing, intensive, on-the-job supervision and feedback has there been a measurable positive impact on interviewing skills. However, Lamb et. Al. found that once the intensive on-the-job supervision was discontinued, child interviewers tended to revert to poor interviewing practices.

The current analysis suggests that the best hope for achieving significant improvements in the overall quality of FCSAEs does not lie with voluntary changes in behavior by practitioners or with that attractive –but expensive and ineffective—panacea, "more training," but rather with the dissemination, adoption, and enforcement of clear practice guidelines and, especially, with the creation and widespread adoption of an empirically-grounded, objective procedure for making substantiation decisions. Only top-down, systemic changes endorsed by scientific and legal experts and mandated by the courts, government policymakers, licensing boards, and professional organizations stand a reasonable chance of significantly reducing the current substantial risks to the public rom poorly conducted FCSAEs.

There are major challenges facing child welfare and juvenile justice systems in the United States (University of Michigan Child & Adolescent Data Lab, 2015):

According to the US Department of Health and Human Services, children's burial, there are over 430,000 children in foster care. According to the Office of Juvenile Justice and Delinquency Prevention (OJJDP), there were approximately 850,000 juvenile arrests and 45,000 juvenile offenders living in residential placements in 2016. Complex family issues, including poverty, unemployment, mental health and the abuse of alcohol and other drugs, interfere with important measures of child safety, family stability and the interruption of offending trajectories.

Rethinking Foster Care: Why Our Current Approach to Child Welfare Has Failed, Vivek Sankaran, Christopher Church, SMU Law Review Forum, April 2020:

Over the past decade, the child welfare system has expanded, with vast public and private resources being spent on the system. Despite this investment, there is scant evidence suggesting A meaningful return on investment. This article argues that without a change in the values held by the system, increased funding will not address the public health problems of child abuse and neglect.

[On] the impact of family separation, one prominent pediatrician stated, "If people paid attention at all to the science, they would never do this."

The National Association of Council for Children created a certification program signifying "an attorney's specialized knowledge, skill, and verified expertise in the field of child welfare law." Since the program's inception in 2006, over 800 attorneys have become certified. In addition to lawyers, each year, more than 85,000 volunteers, court-appointed special advocates or guardians at litem work with more than 260,000 children to make recommendations to juvenile courts about what is in the best interests of those children.

Despite the significant investment of resources discussed, the child welfare system has made little progress in improving justice for children and families involved in the child welfare system.

Only 25% of children referred to CPS ever receive any type of assistance from the agency. Yet we continue to fund this system, which fails to make meaningful progress to protect children from abuse and neglect.

The rate at which the child welfare system protects victims from subsequent harm is also stagnant.

During the most recent annual reporting period, The child welfare system separated more than 1/4 of a million children from their parents. During the 2010 FFY, the average monthly removal rate was 2.98 removals for every 10,000 children in the population. During the 2018 FFY, the average monthly removal rate was 2.9 for 10,000 children.

Despite all the efforts discussed in the previous section, the child welfare system is still identifying and removing victims at rates similar to what they were in 2010 and is not succeeding in reducing the number of maltreated children. As the authors have previously discussed, many of these children may have never needed to be separated from their parents for purposes of placement in foster care [or otherwise]. The trauma of separating children from their families is far more potent when it is laced with the injustice of unnecessary separation.

Children in foster care are prescribed psychotropic medications at significantly higher rates than children in the general population. The overutilization of psychotropic medications for children in foster care negatively impacts their well-being and raises concerns about safety, overdiagnosis, consent, and monitoring. Psychotropic medications raise both clinical and legal concerns.

One state reports that 21.7% of children in care are on an antipsychotic.

Not only has the child welfare system failed in reducing the rate at which it separates families our system has not made progress in supporting families so that children can return home after removal. In fact, between 2007 and 2017, the rate of children in foster care being reunified with their parents dropped from reunification representing 53% of all exits to 49%. Rather than sending more kids home, our system has increased its rate of permanently terminating parental rights over the last decade. The most recent data reveal that the child welfare system now terminates parental rights at a rate of 8.36 per 10,000 children. The increasing rate at which we judicially destroy family bonds is a strong rebuke to our system's goal of keeping children safe with their families whenever possible.

The rate at which children are maltreated has not gone down. The number of children taken from their families and placed in foster care [or otherwise] has increased. Indicators of child well-being for children in foster care are, at best, stubbornly stagnant. Our system continues to increase its rate of terminating parental rights, permanently separating children from their families. We must do better.

We must ensure that the agency caseworker is not the lone decision-maker.

Second, we must ensure that systems treat each family with dignity and respect, regardless of the allegations in the petition. Given that child welfare seeks to reunify families even after children are removed from their parents, it is crucial that we engage families.

To better serve children, policymakers should allocate the majority of funds in a flexible way that allows states to support initiatives that prevent child maltreatment rather than those that simply react to a child who has already been abused or neglected.

The Child Welfare System in U.S. News: What's Missing? (Berkely Media Studies Group, Sarah Han, BA; Laura Nixon, MPH; Pamela Mejia, MPH; Daphne Marvel, BA; & Lori Dorfman, DrPH; January 2019):

When the child welfare system is strong, everyone benefits– not just children but parents, families, and whole communities. One promising approach to strengthen the child welfare system is bridging the disconnect between child welfare and domestic violence services. These services have historically responded to victims separately, although many families who are involved in the child welfare system also experienced domestic violence. In fact, in up to 60% of the families where domestic violence is identified, some form of co-occurring child abuse is also present, and too often, that abuse has fatal consequences.

In recent years, child welfare organizations and domestic violence programs have begun collaborating in order to better meet the needs of adults affected by domestic violence and children experiencing family violence.

If news coverage doesn't illustrate the broader environments that surround a specific incidence of child abuse or neglect, it may be harder for the public and policymakers to see the impact of environments and systems, including the child welfare system.

News coverage also sets the agenda for public policy debates. Journalist's decisions about which issues to cover can raise the profile of a topic, whereas topics not covered by news media may remain outside public dialogue and policy debate.

Only 12% of U.S. news about child welfare from July 1, 2016 -June 30[th,] 2017, mentioned both child welfare and domestic violence.

Predicting and Responding to Physical Abuse in Young Children Using NCANDS; Children and Youth Services Review (Palusci, Smith, and Paneth):

Recurrent rates for child abuse or neglect reported in the literature have ranged from 9% to 67%, depending on the age of the child, length of follow-up, services provided and type of initial or subsequent abuse, and whether the study looked at repeat reports, hospitalizations or actual maltreatment.

Subsequent PA [physical abuse] can occur after any form of original maltreatment, but when the first episode of maltreatment is PA, the risk of repeat PA seems higher than any other form of maltreatment. Even when repeat PA does not recur, neglect and emotional abuse can continue or escalate after investigation and treatment.

National Children's Advocacy Center:

Perpetrators can be anyone, including family members, family friends, coaches, teachers, clergy, babysitters, and any other acquaintance.

Manipulation:

- Perpetrators are patient. They work to gain the trust and friendship of the child and, often, of the entire family.

- Perpetrators pay attention to what a child likes and dislikes to find ways to interact with the child.

- Perpetrators find ways to be alone with the child.

- Perpetrators often "test" a child's ability to protect himself/herself by engaging in touching activities such as hugs and kisses, back rubs, horseplay, etc.

- Perpetrators take advantage of a child's natural curiosity. If the child seems comfortable and/or curious about touching, then slowly increase the sexual contact.

- Listen to and believe children, especially if they are trying to disclose. Children very RARELY lie about sexual abuse.

A History of Child Protection in America (John E.B. Myers, Xlibris Corporation, 2004):

Less Adversarial Protective Services

Efforts are underway to make intervention in families less adversarial. A promising development is "differential response," which reduces reliance on authoritarian intervention. In her book on differential response, Jane Waldfogel describes the current CPS system: "The system focuses on identifying and responding to child victims and adult perpetrators. The initial contact with the family is reactive and investigative, concentrating on gathering information to confirm or disprove the allegations made by the reporter. Investigators and families are also keenly aware that the information being collected during the investigation might be used as evidence in future court proceedings. To the extent that parents are seen as perpetrators, it is assumed that they are part of the problem, not part of the solution. It is also assumed that many parents will not cooperate without the use or threatened use of state authority. Thus, the model for CPS operations, particularly at the investigative stage, is adversarial: it is reactive, investigative, suspicious of parents, and authoritative."

Differential response lessens the adversarial nature of protective work by limiting investigation and authoritative intervention to cases of severe abuse or neglect and to situations where children are at risk of serious harm. In less serious cases, the emphasis is on voluntary assessment and services and on programs that capitalize on parents' strengths rather than their weaknesses. Differential response is based on the assumption that most parents who abuse or neglect their children can be helped and that help is more likely to succeed when it is non-threatening and voluntary rather than when it is imposed from without.

Of course, differential response is no newer than home visiting. Child protection workers have always responded to families on a case-by-case basis. What is promising about today's differential response is its potential to reduce the adversarial relationship between parents and professionals, clearing the way for voluntary services.

Some worry Americans are losing there is sense of community, their desire to get involved, and their willingness to extend a helping hand...... Stronger, more caring communities help struggling parents and lower the amount of child abuse and neglect.

As child protection became a specialized field within child welfare, CPS agencies tended to withdraw from the communities they serve, setting up shops in government buildings far removed- physically and psychologically from clients. CPS workers venture forth to investigate reports, then screw back to the office for paperwork. Ensconced in the safety and order of government buildings, it is easy to lose contact with the people who need help. Fortunately, social workers increasingly realizing that the isolation of the office is comfortable but ineffective. CPS agencies across the country are placing social workers in community centers, schools, and similar locations. CPS professionals are building relationships with citizen groups and community leaders, replacing years of distrust with a sense of shared responsibility for children. Increasingly, CPS professionals realize they cannot do their job alone and that child protection requires the coordinated efforts of government agencies, private organizations, concerned citizens, churches, and many others.

Child Protective Services is in the midst of a revival kindling of the optimism that motivated the "child savers" of the Progressive Era and their descendants in the 1960s who pulled child abuse from obscurity. As social workers returned to communities, I found myself wondering: could we be witnessing the rebirth of the settlement movement? It is possible, though; I'm not holding my breath. Yet, if the spirit that motivated settlement workers should return, what a renaissance we would see in social welfare and social work!

[In Michigan, the Department of Health and Human Services is focusing on Front-End Redesign. The person who heads this is incredible, she is passionate about the work, she is driven, and she genuinely cares. This is in great hands and I hope it remains in her hands. The Guy Thompson Parent Advisory Council is overseen by the same person, but our immediate 'supervisor' is another very passionate and caring individual who is incredibly effective. I feel very blessed for these two individuals simply to be in my life, even more, so that I have the privilege of working with them on what I am most passionate about protecting children. I have made great friends through the Council as well. I feel we all have something in common, and we share a bond in that. Furthermore, I am proud to say that of the various projects and committees I have served on and currently serve on; I am elated at the number of wonderful people who are very devoted to creating positive changes. I have had the honor of meeting and working with some amazing people. Having said that, I am hopeful. My sons and I were destroyed by governmental agencies, many "professionals," and, of course, their paternal family. If I were not part of GTPAC, I wouldn't know of the changes the department is trying to make, and I would still be terribly angry, bitter, and depressed. But knowing that Michigan is trying does at least show there is knowledge that there was/is a problem, and it needs to be fixed. I get to use our (my sons and my) experiences to shed light on where problems existed and might still exist. I will never forget the caseworkers who made such damaging reports and biased decisions (their rudeness and tone with the words they spoke and those they wrote play out in my head over and over), nor all the dominos that fell because of those reports (the judge, police officers, parole officers, etc.), nor will I ever forgive the custody evaluator who got it all so wrong. They all sentenced my sons to a life of pain and horror. For the sake of my sons, and every other child in Michigan, and the rest of the country, I'm going to make a promise to you, my friend, that I will try my hardest to eliminate the hatred in my heart for the current Child Protective Services and do everything in my power to contribute to positive change for children - and humanity].

The Backlash Child Protection Under Fire, John E.B. Myers

Sylvia Pizzini offers a view of the backlash from the perspective of a county child protective services (CPS) administrator. Pizzini describes the legislative framework of the U.S. child protection system, beginning with the Social Security Act of 1935 and working forward to the Adoption Assistance and Child Welfare Act of 1980. Pizzini outlines the value conflicts and inconsistencies inherent in the laws governing child protection. These conflicts and inconsistencies account in considerable measure for the difficulty experienced in implementing effective protective services for children.

Wilson and Steppe describe the backlash from the perspective of state-level CPS administrators. [They] begin by outlining the common elements -and common problems- of CPS agencies. For example, Wilson and Steppe describe the difficulty of attracting sufficient numbers of competent professionals to CPS. [They} go on to define and analyze six criticisms commonly leveled against CPS: (a) CPS accepts anonymous reports and does not adequately screen reports, (b) CPS confuses poverty with neglect, (c) CPS has too much power, (d) CPS staff is not equipped to do the job, (e) reporting laws encourage frivolous reports, and (f) there is a lack of due process protection for individuals names are in the child abuse registries. Wilson and Steppe's analysis is stimulating because they do not make excuses for CPS. On the contrary, they fully acknowledge the many problems plaguing CPS.

[Personally, I think that our mandated reporting laws are lacking in many ways. Sometimes, I think it should be nonexistent. Other times, I think it serves a purpose. However, just because there are laws mandating a report to be made does not mean it will be made. In our case, many members of the school staff didn't report anything as it was a small-town school, and they had a long history with the paternal family. So, it just kept getting swept under the rug. It seems that intake does not properly value anonymous tips because they are anonymous tips, or tips from parents, because they immediately think it is not a legitimate concern, nor mandated reports because the individual was "mandated" to report something, but that does not mean the reporter is legitimately concerned for the child. That sword has a few edges.]

Historically, political progress in child welfare has been linked to the success of feminism (Gordon, 1988).

Social problem movements, even successful ones, face resistance, usually of two sorts: oppositional and inertial. The oppositional form consists of organized opposition groups –an example would be the Tobacco Institute, an organized group that has opposed the movement on behalf of nonsmoker's rights, or the National Rifle Association, which has opposed the gun control movement. The inertial resistance is just as real but more diffuse: it consists of bureaucratic obstacles and delays, professional turf guarding, lack of funding, the pressure of other competing social problems advocates, and public apathy and boredom.

…a countermovement is an opposition that develops in response or in reaction to the success of another social movement…. Phyllis Schlafly and the Eagle Forum represents a countermovement organized in response to the women's movement and the lobbying for the Equal Rights Amendment. What we are calling the child abuse backlash is also such a countermovement.

Organized opposition groups have historical and economic roots –such as those of the tobacco industry. They often have massive resources and a great deal of experience in public relations and political activism.

Already, child advocates have had some success checking the more damaging claims of the backlash through research: for example, the idea that non-abused children can be easily induced to make false allegations of abuse (Goodman & Clarke-Stewart 1991).

County child protective services (CPS) agencies are the most important link in the child protection chain. The other links are medicine, nursing, law, mental health, judiciary, probation, police, and related professions. Although CPS is the most important link in the chain, few would deny that it is the weakest (Hechler, 1988).

The weakness of CPS results from several factors. First, social work is accorded a lower professional status in society than law, medicine, or psychology…. The low social status of social work undermines the fabric of the profession…….It is sadly ironic that the profession with the most complex and demanding responsibilities receives the lowest professional status and remuneration.

Probably the major contributor to the weakness of CPS is chronically inadequate funding….it has always lacked the resources to do the job…..Vincent DeFrancis described a nationwide study of child protective services and lamented that "most disturbing was the finding that no state and no community has developed a Child Protective Services program adequate in size to meet the service needs of all reported cases of child neglect, abuse, and exploitation.

Society's recognition of child abuse as a widespread problem is tenuous, half-hearted, and grudging, and professionals must be alert for rumblings of disbelief. Today, such rumblings are heard across the United States and in Europe. With society predisposed to ignore the uncomfortable reality of child abuse, the escalating backlash places us on the brink of a new era of disbelief.

The war against children. Every year, we let hundreds of children die, force thousands more to live with strangers, and throw a million innocent families into chaos. We call this "child protection.." (Wounded Innocents: The Real Victims of the War Against Child Abuse, Richard Wexler, 1990).

We allow untrained, inexperienced, and sometimes incompetent workers to label parents as abusers and even remove children from their homes entirely on their own authority.

[Or to remove children from their protector and hand them over to their abusers, ignoring the facts and seeing a case through a biased lens].

If the child protection system is out of control, who is to blame? Professionals, of course (Nathan, 1993; von Hoffman, 1992)

And from (Richard, John ?) Gardner:

Thus, among judges, prosecutors, and other professionals, we find unspecified numbers who are sadistic, incompetent, opportunistic, stupid, or *pedophilic*. Gardner (1991) himself assures us that *"there is a bit of pedophilia in every one of us."*

[Really? Because I disagree. I didn't want to include anything from Gardner as he has single-handedly been such a destructive force against women. However, at the same time, you can't fully fight a battle unless you fully know what you're up against.]

The Hostage Child Sex Abuse Allegations in Custody Disputes Leora N. Rosen and Michelle Etlin:

It is comfortable to believe that incest and child sexual abuse need not concern us because we have institutions to deal with these problems. This book disallows that complacency and shows that the system has failed and, worse -that it generated a dangerous atmosphere of denial and cover-up. Focusing on five case studies, Rosen and Etlin expose a systemic breakdown so fundamental, so irrational, and so shocking that the necessity of radical reform becomes apparent.

While explaining the historical, social, and psychological backdrop for this state of affairs, the authors refuse to minimize the problem. They demonstrate that most of the solutions being proposed by professionals in the field are doomed to frustration and failure. In their final chapter, Rosen and Etlin present a proposal for relief [I have ideas about solutions as well!] While it is too late to undo the damage already done by the combined forces of child sexual abuse and institutional denial, this book can at least serve the children now trapped like hostages in this social war.

Scandalous Politics Child Welfare Policy in the States, Juliet F. Gainsborough:

Child welfare policy regulates all stages of a child's contact with state agencies, from the initial charge of abuse and/or neglect to decisions about what forms of intervention are needed to protect the child.

…the fact that the rate at which reports are substantiated has declined over time, from 65% of cases substantiated in 1976 to 27.5% in 2001.

….Changes in the rate at which abuse and neglect reports are substantiated may also reflect changes in how reports are treated by child welfare agencies rather than changes in the degree to which reports of abuse correspond to the real level of abuse and neglect.

…Social programs with a clear focus on helping low-income individuals tend to be the least generous and most politically vulnerable. In addition, linking child welfare policy with antipoverty policy does not necessarily resolve the argument between those who focus on individual wrongdoing as the root of child abuse and those who focus on systemic contributors to abuse and neglect. Antipoverty policy debates feature a similar argument between those who identify individual behavior as the root cause of poverty and those who focus on structural explanations of poverty.

The myth of classlessness may encourage a policy focus on individual pathology rather than on social structure or institutions, but critics of the current child welfare system also suggest that the reality that those involved with the child welfare system are disproportionately poor and African American shape the politics of child welfare......child welfare policy, just like welfare reform, is shaped by "strong and deeply imbedded stereotypes about Black family dysfunction" and "stereotypes of Black maternal unfitness" (Dorothy Roberts, 2002).

...the child welfare system should focus on family preservation rather than child removal.

... In fact, children involved with the child welfare system disproportionately come from poor families.

.......medical professionals may be more likely to accept that injuries to a child are accidental when the family is white and middle-class (Hill, 2006).

... The federal government has passed a number of important pieces of legislation that provide incentives for states to adopt particular approaches to child protection, foster care, and adoption. The most significant are the 1980 Adoption Assistance and Child Welfare Act (AACWA) and the 1997 Adoption and Safe Families Act (ASFA). AACWA focused on encouraging states to move children more quickly out of foster care, with an emphasis on family reunification as the preferred alternative. Receiving federal funds for child welfare was contingent on the state's demonstration that the state agency was making what AACWA called "reasonable efforts" to reunite children in foster care with their biological families (Wilkonson-Hagen, 2004). The policy pendulum swung in the other direction with the

340

1997 passage of ASFA. Although the stated purpose of ASFA was similar, in terms of emphasizing the importance of ending "foster care drift," the focus was now on finding permanent adoptive homes for foster children rather than on family reunification. The timeline for parents to establish their fitness to have their children returned was shortened, and social service agencies were instructed to engage in concurrent planning -that is, developing plans to prepare such children for adoption while their parents' attempt at reunification was ongoing. Receipt of federal incentives was now tied to the state's success at increasing the number of adoptions of foster care children. Additional financial reward was attached to the return of the child to his or her biological family. By requiring states to meet changing federal standards and attaching financial incentives to compliance, these pieces of legislation can be expected to significantly shape state policy. Furthermore, some observers of child welfare policymaking at the federal level suggest that national legislation is also shaped by scandal.

In addition to the effect of national policy on state behavior, another dimension to consider in a federal system is the relationship between state action and local government.

In ASFA's view.....AACWA had focused states too much on efforts to reunify families. Instead, ASFA was designed to speed up the process of terminating parental rights by placing time limits on the efforts to reunify families, delineating instances in which states need not make reasonable efforts to reunify families, and allowing states to make concurrent plans for termination of parental rights while efforts to reunify were in progress. In addition, the legislation created financial incentives for states to increase the number of adoptions and established "a state accountability system, whereby states face financial penalties for failure to demonstrate improvements in child outcomes" (Murray and Gesiriech, 2008; Stein, 2006).

Interviewing Children About Sexual Abuse Controversies and Best Practice, Kathleen Coulborn Faller

Dr. Kathleen Faller is the Director of the Family Assessment Clinic, which is a part of the U of M School of Social Work:

Child sexual abuse was "rediscovered" in the late 1970s and early 1980s. At that time, several influential professionals argued for a believing stance toward sexual abuse allegations. Sgroi (1980), a pioneer in the sexual abuse field, wrote, "Recognition of sexual molestation in a child is entirely dependent on the individual's inherent willingness to entertain the possibility that the condition may exist." Herman (1981) and McCarty (1981) took a priori position that most accounts are true. Drawing upon clinical experience and research, Faller (1984, 1988a) asserted that false allegations are quite rare and pointed out that children have little motivation for making a false allegation, but offenders have considerable motivation for persuading professionals that children are either lying, mistaken, or crazy. Similarly, in his conceptualization of the Child Sexual Abuse Accommodation Syndrome, Summit (1983) assumed that children were suffering because of actual abuse but, because of their powerlessness, accommodated themselves to the abuse, delayed disclosing it, and sometimes recanted after disclosure.

Very young children pose a special challenge for interviewers, especially interviewers working in a forensic context. Very young children lack the language to communicate, have greater difficulty using media, and are more suggestible than older children. These characteristics, coupled with their greater vulnerability, make their assessment especially difficult for professionals.

Although there are challenges to assessing very young children for sexual abuse, there are some strategies interviewers can use. These include gathering data from a range of sources, taking time over several sessions to understand the child's communications, using developmentally appropriate questions and media, carefully considering all information during decision-making, and structuring safety plans for very young children.

Despite the fact that very young children less frequently disclose and provide fewer details when they do, compared with older children, there is evidence that they also are sexually abused (National Child Abuse and Neglect Data System, 2005 a and b). Interviewers, therefore, are advised to use the special methods necessary with young children in order to provide them protection and justice.

[An] Important factor that predicts disclosure is whether or not the child has a supportive caretaker....Of 12 children who disclosed sexual abuse when interviewed, 10 had supportive caretakers.

Recantation often occurs after substantiation (Jones & McGraw).

...research indicates that, for many children, disclosure is a process that may involve initial disclosure of abuse and later retraction.

Unfortunately, some authors (e.g., Besharov, 1990; Gardner 1991, 1992, 1995; Wexler, 1990), referring to the proportion of cases that are not substantiated, imply that an unsubstantiated case is the equivalent of a deliberate false allegation. Based upon this distortion, these writers have asserted that there is an overwhelming flood of false, maliciously made reports of child maltreatment. The implication of this assertion is that at least a million calculated false reports are made every year. As noted above, based upon the 2003 official reports, which are limited by the number of states that report deliberate false reports, the actual number (n=436) is 0.04% of the more than one million reports suggested by some writers (e.g., Besharov, 1990). To arrive at the 0.04% estimate, a number of assumptions were made, which potentially limits its accuracy.

Nevertheless, existing data suggests that calculated false reports represent quite a small percentage of reports of child maltreatment.

Courts and child protection agencies often assume that the retraction of an allegation is a signal that the original allegation was false….Researchers have found that a proportion of children recant in actual cases of sexual abuse…..In some of these studies, sexual abuse is documented by another indicator of abuse, such as medical evidence or offender confession.

The practice of making inferences about the likelihood of sexual abuse from behaviors during interactions between the child and the accused parent has been challenged.

Polygraph results have been used as one of the several measures by one team of practitioners/researchers, and the polygraph is often used by law enforcement to screen cases for criminal prosecution. If the suspect passes the polygraph, the veracity of the allegation is questioned. Conversely, if the suspect fails a polygraph, this failure adds credibility to the allegation. Although the polygraph has its proponents, the scientific validity and reliability of the polygraph have yet to be demonstrated……the properties of the polygraph, in that it measures autonomic nervous system response when responding to questions, make it particularly problematic in sexual abuse cases.

Despite the evident focus of the American Academy of Child and Adolescent Psychiatry (1997) practice parameters on false allegations, its list of causes of false allegations is prefaced by a statement that most allegations are true.

Mandated Reporting:

In Michigan, Few Prosecuted for Failure to Report (Ross Jones, posted February 8, 2018, WXYZ Detroit 7 ABC):

Adults who failed to report suspected abuse of children are seldom punished in Michigan, a 7 Action News investigation has found. Michigan's mandatory reporter law, which requires teachers, doctors and other professionals that regularly interact with children to report suspected abuse, has led to charges only 69 times since 1990 statewide-not even 3 prosecutions per year. Of those cases, only 17 have led to a conviction.

While the law lists more than 20 other professionals as mandated reporters, positions like coaches and trainers are never mentioned. That means the Michigan State coaches and trainers alleged to have been told about Nassar's abuses may not, under Michigan law, have had to report them.

"We're talking about children," Seikaly said. "You would think those would be the people we most want to protect."

[I have been and remain conflicted regarding Michigan's Mandated Reporter Law. There were a plethora of school staff that *should have* reported suspected abuse of my children but didn't. Nothing ever became of that because nothing ever came of the reality of my sons having been continuously abused. I also think it's a double-edged sword, in that when a 'professional' hears something that could mean many other things, but they feel they *have* to report it because of the law, so they do, that could turn into disruption for the family when there should not have been any, it also may be completely blown off by Intake because the Reporter thought it was nothing but they *had* to report it, and conversely it was something that needed to be investigated. However, it was not investigated because of the minimization of the mandated reporter role. It also, is a crying shame that Intake does not take seriously calls from parents. When children are very young, infants, toddlers, and the like, parents are typically the only ones who will see disturbing behaviors and hear disturbing comments. In the world of Michigan CPS, it's as if a child doesn't count until they go to school. So, who collectively would be responsible for the fact that the first year of life for a child in Michigan is its most dangerous?]

Small Town Public School:

Porn searches that were found on my youngest son's school-issued computer that wasn't successful because of internal blocks. He was in the first grade. Principal PennyWise blew it off and swept it under the rug, "boys will be boys," she said. PennyWise said that about almost everything, other than behaviors, she thought she could blame me -even though I could barely see them. She excused much of their sexually explicit behaviors (in 1st, 2nd, and 3rd grades and continuing). She also called my sons thugs.

My sons were abruptly picked up from Lexington, KY, and taken to a hotel room to wait until the ex parte motion to change custody motion was heard by a judge in Lexington the next day. Unfortunately, that judge -only knowing the details they were fed to him/her, upheld the motion. So, on that day -which would have been the 16th of January, 2008, my sons were driven north to Michigan. What I know of that trip is devastating to me; they were both crying, they were throwing up, and with grandparents, they had not seen in about a year and a half, whom they did not wish to see, much less have to live with them. Gabriel spoke for Castiel because only he and I could clearly understand him. It was a culture shock to go into that family for them. I'm sure they were met with a lot of people when they arrived, none of them having any boundaries. Most are loud, bossy, controlling, very strict, see children as property, and are bombastic. Our home was none of that. Granny's (my mom) home too, was always safe, loving, caring, and fun, but never crazy. My very young sons were taken from me -their primary caregiver, trusted, safe, gentle, and loving. Also, from their granny, whom they adored, who always was very loving and caring to both boys. And their papa (granny's husband then), who they never saw again.

They were soon enrolled in a very small-town school system (with small-minded people). Gabriel was taken from a kindergarten he really enjoyed in Lexington, where he had already made a friend and was placed into a school that was completely different. The teachers were old-fashioned and mean, and the kids weren't that great either. The teacher, Gabriel, was one of the worst. She was temperamental, she yelled a lot, she was very short on patience and kindness, and she didn't even have a teaching degree. Castiel was enrolled in a preschool, which was a very negative experience as well. It was a co-op, so every day, there were different parents there. Many of those parents had complained a lot about Castiel's behavior, and they clearly did not like him. Some had petitioned to have him removed. Also, Castiel's grandmother would be there some days, which I can't imagine as making for a great day there, or a great day when he got to X's either. This school system was the one that their great-grandmother (at least that I know of, but probably went back for generations) and grandparents had attended, as well as their father and his sister. Everybody knew everybody else, and if you were an outsider, someone would create a story about you that others would now 'know,' that generally was never positive. X and his family had lots to say about me, they even had some documents to back many of their lies up with (for instance, the custody evaluation, which they threw in everyone's faces). Thereby beginning years of nightmarish school experiences for my sons and my "Hester Prynne" years. During all the school years - as I could never get X to agree to change schools (Why would he do that? This entire system worked to placate him.) so, the boys and I were stuck with the Confederate flag waving, backward, redneck, racist, biased, judgmental, gossipy, rude, and teeny-tiny narrow-minded staff and parents, who gleefully glared at me - or wouldn't look at me at all, while they whispered to each other as I walked by. I always thought of Hester Prynne and how graceful and dignified she carried herself wearing her embroidered Scarlet Letter on her dress while the townspeople glared and gawked at her, and I would try to emulate that, looking them dead straight in the eyes, right through them, or not acknowledging them at all. Even though I was sure my sons could pick up on how they treated me, and that was the worst part, those people were never worth a damn to me. It was ironic that we were all standing there waiting to pick up our elementary school children, and we were supposed to be the adults. But for so many of them, they chose to be petty and childish, so much so that their children appeared to be the adults in the family. If they wanted to focus on me, ok, have at it. I was watching the door, because I just couldn't wait a second more to see my favorite two people in the entire world!

We had joint legal custody, which meant every doctor's appointment, every permission slip, every I.E.P. meeting, every 'meeting' at school, and if something happened to them at school, I was supposed to get a call. This did not happen. I never knew of psychological tests conducted or I.E.P. meetings or that my youngest child even had an I.E.P., then was taken off, then was placed back on again. I never knew because I was never invited to these meetings, nor was I ever made aware of them. The same was true of doctor's appointments and the like.

Once I finally was made aware of the meetings, and of course attending them - the boys were in high school. I was not listened to. My opinion did not matter. X rambled on about how at *his* house, it was very structured, that Castiel enjoyed "family game night" and "family time"-all complete bullshit, but the idiotic principal and staff ate it all right up. It was because of the fraction of time my sons spent with me and 'everybody knows how unstructured my home was' (right?) that the boys, especially Castiel, had such difficulty in school. Incidentally, every single one of the behavior issues that were stated by them to be either laziness, uncontrollable and oppositional, defiant, 'boys will be boys' type behavior (sexualized), disruptive, ADHD, not trying hard enough, and aggressive is all very well explained as to what those roots are in this section. But, the teachers apparently could never get the wool off of their heads that X and his family had wrapped so tightly. They never questioned the sexualized behaviors or the porn searches by a first grader on a school-issued iPad. They never wondered why there was poop smeared on the bathroom walls across from one of their classrooms on several occasions or pee everywhere (elementary school). They didn't think twice about this young child mooning other children or making sexual comments -also kindergarten and beyond, never thought twice about the swearing and the incredibly demeaning vicious name-calling or the outrageously aggressive behavior and statements made by these children. No, these were just swept under the rug as 'typical kindergarten, first grade, etc., boy behavior'. Even stepping back, knowing this and having experienced years of these behaviors, they continued to punish my sons with detentions, in-school suspensions, and school suspensions, loss of privileges, placing them in a corner or in the front or back of the room, always being sent to the office, and so on. To me, one does not need training or books to see this for what it is. My sons were being terribly abused by their father; like most abusers, he put on a show, or even when he didn't put on a show -it didn't seem to matter. They continued to only see what they wanted to see and chose to ignore my son's screams for help.

Right from the start, the school took X's word for the name changes he and his family made. Until I corrected their last names, at the very least. There was nothing I could do about their first names at that point.

I never knew of events - field trips, Christmas shows the children put on. The teachers never informed me of anything, and I could never get any of them to call me back. I grew tired of leaving messages. I think of my sons at a Christmas party or school event and looking for me in the crowd (their father is a sick man, and most likely told them he told me about it -when he didn't), when they didn't see me (because I didn't even know about it) how do you think they felt? It's just more anti-mom propaganda.

PennyWise forbade me to allow my 5-year-old son to sit on my lap when I visited my sons for lunches, then strictly limited my lunchtime visits, who then went on to middle school the very same year Castiel did, then forbade me to bring lunches to them in middle school, for the reason she told me, and the then probation officer (they both had each other's backs) for Castiel that my coming there to bring them lunches is disruptive, and that it makes the other children feel bad, that they aren't having lunches brought to them. Seriously.

Teachers regularly said my sons were not trying hard enough -that they understood and knew the material, they just weren't doing the work. That, too, is bullshit. The teachers were lazy and didn't want to do their jobs. I have a 22-year-old son who has difficulty with reading, spelling, and writing. For my 19-year-old son, his math teacher repeatedly expressed his disapproval of Castiel and his just not trying. Castiel did not understand the material and I know this to be true, as when Covid happened and he began to homeschool with me, I discovered exactly what level he was at in every subject, including math.

Both boys were followed around by staff members in the school, especially if they were out of the classroom during class time. If either of them needed to use the bathroom, a staff member would follow him into the bathroom.

In the fall of 2008,- Gabriel would have been in first grade. Apparently, he had an eye 'exam' through the school. I only recently discovered going through some of the documents I was sent by the school after I repeatedly requested the entire files for both of my sons (which I never got). He had failed his eye exam and needed to go to an eye doctor. I never received this information, and of course, X never took him to have his eyes checked or to get him glasses. Gabriel finally just got eye insurance, so he went to the eye doctor, and what do you think they found? He needs glasses. He has been struggling to see all these years because of the neglect and intimidation of his father. Unbeknownst to me - Gabriel has been struggling at work to do his job because of his vision.

Before the boys were taken from Kentucky, I had taken Gabriel to have his eyes checked. He needed glasses then (he was 5), so I got him a pair that he wore in Kentucky, and he really liked them. However, as soon as he was in Michigan with the X's, the glasses went away right along with his hair and his name. My best guess -and most likely spot on, is that he was teased and mocked by them when he wore them.

Incidentally, regarding the records from the incompetent and secretive repugnant schools; I had requested several times to get their records. The reason for my repeated requests is that I knew I was not getting everything in the files -there were documents I knew they had, so what happened to them if they weren't in the boys' files? The last time I requested them, they didn't send me a thing, they didn't respond to my emails or voicemails - nothing. The two times I received the "files," there were repeated documents over and over again, there were blank pages, and a lot of non-information information. I knew they were covering their butts because they had broken the law when it came to the rights of my sons, as well as myself, and they knew it too.

They enrolled Castiel in two gym classes a day for several semesters: in elementary school, middle and high school.

School, for them, was very similar to being at their father's, which is exactly the way X wanted it.

This little school system added massive amounts of damage to my already destroyed sons. They failed them miserably academically, personally, and psychologically.

Child Abuse and Academics:

Early Exposure to Child Maltreatment and Academic Outcomes (U of M Child & Adolescent Data Lab, Joseph P. Ryan, Brian A. Jacob, Max Gross, Brian E. Perron, Andrew Moore, Sharlyn Ferguson, November 2018):

Early childhood trauma increases the risk of academic difficulties.

African American and poor students were more likely to be investigated for maltreatment. Children associated with maltreatment investigations scored significantly lower on standardized math and reading tests, were more likely to be identified as needing special education, and were more likely to be held back at least one grade. Involvement with CPS is not an infrequent event in the lives of young children, and … within some school districts, maltreatment investigations are the norm. Child welfare and educational systems must collaborate so that the early academic struggles experienced by victims of maltreatment do not mature into more complicated difficulties later in life.

Identification of Domestic Violence Service Needs Among Child Welfare-Involved Parents with Substance Use Disorders: A Gender-Stratified Analysis (U of M Child & Adolescent Data Lab, Bryan G. Victor, Stella M. Resko, Joseph P. Ryan, Brian E. Perron, April 2018)

Approximately 42% of mothers and 33% of fathers with a substance use disorder had a concurrent need for domestic violence services. For both mothers and fathers, the strongest association was an additional need for mental health services.

Domestic violence is a commonly Co-occurring service need for child welfare-involved parents with identified substance use disorders, and associations with this need vary by gender.

Principals: More of Your Students Might Be Abused or Neglected than You Think (U of M Child & Adolescent Data Lab, Sarah D. Sparks, March 2018):

Generally, principals and teachers are not notified of child welfare investigations. Even if there is a formal confirmation of abuse or if the child is removed from the home, the effects do make themselves known. This study looked only at Michigan. It is in line with other studies that suggest about 20% of children experience this sort of trauma. As The Every Student Succeeds Act requires states to track the educational progress of vulnerable students like those in foster care, more states may begin to look at the rates of abused children in their own districts. The results of this study may make policymakers and educators rethink the structure of initiatives such as retaining students who cannot read proficiently by the end of grade three. Falling behind may be a warning sign that these students need counseling or other emotional support, not just academic enrichment.

How Child Abuse Affects Academic Achievement (CASA, Court Appointed Special Advocates for Children, Child Advocates of Montgomery County):

Unfortunately, it is a largely accepted fact that abused and neglected children are at higher risk for lower academic achievement… mistreated children have a greater instance of exhibiting poor social skills and classroom behavior problems. Maltreatment in the first five years of life nearly triples A child's likelihood of having academic problems. These children are far likelier to drop out of school before completing high school. According to research, children with special educational needs are more than seven times more likely to suffer physical abuse and neglect. Lower academic success can cause lifelong, negative psychosocial and economic consequences.

And sexually abused children, cognitive ability and memory scores, as well as academic achievement, are lower than their peers.

Most people do not realize that child sexual abuse is one of the most significant risks facing children today. One in 10 children is the victim of sexual abuse.

Texas law requires that all school employees participate in training concerning prevention techniques for and recognition of sexual abuse and other maltreatment of children, and free training is available. Early identification can help prevent or minimize the damage the child suffers. Multiple victimizations substantially increase the child's risk of poor academic functioning.

CASA (Court Appointed Special Advocates) How Child Abuse Affects Academic Achievement:

......It is a largely accepted fact that abused and neglected children are at higher risk for lower academic achievement. Additionally, studies show that children who have suffered from neglect exhibit lower academic achievement [than] children who were physically abused. Mistreated children have a greater instance of exhibiting poor social skills and classroom behavior problems. Maltreatment in the first five years of life nearly triples a child's likelihood of having academic problems. These children are far likelier to drop out of school before completing high school. According to research, children with special education needs are more than seven times more likely to suffer physical abuse and neglect. Lower academic success can cause lifelong, negative psychosocial and economic consequences.

In sexually abused children, cognitive ability and memory scores, as well as academic achievement, are lower than their peers. Most people do not realize that child sexual abuse is one of the most significant risks facing children today. One in ten children is a victim of sexual abuse.

Early identification can help prevent or minimize the damage the child suffers. Multiple victimizations substantially increase the child's risk of poor academic functioning.

Early Exposure to Child Maltreatment and Academic Outcomes (Ryan, Jacob, Gross, Perron, Moore, and Ferguson):

Regarding school success, the findings in the current study clearly indicate that early involvement with CPS is associated with a range of negative academic outcomes.

On average, students with a history of child protection involvement score at approximately the 30th percentile [or much lower]. These effects remain even after controlling for a wide range of important covariates, including race, gender, and poverty.

Brainwashing:

How Brainwashing Works (Julia Layton & Alia Hoyt, How Stuff Works, Updated September 7, 2023):

Brainwashing is a term that refers to both coercive persuasion and a systematic process aimed at altering an individual's beliefs, attitudes and behaviors through various psychological and manipulative means. This process often involves isolation, indoctrination, threats, rewards and the use of propaganda to remove free will.

In psychology, the study of brainwashing, often referred to as thought reform, falls into the sphere of " social influence." This type of influence happens every minute of every day. It's the collection of ways in which people can change other people's attitudes, beliefs and behaviors.

Brainwashing is a severe form of social influence that combines…..[a variety of] approaches to cause changes in someone's way of thinking without that person's consent and often against their will.

Because brainwashing is such an invasive form of influence, it requires the complete isolation and dependency of the subject…

The agent (the brainwasher) must have complete control over the target…

In the brainwashing process, the agent systematically breaks down the target's identity to the point that it falls apart. The agent then replaces it with another set of behaviors, attitudes and beliefs that work in the target's current environment.

There is often the presence or constant threat of physical harm, which adds to the target's difficulty in thinking critically and independently.

This is a systematic attack on a target's sense of self (also called the identity or ego) and their core belief system. The agent denies everything that makes the target who they are.. The target is under constant attack for days, weeks or months, [years]to the point that they become exhausted, confused and disoriented. In this state, their beliefs seem less solid.

[So, for Gabriel and Castiel, they were called names, everything they did was bad/wrong, they were humiliated and made fun of -they were shamed and shunned. Also, suddenly after custody was gained by them (all of this was done by all of the paternal family, which is why I frequently say "they") their heads were shaved, they changed their first and their last names, they lived with completely different 'rules' and received harsh punishments, in a completely different environment, they were cut off from having any access to me and any of their maternal family - including their granny of whom had played a very significant role in their lives up to that point, they had a completely different way of life - those people are very different from us (they are loud and bombastic, they drink somewhat heavily, there are absolutely no boundaries, nor privacy, they treat children, as well as animals as 'less than' - the adults are 'kings'), they had none of their former belongings, nor could they ever keep anything that I gave them or purchased for them for the following years, the school was in that family's pocket as the entire family had been enrolled in that school system for generations. In short, it was a culture shock -the family worked as a united front to cast me out and make sure they bombarded the boys with untruths such as I was 'crazy' and that the reason for any and all of their problems was because of me, they united in harsh punishment, and the humiliating and indoctrination of my sons. Every brief encounter I had with my sons -when and once I had them, each and every time was a bit more devastating than the last. I kept losing more and more of them.]

Brainwashing entails: 1. Isolation from the familiar, inclusive of, but not limited to, colleagues, family or the environment; 2. Absolute submission, and 3. A rigid system of reward and punishment in terms of obedience and unwillingness to cooperate, respectively. [As far as rewards are concerned, the boys have frequently mentioned that X made a lot of promises, but he never followed through on any of them].

Brainwashing is perhaps best known in the context of prisoners, war criminals, cults and, more recently, child custody cases. It is well recognized as a war crime and is deemed impermissible according to the Geneva Conventions. However, it isn't technically illegal in the United States, though there are some laws regarding manipulation.

Someone is said to be brainwashed when their mind is controlled or altered by force, changing what they believe, think, value and do.

Gaslighting:

Gaslighting (GoodTherapy, 10/15/2019):

Gaslighting is a type of emotional abuse. Someone who is gaslighting will try to make a targeted person doubt their perception of reality. The gaslighter may convince the target that their memories are wrong or that they are overreacting to an event. The abuser may then present their own thoughts and feelings as "the real truth."

The abuse is often subtle at first....over time, the person may second-guess their own emotions and memories. They may rely on the abuser to tell them if their memory is correct or if their emotions are "reasonable."The abuser uses this trust to gain control over their target.

A gaslighter often uses the target's "mistakes" and "overreactions" to cast themselves as the victim. For example, an abuser may scream accusations at a person until the other party must raise their voice to be heard. The abuser may then cut the conversation short, claiming the other person is "out of control" and "too aggressive." In some cases, the abuser may accuse the other person of being the true gaslighter.

Gaslighting is an insidious form of abuse that thrives on uncertainty. A person can grow to mistrust everything they hear, feel, and remember.

Gaslighting can also affect a person's social life. The abuser may manipulate them into cutting ties with friends and family. The person might also isolate themselves, believing they are unstable or unlovable.

Even after the person escapes the abusive relationship, the effects of gaslighting can persist. The person may still doubt their perceptions and have trouble making decisions. They are also less likely to voice their emotions and feelings, knowing that they are likely to be invalidated.

8 Signs That Someone Is In a Relationship With a Gaslighter (Verified by Psychology Today, Feb. 15, 2017)

If you repeat a lie often enough, it becomes accepted as the truth.

-attributed to various sources

Gaslighting is a form of persistent manipulation and brainwashing that causes the victim to doubt her or himself and ultimately lose his or her own sense of perception, identity, and self-worth. Gaslighting statements and accusations are usually based on blatant lies or exaggeration of the truth.

- 1. You are constantly reminded of your flaws.

- 2. You often feel insecure and uncertain.

- 3. You feel like you're walking on eggshells.

- 4. The gaslighter rarely admits flaws and is highly aggressive when criticized.

- 5. You make self-disparaging remarks.

- 6. Despite poor treatment, you look to the gaslighter for acceptance, approval, and validation.

- 7. You hide and excuse the gaslighter's coercion.

- 8. You feel stuck and/or alone.

Sadistic Abuse:

Sadistic Abuse: Definition, Recognition, and Treatment (Jean M. Goodwin, M.D., M.P.H.):

The term "sadistic abuse" Is proposed to designate extreme adverse.. experiences, which include sadistic sexual and physical abuse, acts of torture, over-control and terrorization, induction into violence, ritual involvements, and malevolent emotional abuse………describing torture, the Holocaust, prostitution, pornography and sex rings, cult abuse, and sadistic criminals.

… severe abuse, often occurring in childhood, may include torture, confinement, extreme threat and domination, overlapping physical and sexual abuse, and multiple victims or multiple perpetrator patterns of abuse. The term focuses on the presence of sadistic behaviors, exhaustively cataloged in the works of the Marquis de Sade (1789/1987).

Sadism was defined by Freud's mentor Kraft-Ebing (1894/1965) in the Nineteenth century as follows: "The experience of sexual or pleasurable sensations… Produced by acts of cruelty, such as bodily punishment inflicted on one's own body or witnessed in others, be the animals or human beings. It may also consist of the innate desire to humiliate, hurt, wound, or even destroy others…"

As Kraft-Ebing noted, emotional terror and successful deception are as important to sadists as the infliction of bodily harm. One study found that the victim's facial expression of pain and terror, achieved by whatever means, provided the sadist's most direct source of satisfaction (Heilbrun & Seif, 1988). As a sadistic serial killer put it: "The pleasure in the complete domination over another person is the very essence of this sadistic drive" (Deitz, Hazelwood, & Warren, 1990).

…in mnemonic form elements in a patient's account of childhood adversity that may alert the clinician to the possibility of sadistic or severe abuse in the developmental history. Such experiences may remain closely guarded secrets or confused mysteries even in those patients whose abuse was disclosed in childhood. Identification of extreme cases will become a priority as research in this area begins to quantify and differentiate the developmental impacts of different types of childhood adversity.

"sadistic abuse" emphasizes the severity of childhood adversity and the possibility of sadistic or sadomasochistic types of reenactments and transference.

Treatment of patients who present with histories of sadistic abuse involves trauma-based principles well described in the treatment of other child abuse survivors. Symptom variety, severity, and duration seem to reach higher levels in this group, and there are risks of complication and relapse in every phase of treatment.

Stockholm Syndrome:

Stockholm Syndrome (Good Therapy, goodtherapy.org):

Stockholm syndrome refers to symptoms that may occur in a person who is in a hostage situation or otherwise held prisoner. Typically, these feelings can be described as sympathy toward captors or the development of a bond with the captor or captors. This reaction can also be recognized in those who have left abusive relationships or other traumatic situations.

A person who develops Stockholm syndrome often experiences symptoms of post-traumatic stress: nightmares, insomnia, flashbacks, a tendency to startle easily, confusion, and difficulty trusting others.

From a psychological perspective, this phenomenon can be understood as a survival mechanism….. A connection with the perpetrator can potentially make the situation more bearable for the victim, and they make the captors more inclined to meet the captive's basic needs.

Why Stockholm Syndrome Happens and How to Help (Sharie Stines, PsyD., Good Therapy, goodtherapy.org, September 26, 2018):

Stockholm syndrome is a psychological condition that occurs when a victim of abuse identifies and attaches, or bonds, positively with their abuser.

Professionals have expanded the definition of Stockholm syndrome to include any relationship in which victims of abuse develop a strong, loyal attachment to the perpetrators of abuse; some of the populations affected by this condition include abused children, such as survivors and victims of domestic violence.

How Stockholm Syndrome Works

A condition can develop when victims of abuse believe there is a threat to their physical or psychological survival, and they also believe their abusers would carry out that threat.

When victims of kidnapping are treated humanely or simply allowed to live, they often feel grateful and attribute positive qualities to their captors, believing that they are, indeed, good people.

Intermittent good/bad behavior can create trauma bonds. Stockholm syndrome is a form of trauma bond. We're victims "wait out" the bad behaviors for the "crumbs" of good behaviors bestowed on them.

Victims are isolated from others. When people are in abusive systems, such as a kidnapping situation, access to outside input and communication is limited or even nonexistent. This way, only the perpetrators' input is allowed.

Stockholm Syndrome:

Bonding with the abuser is now seen as a common phenomenon by professionals who work with victims and hostages and maybe a universal survival strategy for victims of interpersonal violence.

The Stockholm Syndrome provides an explanation for the reluctance of both child and adult victims of child sexual abuse and, when already disclosed, to recant (later deny) that it occurred. Because of the close relationships between parent and child, betrayal bonds are present when abuse occurs. Dissociation is a central mechanism in betrayal theory, allowing victims to be unaware of information that may threaten the relationship with a trusted other or someone upon whom they depend for survival.

When discussing domestic violence or child sexual abuse, the dynamics of the Stockholm Syndrome can be helpful in understanding the behavior of child victims. The process that brings about this change in victims includes specific stages. These are:

- Compliance and denial—inability to get away.
- Coping with fear and anger—coping with emotions.
- Hope and Gratitude—change in thought process about the perpetrator.
- Self-deprecation and depression—change in self-perception
- Accepting and adapting –coming to terms with reality.

Accommodation Syndrome
- Secrecy
- Helplessness
- Entrapment and accommodation
- Delayed and unconvincing disclosure
- Retraction [recantation]

…If the abuse is disclosed, the child has to cope with the chaos that follows. The perpetrator denies it, adults do not believe them, and children retract their disclosures. They say it really did not happen, change their stories, or just shut down and say nothing. In shutting down and no longer talking about the abuse, the child has found a way to survive.

Sociopaths/Psychopaths:

How Sociopaths Are Different from Psychopaths: Both are forms of antisocial personality disorder (Marcia Purse, November 14, 2022):

Although sociopath and psychopath are often used interchangeably and may overlap, each has its own clear lines of distinction. For example, sociopathy is the unofficial term for antisocial personality disorder (APD), while psychopathy is not an official diagnosis and is not considered an APD.

Psychopaths are classified as people with little or no conscience but are able to follow social conventions when it suits their needs. Sociopaths have a limited, albeit weak, ability to feel empathy and remorse. They're also more likely to fly off the handle and react violently when confronted by the consequences of their actions.

Sociopath:

Make it clear they do not care how others feel

Behave in hot-headed and impulsive ways

Prone to fits of anger and rage

Psychopath:

Pretend to care

Display cold-hearted behavior

Fail to recognize other people's distress

Sociopaths have a conscience, albeit a weak one, and will often justify something they know to be wrong. By contrast, psychopaths will believe that their actions are justified and feel no remorse for any harm done.

Violence, while certainly possible, is not an inherent characteristic of either sociopathy or psychopathy.

With that being said, people with APD will often go to extraordinary lengths to manipulate others, whether it be to charm, disarm, or frighten them, in order to get what they want. When psychopaths do become violent, as in the case of Jeffrey Dahmer, they're just as likely to hurt themselves as others.

Narcissism:

Narcissistic Personality Disorder, (The Mayo Clinic, April 6, 2023):

Narcissistic personality disorder is a mental health condition in which people have an unreasonable high sense of their own importance. They need and seek too much attention and want people to admire them. People with this disorder may lack the ability to understand or care about the feelings of others. But behind this mask of extreme confidence, they are not sure of their self-worth and are easily upset by the slightest criticism.

Symptoms:

- Have an unreasonably high sense of self-importance and require constant, excessive admiration.

- Feel they deserve privileges and special treatment.

- Expect to be recognized as superior even without achievements.

- Make achievements and talents seem bigger than they are.

- Be preoccupied with fantasies about success, power, brilliance, beauty, or the perfect mate.

- Believe they are superior to others and can only spend time with or be understood by equally special people.

- Be critical of and look down on people they feel are not important.

- Expect special favors and expect other people to do what they want without questioning them.

- Take advantage of others to get what they want.

- Have an inability or unwillingness to recognize the needs and feelings of others.

- Be envious of others and believe others envy them.

- Behave in an arrogant way, brag a lot and come across as conceited.

- Insist on having the best of everything –for instance, the best car or office.

At the same time, people with narcissistic personality disorder have trouble handling anything they view as criticism. They can:

- Become impatient or angry when they don't receive special recognition or treatment.

- Have major problems when interacting with others and easily feel slighted.

- React with rage or contempt and try to belittle other people to make themselves appear superior.

- Have difficulty managing their emotions and behavior.

- Experience major problems dealing with stress and adapting to change.

- Withdraw from or avoid situations in which they might fail.

- Feel depressed and moody because they fall short of perfection.

- Have secret feelings of insecurity, shame, humiliation and fear of being exposed as a failure.

Stalking:

Stalking Know it. Name it. Stop it. (Advocacy, Education & Community Awareness):

Stalking is a serious issue affecting more than 6 million people each year.

It can be a terrifying crime for those who experience it, and it is often one of the many tactics that abusers use in order to maintain power and control over a current or former intimate partner.

Effects of stalking

Job loss and/or changing jobs due to stalking behavior

Feeling trapped in their own home and fear of leaving their home

Relocating and moving in secret

Fear, humiliation and/or depression

Distrust of others

Many behaviors that are often described as "emotional abuse" are also stalking behavior. Often, victims and service providers do not identify the behavior as "stalking" when it happens during a relationship. The constant contact, surveillance and threats that may be part of an abusive relationship are also stalking behaviors.

87% of stalkers are men.

Roughly half of all stalking victims report their stalking to the police.

1/4 of stocking cases reported to the police result in an arrest.

28% of female and 10% of male victims obtain protective or restraining orders against their stalkers.

87% of all restraining orders against stalkers are violated.

Domestic Violence and Stalking – A Potential Deadly Combination

... Women murdered by a former intimate partner who is subjected to physical abuse, 90% of those women had been stalked.

[X used stalking behaviors to intimidate, threaten, and harass Gabriel, Castiel, as well as me. He had cameras that I did not know about -they were hidden until I found one of them in the house in Bellaire. In that house, he also used the baby monitors to listen to what I was saying and doing and what Gabriel was saying (he turned them around, so I couldn't see the light and had no idea they were on -until I saw one partially hidden in his office), he checked my rare internet usage thereby checking the history and then asked me why I looked at certain things, he went into my email account, he checked all incoming and outgoing phone calls and would ask me about those he didn't know who they were, he purchased a police scanner after the boys, and I left. When he got the boys to 'his' house, he had cameras installed in that house, specifically to watch the boys, he had a very tall privacy fence installed around the yard, once they got phones he had the 360 app installed and monitored everywhere they went and everything they did and questioned them about it when they got back, he'd check every incoming and outgoing phone calls, if there were any to me, they lost their phone for a certain amount of time, he had 'friends' at the school keeping watch of them and reporting to him - they reported about my comings and goings as well, he didn't let them ever stay at friend's houses, he only let one friend of Castiel's come over one time in all the years they were there, they very rarely let them go any place - unless it was with them, he'd regularly search their rooms, either when they were in school or at our house; he flip the beds, tear out drawers and dump them, throw everything all over the place and leave it for the boys to clean up, he did the same thing with their backpacks - but this was everyday and whenever they came back from my place; he dump everything out of all of the packets - everything].

Economic Abuse:

4 Warning Signs Of Financial Abuse – And How Victims Can Recover (Kelly Anne Smith, Oct 11, 2022, Forbes Advisor):

A 2011 Center for Financial Security study of 103 women who had suffered domestic violence found that 99% of them also reported experiencing economic abuse, defined as a partner taking control over a significant other's ability to acquire, use and maintain economic resources.

Financial abuse is a tactic used by abusers to increase control over their victims through maneuvers like reducing the victim's access to bank accounts and assets or forcing them to quit their jobs.

"When we look at a list of red flags, they seem really obvious to us. But for a lot of women, it's very incremental how an abuser goes from someone you feel is taking care of you and is doing all of these things because they love you to someone who's taken complete control over your finances and your life," Scouller says.

4 Types of Financial Abuse:

1. The Abuser "Takes Care" of the Finances.

2. Employment Sabotage.

3. Economic Exploitation.

4. Coerced Debt.

Leaving an abusive relationship is the most dangerous time for the victim. Eric Scott, executive director at the Family Violence Law Center, stresses the importance of creating a safety plan before physically leaving an abusive situation.

If you're worried about finding legitimate shelter on your own, you can call the U.S. National Domestic Violence Hotline at 1-800-799-7233 for recommendations of where to go.

Emotional Abuse: Economic Abuse: The Invisible Form of Interpersonal Violence How domestic abusers inflict more than physical and emotional abuse (Wendy L. Patrick, J.D., Ph.D., June 26, 2021, verified by Psychology Today)

- Interpersonal abuse is emotional, physical, and also financial.

- Because intimate partner violence is about power and control, this often extends to control over money.

- Economic abuse is often manifest through daily methods of depriving a victim of necessities.

…note how common economic abuse is within abusive relationships. One study showed 94% of survivors as having experienced some form of economic abuse, 79% reported economic control, 79% reported economic exploitation, and 78% reported some form of employment sabotage.

[I found conversations between X and his father where his father asked him if he "still had control of the money," I never saw any money or bank accounts. He always beat me out to get the mail -he saw when it came from his upstairs office -so I never saw any bank statements. He certainly had 'control' of the money].

Pathological Liar:

How to Cope With a Pathological Liar (Sanjana Gupta, December 25, 2023)

While a pathological liar is not a mental health diagnosis on its own, according to the Diagnostic and Statistical Manual of Mental Disorders, Fifth Edition (DSM-5), it can be a feature of mental health conditions.

Some providers have suggested that pathological lying is different from other types of lying because it's excessive (a person tells multiple lies a day and has gone on for at least six months).

Like other problematic lying, pathological lying can be unconscious and without any obvious gain. However, it can be intended to manipulate others.

While some people who lie will feel remorse and even guilt and shame when caught, pathological liars may not feel bad about it or have any inclination to stop.

You'll feel confused around a person who lies pathologically because you don't know what to believe.

--Aimee Daramus, PSYD

Being lied to can feel a lot like gaslighting, says Daramus. The difference is that someone who's gaslighting you has a strategy. While the actions of a pathological liar may be clearly intentional at times, they can be seemingly random at others.

Pay attention to their actions instead of their words: since it can be hard to trust the words of a person who lies pathologically, "one of the most effective things you can do is read the person's actions. Actions don't lie, and over time you'll spot patterns that will help you predict their future behavior," says Daramus.

Polygraph:

How Credible are Lie Detector Tests? October 4, 2018 BBC News:

So, do they work?

The credibility of the polygraph was challenged almost as soon as it was invented in 1921, and there is much debate about its accuracy.

Some experts say the fundamental premise is flawed.

"It does not measure deception, which is the core problem," says Prof. Aldert Vrij, who has written extensively on the subject. "The idea is that liars will show increased arousal when answering the key questions, whereas truth tellers will not.

"But there is no sound theory to back this up."

Dr. Van Der Zee says that because taking a lie detector test can be a stressful experience, it can …….. present innocent people as guilty.

This means a victim, especially one recounting a traumatic experience, may appear as if they are lying because they are in an emotional state.

Ultimately, experts say there are many caveats to polygraphs and a number of different factors that can lead to inaccurate results.

Why Lie Detector Tests Can't Be Trusted

Federal agencies embraced the polygraph in the 1950s to reassure the public that they could unmask spies.

John Baesler, Zocalo Public Square July 25, 2019

Polygraph measurements derived from changes in blood pressure, breathing depth, and skin conductivity of an electric current --have never been proven to be reliable indicators of deception.

In large screening tests, significant numbers of "false positives" (innocent people being labeled deceptive) are unavoidable.

The Truth About Lie Detectors (aka Polygraph Tests)

www.apa.org/topics/cognitive-neuroscience/polygraph:

The National Research Council found the high accuracy claims of polygraph exams to be without scientific validity. Polygraph tests aren't psychic tools that can tell beyond any doubt that someone is lying.........A false positive can occur when someone telling the truth triggers the device, which then may indicate he's lying even if he isn't. Because of this, polygraph results aren't admissible evidence in any state.

The reason the polygraph is not a lie detector is that **what it measures--changes in heartbeat, blood pressure, and respiration--can be caused by many things**. Nervousness, anger, sadness, embarrassment, and fear can all be causal factors in altering one's heart rate, blood pressure, or respiration rate.

Polygraph-lie-detector The Skeptic's Dictionary www. skepdic.com/polygraph.html The Lie-Detection Myth:

Why polygraph tests should not be used in criminal trials and security screening Gershon Ben-Shakhar Ph.D Memory detection October 31, 2019:

The main assumption behind this method [CQT- Comparison Question Test Method] is …. This assumption-which is not supported by theory or by solid research on shaky ground..........whether guilty or innocent, is likely to be more aroused by the relevant, crime-related question than by the unrelated comparison question. This implies that innocent suspects tested by this polygraph method may be misclassified, which contradicts the most important goal of a criminal investigation -protecting the innocent.

In addition, the assumption that the physiological responses measured by the polygraph cannot be controlled has been refuted by research. With minimal training, guilty suspects can avoid being detected.

Thus, the idea that a machine can detect deception and differentiate truthful from deceptive individuals is a myth.

The Lie Behind the Lie Detector (5th Edition, George W. Maschke & Gino J. Scalabrini, AntiPolygraph.org):

Little-known truths:

- Polygraphy is not science

- Our government's reliance on unreliable polygraphy serves to protect spies, undermining – not enhancing –our national security.

- Polygraph "tests" are actually interrogations.

- Polygraphy depends on your polygraph operator lying to and deceiving you.

- Polygraphy is biased against the truth.

- Polygraphy "testing" can be (and has been) easily defeated through countermeasures.

Polygraphy is still relied upon by the American criminal justice system. While the results of the polygraph "tests" are disallowed in an overwhelming majority of the courts, the polygraph is routinely employed by federal, state, and local law enforcement agencies during the interrogation of criminal subjects.

When we lie, our blood pressure goes up, our heart beats faster, we breathe more quickly (and our breathing slows once the lie has been told), and changes take place in our skin moisture. ... An examiner can tell from those mechanical scribbles whether or not you've spoken the truth. --polygraph examiner Chris Gugas

The Silent Witness, 1979

Whoever undertakes to set himself up as a judge in the field of truth and knowledge is shipwrecked by the laughter of the Gods.

--Albert Einstein

Polygraphy is not science....it is codified conjecture masquerading as science. Polygraph "testing" is an unstandardizable procedure that is fundamentally dependent on trickery.

The dirty little secret behind the polygraph "test" is that while the polygraph operator admonishes the examinee to answer all questions truthfully, he secretly assumes that denials in response to certain questions —called "control" questions -will be less than truthful.

The examiner's subjective opinion may influence the outcome.

[When neither Michigan CPS nor Kentucky CPS would investigate the sexual abuse allegations....-again, it went to Michigan State Police. They (the officers on our particular case, anyway) were no more qualified to investigate a child sexual abuse case than a dandelion. X and his parents went to Grayling to "talk" to the officer investigating the case (I was in Kentucky and had all of one brief telephone conversation with her, in which she was very rude). In the brief interaction that I'd had with her, she told me she "didn't believe the allegations," which is hardly neutral and wouldn't impinge on the outcome of the case at all, and that she was going to give him a polygraph to "prove" he was innocent. I knew right then and there that she would find that in the polygraph for many reasons; that was what she wanted to find. X lied all the time, and I'm certain he would have searched how to beat a polygraph just to be sure, and polygraph screening is a bunch of bunk].

[Polygraph screening] is completely without any theoretical foundation and has absolutely no validity. …..there is almost universal agreement that polygraph screening is completely invalid and should be stopped…..the diagnostic value of this type of testing is not more than that of astrology or tea-leaf reading.

……anyone can be taught to beat this type of polygraph exam in a few minutes.

……One area of special concern…..is the incorrect identification of innocent persons as deceptive. All other factors being equal, the low base rates of guilt in screening situations would lead to high false positive rates, even assuming very high polygraph validity.

[The National Academy of Sciences; Committee to Review the Scientific Evidence on the Polygraph found:]

- Almost a century of research in scientific physiology provides little basis for the expectation that a polygraph test could have…high accuracy.

- The theoretical rationale for the polygraph is quite weak, especially in terms of differential fear, arousal, or other emotional states that are triggered in response to relevant or comparison questions.

- Research on the polygraph has not progressed over time in the manner of a typical scientific field. It has not accumulated knowledge or strengthened its scientific underpinnings in any significant manner.

- The inherent ambiguity of the physiological measures used in the polygraph suggests that further investments in improving polygraph technique and interpretation will bring only modest improvements in accuracy.

Polygraph is more art than science, and unless an admission is obtained, the final determination is frequently what we refer to as a scientific wild-ass guess (SWAG).

Polygraph testing yields an unacceptable choice for….employee security screening between too many loyal employees falsely judged deceptive and too many major security threats left undetected.

Its accuracy in distinguishing actual or potential security violators from innocent test takers is insufficient to justify reliance on its use……(National Research Council, 2003, National Academy of Sciences). [NAS further warns]… Overconfidence in the polygraph -a belief in its accuracy not justified by the evidence -presents a danger to national security objectives.

Racial bias also plays a significant role in polygraph outcomes………..[in one DOD study], only 23.5% of innocent black subjects were correctly classified as being non-deceptive, which is considerably less than the 36.9% of whites correctly classified.

Polygraph operators have been known to inflate or even fabricate admissions…

Government officials have also used polygraph "testing" as a pretext for adverse action in the absence of supportive evidence. Polygraph "tests" may be deliberately rigged to increase the likelihood of the subject "failing."[or "passing"].

Polygraph research (direction, funding, and evaluation), training, and operational review are controlled by those who practice polygraphy and depend upon it for a living. This is tantamount to having the government's cancer research efforts controlled by the tobacco industry. Independent scientific experts must be (and have not been) consulted to obtain an objective view of polygraphy.

The fact that human physiology is marvelously wonderful and complex, that polygraph methods have been able to accurately record this physiology for most of this century and beyond, and the fact that computerized acquisition and evaluation of this data is now available in no way compensates for the vast shortcomings of polygraph applications and questioning formats. State of the art technology utilized on faulty applications amounts to nothing more than garbage in, garbage out.

The polygraph operator is making believe. His explanation [of polygraph] is deliberately false and misleading: telling a lie may or may not result in physiological changes measurable by the polygraph. When the polygraph operator says, "It is important for you to understand that even though a lie might be socially acceptable or a small lie, or a lie by omission, your body still responds," he really means, "It is important for me that you believe this to be true." Fear is an essential element of all polygraph "tests."

The whole process smacks of 20th-century witchcraft.

--Senator Sam J Ervin, Jr.

Substance Use Disorder:

Substance Use Disorders and Cross-System Collaboration, Child Welfare Information Gateway:

Substance use disorders are complex. Parents who are affected by substance use disorders while also being involved with the child welfare system can benefit from a cross-collaborative team of supportive people and services –such as substance use treatment, education, family court, or recovery coaches and therapists – as they navigate a path to recovery.

Impact of Substance Use on the Child Welfare System, Child Welfare Information Gateway:

Many families and children receiving child welfare services are affected by parental substance use. A substance use disorder is a risk factor for maltreatment, as it may affect a parent's ability to function as a caregiver and provide for their children's basic needs, such as safety, security, and permanency. For these reasons, child welfare professionals must understand the intersection of child welfare and substance use disorders to assess and intervene in affected families effectively. Child welfare practitioners should be aware that families of color are disproportionately represented in the child welfare system. Families from diverse racial and ethnic backgrounds involved with child welfare also experience the disproportionate effects of substance use disorders while facing disparate access to substance use disorder treatment. [Child welfare professionals have regularly taken children out of the home, placed the child in foster care and waited for the parent to jump through many hoops, as well as recover from substance use disorder, for the chance of getting their child back home. I believe there can be a compromise; I feel that a child should only be removed from their home in very extreme situations, and then only if in-home services are unable to remedy the situation. Outpatient services, recovery coaches, and all in-home services should be exhausted prior to considering temporary child removal, as there are many alternatives over further damaging the family -as would be the case with placing the child in foster care -to both the child and recovering parent/caregiver.

<u>A final note from me:</u>

Every one of these above-mentioned 'issues' was a part of our long, drawn-out, painful case, which really began for me when I began dating X, and then I was foolish enough to marry him. Everything above is real, and they damage and/or destroy people's lives on a daily basis. The affected people are from all over the world, people of many different ethnicities and cultures, and speak a variety of languages; they are straight, they are gay, they are of all religions, they are agnostic, they are high school drop-outs, and college-educated. However, most important to me are the children. These children are from the same variety of families all across the world, and they are of all ages, from infant to adulthood - but they are considered children only until they are 18. Infants, toddlers, and children die at the hands of murderous abusers. Surprisingly, I remain an idealist, and this may be a pipe dream even for an idealist, yet humanity still has the chance to come together for the sake of our children. We have to try to put aside political differences, religious differences, and all the things we try to force others to believe because it's how we believe, because after all; this is not a time to be arguing about such things. Come on, focus. Children need adults to be adults and to protect them how they should be protected. I'm sorry if you interpret your God as punishing your children harshly. I don't believe my God wants precious children to be hurt. Taught and well-modeled for -yes, but never abused in any way. So, please do your part. Do not hurt your child. Be a respectable, peaceful, and considerate role model to all around you. Speak up for every and any child you can -whether they are "yours" or not. Look to see if there are any committees, councils, and/or community centers you can get involved in where your voice advocating on behalf of the safety of children will be heard.

Thank you for all you do as a carer for children. Also, my friend, if you've come this far, thank you very much for your time and your interest. May peace find you wherever you may go.

Bibliography:
Books, Resources, Websites, Organizations, Phone Numbers:

Books:

1. Neustein, Amy, and Lesher, Michael. *From Madness to Mutiny: Why Mothers Are Running from the Family Courts - and What Can Be Done About It.* Northeastern University Press, 2005.

2. Myers, John E. B. *The Backlash: Child Protection Under Fire.* Sage Publications, 1994.

3. Myers, John E. B. *A Mother's Nightmare - Incest: A Practical Legal Guide for Parents and Professionals.* Sage Publications, 1997.

4. Myers, John E. B. *Child Witness Law and Practice: 1990 Cumulative Supplement.* Wiley Law Publications, 1990.

5. Faller, Kathleen Coulborn. *Interviewing Children About Sexual Abuse.* Oxford University Press, 2007.

6. Pipe, Margarate-Ellen, Lamb, Michael E., Orbach, Yael, and Cederborg, Ann-Christin. *Child Sexual Abuse: Disclosure, Delay, and Denial.* Taylor & Francis Group, LLC, 2007.

7. Monahon, Cynthia. *Children and Trauma: A Guide for Parents and Professionals.* Jossey-Bass, 1993.

8. Brohl, Kathryn, with Potter, Joyce Case. *When Your Child Has Been Molested: A Parent's Guide to Healing and Recovery.* Jossey-Bass, Revised Edition, 2004.

9. Hunter, Mic. *Abused Boys: The Neglected Victims of Sexual Abuse.* The Random House Publishing Group, 1990.

10. Reeves, Claire R. *Childhood: It Should Not Hurt.* C.C.D.C., CTI Publishing, 2003.

11. Mather, Cynthia L., with Debye, Kristina E. Forward by Eliana Gil. *How Long Does It Hurt? A Guide to Recovering From Incest and Sexual Abuse for Teenagers, Their Friends, and Their Families.* Jossey-Bass.

12. Butler, Sandra. *Conspiracy of Silence: The Trauma of Incest.* Volcano Press, 1985.

13. Goodwin, Jean M. *Sexual Abuse: Incest Victims and Their Families.* 2nd Edition. Year Book Medical Publishers, 1989.

14. Angelica, Jade Christine. *We Are Not Alone: A Teenage Boy's Personal Account of Child Sexual Abuse from Disclosure Through Prosecution and Treatment.* The Haworth Maltreatment and Trauma Press, 2002.

15. Marcy-Webster, Susan, and Philips, Emily. *If I Tell: Kid's Rights Pamphlet.* Published by Kid's Rights, 2007.

16. Adams, Caren, and Fay, Jennifer. *Helping Your Child Recover from Sexual Abuse.* University of Washington Press, Updated 1998.

17. Bancroft, Lundy. *Why Does He Do That? Inside the Minds of Angry and Controlling Men.* Penguin Random House, 2002.

18. Bancroft, Lundy. *When Dad Hurts Mom: Helping Your Children Heal the Wounds of Witnessing Abuse.* Berkley Books, 2004.

19. Faller, Kathleen Coulborn. *The Batterer as Parent 2: Addressing the Impact of Domestic Violence on Family Dynamics.* [This is an article but can be found online.]

20. Winner, Karen. *Divorced from Justice: The Abuse of Women and Children by Divorce Lawyers and Judges.* Harper Collins Publishers, 1996.

21. Gainsborough, Juliet. *Scandalous Politics: Child Welfare Policy in the States.* Georgetown University Press, 2007.

22. Rosen, Leora N., and Etlin, Michelle. *The Hostage Child: Sex Abuse Allegations in Custody Disputes.* Indiana University Press, 1996.

23. Paul, Annie Murphy. *The Cult of Personality: How Personality Tests Are Leading Us to Miseducate Our Children, Mismanage Our Companies, and Misunderstand Ourselves.* FP Freepress Publishing, 2004.

24. Wood, James M., Nezworski, M. Teresa, Lilienfeld, Scott O., and Garb, Howard N. *What's Wrong with the Rorschach?* Jossey-Bass, 2003.

25. Myers, John E. B. *A History of Child Protection in America.* Xlibris Corporation, 2004.

26. Bennett, Jeffrey P., with Phillips, Francine. *Breaking the Bonds of Child Abuse: A Guide to Political Action,* 1995.

27. Van Der Kolk, Bessel, M.D. *The Body Keeps the Score: Brain, Mind, and Body in the Healing of Trauma.* Penguin Books, 2014.

28. Chapman, Gary, Ph.D., and Campbell, Ross, M.D. *The Five Love Languages of Children: Includes the Five Love Languages Assessment Tool for Children.*

There are many books that cover these subjects incredibly well and are deeply detailed and intensive. The authors I recommend most regarding domestic violence, all forms of child abuse, and sexual abuse are Kathleen Coulborn Faller, Lundy Bancroft, and John E.B. Myers. If affordability is an issue, I recommend checking your local library, which may have or can obtain these titles.

Websites, Organizations, Phone Numbers, etc.:

1. RAINN: Rape, Abuse, and Incest National Network. Available 24/7 for help. Call 800-656-HOPE (4673) or visit online.rainn.org.

2. SPARC: Stalking, Prevention Awareness, and Resource Center.

3. National Domestic Violence Hotline: Call 800-799-7233 (SAFE), Text "START" to 88788, or TTY 800-787-3224. Available 24/7.

4. NNEDV.org: National Network to End Domestic Violence. Ph. 202-543-5566, F. 202-543-5626.

5. Womenslaw.org

6. Techsafety.org: Protecting yourself from stalking through technology.

7. Domestic Violence Crisis Center (Connecticut only): Call or text 24-hour hotline 888-774-2900.

8. ProtectionFromAbuse.org: Email at email@ Protectionfromabuse.org.

9. CASA: Court Appointed Special Advocates.

10. ESSA: Every Student Succeeds Act.

11. The Advocacy Institute in Washington D.C.: Advocates for disabled people.

12. Psychological Harassment Information Association.

13. Working Psychology.

14. HowStuffWorks.

15. Straightdope.com.

16. PETA: peta.org and peta.org/wp-content/uploads/2021/06/AnimalAbuseHumanAbuse.pdf.

17. Ladyfreethinker.org: The Link Between Animal Cruelty and Human Abuse.

18. Violence Against Women.

19. International Journal of Environmental Research and Public Health.

20. Animallaw.info.

21. The Journal of Interpersonal Violence.

22. Americanhumane.salsalabs.org.

23. American Psychological Association: apa.org.

24. American Psychiatric Association.

25. Family Violence Law Center.

26. Freeform.org: Helps survivors build financial security.

27. The Verywell Mind Podcast.

28. Child Welfare Information Gateway: childwelfare.gov.

29. National Center on Substance Abuse and Child Welfare.

30. Children and Family Futures: Family-centered approach to drug intervention services.

31. Children's Bureau.

32. Administration for Children and Families.

33. U.S. Department of Health and Human Services: hhs.gov.

34. Mayo Clinic: mayoclinic.org.

35. Childhelp.org: To report child sexual abuse, whether in-person or online.

36. Childwelfare.gov Resources:

    • Recognizing the signs and symptoms of child abuse and neglect.

    • Definitions of child abuse and neglect.

    • Effects of maltreatment on brain development.

    • Cost of injury to society analysis.

    • Social and economic consequences of child abuse.

37. CDC: cdc.gov/violenceprevention/acestudy/.

38. Harvard: Developingchild.harvard.edu.

39. Acesconnection.com: Community for adverse childhood experiences research.

40. Cahmi.org: ACES Brief Final.

41. Childtrends.org: Prevalence of Adverse Childhood Experiences.

42. Dr. Nadine Burke-Harris TED Talk (2014): "How Childhood Trauma Affects Health Across a Lifetime."

43. Rwjf.org: The Truth About ACEs.

44. Acestoohigh.com: "Got Your ACE Score?"

45. SAMHSA: samhsa.gov/nctic/trauma-interventions.

46. Childhelp.org Resources:

    • Handling child abuse disclosures.

    • Risk Factors.

    • Perpetrators.

47. National Child Traumatic Stress Network: nctsn.org.

48. Preventchildabuse.org: Prevent Child Abuse America.

49. Nature: Adverse Experiences and the Developing Brain.

50. NCADV: National Coalition Against Domestic Violence: ncadv.org.

51. Promising Futures: Best practices for trauma-informed care.

52. Futures Without Violence: List of resources for families and front-line workers.

53. Quality Improvement Center on Domestic Violence in Child Welfare.

54. CPTSD Foundation: cptsdfoundation.org.

55. The Collins Center: Previously known as Citizens Against Sexual Assault: thecollinscenter.org.

56. Darkness to Light: darkness2light.org.

57. Google Scholar: googlescholar.com.

58. Child Welfare Outcomes Report to Congress.

59. Michigan League for Public Policy: mlpp.org.

60. Kids Count in Michigan: Data on child welfare.

When I went back to school and finally earned my Bachelor's Degree from U of M in April 2012, I was very fortunate. First, I had the honor of working with excellent professors. I was older, I wasn't there to screw around, I wanted to learn and earn a degree, so I think I was given a little bit more respect from most of the professors. I was able to work on one with a variety of professors and created my own independent studies. My main focus was child welfare and child welfare reform locally (Ann Arbor), county-wide (Washtenaw County), state (Michigan), nationally (U.S.), and globally (focused on Sweden, Denmark, Finland, U.K., African countries, China, and some middle-eastern countries). I couldn't focus a lot on global child welfare and welfare reform because I simply didn't have the time; I had spent so much time at the local-national level). The United States is the worst country of developed nations for how we take care of our children, and at that time, Michigan was ranked very low as well. This was extremely infuriating, yet interesting to me, and also very difficult, as I was going through excruciating pain because of our local child welfare and legal failures. I learned a lot during that time. The U of M had the best search engines (I miss those!), so I found a wealth of great information on the subjects I was searching. This book began from that research in 2010-2011. So, clearly, this has taken me a long time, but this hasn't been just about 'writing a book'; it's been a process. And I could not have completed this 16 or 17 years ago. It was too painful then and was painful at this time as well. I was not able to think clearly enough for years. I still am triggered, have nightmares, and have flashbacks on a daily basis. But I saw the light at the end of the tunnel, and this time, it wasn't a train coming towards me -it was freedom.

www.ingramcontent.com/pod-product-compliance
Lightning Source LLC
Chambersburg PA
CBHW061550120626
46550CB00004B/1432